TALES FROM THE HOME FARM

MICHAEL KELLY is the bestselling author of *Trading Paces* and writes features on health, lifestyle, food and travel for *The Irish Times*. He is a regular contributor to RTÉ programmes on the subject of self-sufficiency and growing your own food. Michael is the founder of GIY Ireland, a network of local food groups where back-garden growers get together to exchange tips, suggestions and war stories. For more tips and anecdotes about growing your own grub, visit his blog at www.michaelkelly.ie

PAULA MEE BSc, Dip Dietetics, MSc in Health Sciences, Dip Allergy, MINDI Diploma in Allergy from Southampton University, is a current member and past president of the Irish Nutrition and Dietetic Institute and runs her own nutrition consultancy. She is on the board of Consumer Foods at An Bord Bia and was one of the presenters of RTE TV's *Health Squad* programme which ran from 2002 to 2006. She makes regular appearances on TV and radio programmes, advising on nutrition and health issues.

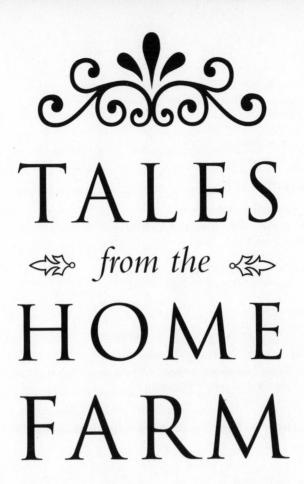

TALES

from the

HOME

FARM

Michael Kelly

THE O'BRIEN PRESS
DUBLIN

First published 2009 by The O'Brien Press Ltd.
12 Terenure Road East, Rathgar, Dublin 6, Ireland.
Tel: +353 1 4923333;
Fax: +353 1 4922777
Email: books@obrien.ie
Website: www.obrien.ie

ISBN: 978-1-84717-168-9

1 2 3 4 5 6 7 8 9 10

09 10 11 12 13 14 15

Typesetting, editing, layout and design: The O'Brien Press Ltd
Printed and bound in the UK by J F Print Ltd, Sparkford, Somerset.

The paper in this book is produced using pulp from managed forests.

Cover photograph of author by Nicky Fortune
Cover images courtesy of iStockphoto and the author

ACKNOWLEDGEMENTS

I am a great believer in the idea that if you 'follow your bliss' and do the things you are meant to do in this life, *something* seems to take over and order your affairs for you. Call it synchronicity, luck, coincidence – whatever. Things just seem to work, the ducks are put in a row, doors open, it seems almost *too easy*.

Setting up GIY Ireland was a case in point. From the very start, people got involved who seemed to know what to do next, when I most assuredly didn't. We have made so many new friends in the past year among the GIY groups already in existence – thank you, one and all! Special thanks to all those who were involved in getting GIY Ireland off the ground for giving their time, passion and great ideas so generously. Thanks to our fellow *meithealers* – Feargal, Dave, Bryan, Ciaran, Caoimhín and Nicky – I can't tell you how enjoyable you have made the past year.

I am enormously grateful to my publisher, Michael O'Brien, who shared a clear vision of where this book needed to go and continues to be such a supportive advocate. My wonderful editor, Ide Ní Laoghaire, once again showed razor-sharp insights in helping me convert manuscript into book – I think she may even have caught the growing bug herself along the way!! Thanks to all at The O'Brien Press for their unstinting support and hard work.

To Anne Cullen for helping me with the monthly Grower's Calendars, and Paula Mee for her input on the nutritional value of vegetables. To my sister and organic grower extraordinaire, Niamh, at Maybloom Farm, for taking long, meandering phone calls from me when she should have been working!

If you like what you read in these pages there's plenty more on offer on my website (www.michaelkelly.ie) – the reason it looks so professional is down to the sterling efforts of the team at Emagine Media, particularly Aaron Jay. Thanks also to Mick Brown for his unheralded work on the GIY site (www.GIYIreland.com).

Thanks to my friends, family and extended family for their continued support and encouragement. After all, what is life really worth unless you surround yourself with people you love? The greatest debt of thanks, as ever, is due to the person whom I am so incredibly lucky to share this life's journey with – so, to Eilish, my *anam cara*, thank you.

CONTENTS

PREFACE

I swear to God, I nearly fell off my chair. I was listening to the radio the other day and I heard an economist advising people to go out and start growing their own vegetables! I did a double-take at first, wondering had I heard him right – but yep, this expert in the study of supply and demand appeared to be touting vegetable growing as the only guaranteed way to survive the global economic downturn. If you grow your own vegetables already, as we do, you should feel pretty smug when you hear things like that, because it means that you are well ahead of the curve. *A-ha*, you might say, *I have been growing vegetables for years!! At last, people have seen the light! Victory is mine!* But strangely, instead of feeling smug, I felt absolutely terrified – if we're relying on my vegetable-growing skills in order to survive in a world where even economists are advising us to grow our own, we are, pardon my French, completely shagged.

Let's not even try to establish whether our economist friend is correct in his assessment because discussions of macro economics are just too depressing and this is not going to be a depressing book. Promise. It's probably fair to say, however, that after years in which growing your own food was dismissed as a hobby for middle-class folk with too much time on their hands, there's a feeling in the air that a revival is underway. The ability to produce food in your own garden (or allotment or community garden) is simply more useful than it used to be now that money is tighter. Growing your own vegetables has always been fun. It's always been good for your body, mind and soul. It's always made sense in terms of the flavour and the variety of your food, and it's always been a good thing for the environment. But it hasn't, for a long time, been *necessary*. I find it enormously comforting that in our hour of need these ancient skills are there for us to fall back on. They have been waiting patiently in the wings, smiling quizzically while we indulged our fascination with convenience foods, 24/7 Tesco and low-fat dairy spreads. They are not annoyed that we've been away for so long – in fact, they're *happy to see us* even though they are acutely aware that the economic downturn will assuredly pass in due course and we will become obsessed with other, more trivial stuff, all over again.

Our Home Farm is a windswept acre in rural Waterford in the southeast corner of Ireland. We moved out of the big city about five years ago, turning our backs on the insidious clutter and stresses of the rat race to go in search of a gentler, more simple way of living. We found 'the good life' almost by accident. It started with us sowing a few vegetables – garlic, onions and potatoes – in our first spring here, just for something to do, really, and it basically snowballed out of control from there. Before we knew what was happening, our vegetable patch seemed to be taking over the garden and our lives, like a particularly aggressive weed, and we seemed to have accumulated an array of farmyard-type animals – pigs, ducks, chickens and hens. And so, out of fairness to you, dear reader, I should mention right here in this opening gambit just how addictive the whole thing is. Once you've tasted the magic, there's just no going back. If you are not currently producing any of your own food, it's still not too late. You can put this book down right now and go and watch TV or take a nap – and save yourself a whole lot of bother. No harm done.

Still here? All righty then!

For us, abandoning the rat race was about trying, in some small way, to turn our backs on a society that is relentless in its pursuit of *things*. A society where marketeers continuously hold up the prospect that happiness is within our grasp if we would only consider shelling out some money on their particular product. We are bombarded with messages to this effect, morning, noon and night, on TV and radio, on the internet, on billboards. Driven half-mad with acquisitiveness, with the desire *to have, to acquire, to possess*, we spend our lives killing ourselves working at jobs we often despise, so that we can earn the money we need to fund these trophies – and, of course, along the way we become completely detached from what's important and from the things that can really make us happy. We forget that we can be happy simply by *being*. I don't claim to be completely fulfilled, or enlightened in these matters, but I do think that real happiness comes, not from owning stuff, but from not even wanting the stuff in the first place. It comes from being happy with what we have NOW, even if it's not a lot. It comes from accepting things as they are. None of this is easy, of course, and to choose to live that way is to place yourself at odds with society as a whole.

When we moved here, we both gave up good, solid corporate careers to pursue our dream jobs – in my case, writing; in Mrs Kelly's case, teaching nippers in the local school. The result was (eventually) a very welcome change of pace and a sense of fulfilment in our working lives. But there was also, of course, a dramatic downward shift in our income, mainly because writing doesn't pay very well. It has taken a considerable adjustment in our thinking to deal with that change in our standard of living. But, thankfully, though our earnings are a little emaciated compared to what they used to be, we have found happiness in having *more than enough*. There is not even a sniff or a hint of self-denial about the way we live – quite the opposite, in fact. I like the term 'elegant frugality' as a way to describe a simpler and yet, ultimately, far more fulfilling way of life. When people think about 'the good life' they often think of poor old Barbara sewing a new leg on to her dungarees, and they assume that this way of life is about destitution and grinding poverty. Nothing could be further from the truth.

This life gives you something *real* – something that no government or boss or bank or bureaucrat can ever take away from you. It will stay with you long after our economist friend has decided that the solution to our economic woes is not vegetable growing, after all, but some other soundbite he is keen to bandy around to anyone who will listen. This lifestyle is about *really* living and being incredibly wealthy in all the things that are important. It is about trying to make sure that simplicity reigns in all things. It is about being happy and grateful in your work, in your partner, in your family, in your leisure time. It is about trying to be perpetually thankful for just having the ability to breathe in and out, or to get out of bed in the morning. It is about being grateful for the earth's spectacular largesse and being in tune with the ancient rhythms of nature. It is about taking a childlike delight in the abundant variety of life – the sounds, the smells and the sights. It is about enjoying great food that you have plucked from the earth yourself and seeing food for what it really is: not a raw material to be thrown, unthinking, into the body, but a life-giving part of who we are, to be savoured and relished. This life is about enjoying the company of good friends, family and neighbours – helping them and being helped, giving our time and gratefully receiving the time of others. When a huge part of your life revolves around producing your own food, you are *forced* to slow down and be patient, because nature, as we know, simply refuses to be rushed. She moves along at her own inexorable pace and you have no choice, really, but to slow down with her. And, of course, in slowing down, you learn to appreciate. In appreciation you learn to be grateful, and in gratitude there is happiness.

So why do I call it the *Home Farm*? Well, basically, I suppose I am a frustrated farmer. In addition to our vegetable growing, at the time of writing there are thirty-three creatures to feed, morning and evening, around these parts – thirty-five if you count Mrs Kelly and myself as creatures, which I suppose we are. Though we have crammed our little acre with more growing/rearing enterprises than is really sensible or advisable, what we have here doesn't constitute a proper farm by any stretch of the imagination. I don't think I am quite at the level where I can be described as a smallholder either. I don't know how exactly you would define a smallholding, and I know there are small-holdings out there that would be similar in size to our garden, but still, the term just doesn't really fit what we do here. To my mind, a smallholding is a fulltime project, with either a commercial aim or a view to complete self-sufficiency. The food producing that we do here is a way of life, but it is essentially a hobby – an incredible, life-changing hobby – but a hobby, nonetheless. We both have jobs to do each day and we have a mortgage to pay, and we cram in our 'Home Farming' around that whenever we can. In any case, we don't have enough land dedicated to food production within our acre for it to be considered a smallholding. It's more a regular garden with some food production going on within it – and I presume, since you are reading this book, that yours is similar or perhaps you would like it to be. In addition to our veggie patch, we keep some ducks and hens, and once or twice a year we get some chicks and fatten them for the table. For a number of years, now, we have also fattened a pair of weanlings (piglets) for six months or so each year. As far as I'm concerned, having a few animals around the place gives me licence to call it a farm, and because people usually laugh when I call it that, I add in the word 'home' just to put things in perspective. Whenever I go away for a few days I like to call Mrs Kelly and ask, 'How are things on the Home Farm?' I'm a strange boy, I know.

Ultimately, we are in a very fortunate position – we have an alternative source of income and so we don't depend totally on what we produce, like real farmers do. It's a terrible pity when a crop fails on us (as they often do), but we won't starve. I would like us to be as self-sufficient as we can, but there's also a part of me that recognises that trying to achieve a hundred percent self-sufficiency could be a straitjacket just as tight as the corporate life we left behind us. I love the work I do on the Home Farm and I don't ever want it to become a chore. We don't lose sleep over the fact that we will probably never completely achieve the aim of self-sufficiency. We frequent supermarkets more than occasionally – admittedly, less than we used to, and still more than we would like to. We buy things like oranges and bananas that have been shipped half-way around the world and we usually feel pretty bad about that – but we still buy them. Like a growing number of people out there, however, we see tremendous value in being able to sit down to a home-grown meal or even a meal that is partly home-grown. We worry about the quality and integrity of the food we buy in the shops, so we think that growing our own is good for our bodies. I think that having spent five years or so working the soil here and loving the produce that comes out of it, we have a better understanding of the relationship between good soil, good vegetables and good health. There are loads of layers in between, but essentially the link is direct – if you have good soil you have good plants, which lead to nutritious vegetables, which in turn leads to a healthy body. I can also vouch for the fact that producing your own food is incredibly good for the soul. I talked in my first book, *Trading Paces*, about how the Home Farm has been the location for some of the most enjoyable, honest moments of my life. Scientists now believe that soil actually releases endorphins when you dig it, which might explain why us food growers get so much satisfaction out of spending time with a spade – we are basically high all the time.

Now, you might be thinking: *Hold on a minute, this guy has only been producing his own food for five years, what makes him think he's qualified to write a book on the subject?* This is, indeed, a very good question and one I have asked myself many, many times while writing it. It's really important to mention, up front, that we are not experts and this is not an expert guide, so if it's an expert guide you're after, I'm afraid you have bought (or borrowed, or stolen) the wrong book. Don't worry, there are loads of expert guides out there and I am sure if you talk nicely to your better half, or a family member or friend, they might get you one for Christmas. I have a shelf-load of them that range from the exceptionally useful to the not-so-useful, and I have to admit that sometimes I find the information in them a little daunting. The good news, however, is that you don't need to absorb any or all of the information in those books before you get started. What you actually need to do is *just get started*. I mentioned in my first book that a good way to describe us is that we are waiting for our expertise to catch up with our enthusiasm – sadly, the wait goes on but, in the meantime, blind enthusiasm continues to make up for our lack of know-how. I like to think that the fact that we still manage to produce wonderful food for ourselves every year, even though *we are not experts*, will make most of the growing achievements in this book accessible to most people. It must be said, however, that in some cases there is probably a severe mismatch between the *best way* to do things and *our way* of doing things, as outlined in this book. In other cases, I do try to outline the best way of doing things, but you can be fairly sure that our own conduct on the matter probably falls far short of this ideal. So, essentially, I am a flawed messenger bringing you what I think is a really, really worthwhile message.

Thankfully, I had a lot of help in putting together the more instructive, authoritative parts of this book. Nutrition consultant Paula Mee was good enough to come on board to put some much-needed scientific meat on the bones of my amateur musings – you will find her contributions about the nutritional value of the key vegetables you can grow on your Home Farm in each chapter. Anne Cullen, from GIY (Grow It Yourself) Waterford, helped me put together the hugely informative and useful Grower's Calendars which appear at the end of each chapter and the seed-sowing guide at the end of the book.

The million-dollar question, I suppose, is: what's the motivation? Why bother with growing your own? Isn't it just easier to buy food in the supermarket? Well, yes, it most definitely is. But before we go any further, let's take a step back and take a look at some of the problems that exist within our food chain. Most readers would, I am sure, be familiar with the concept of 'food miles', which describes the journey your food has had to endure to get from the place it was grown to the place it will be eaten. The common way of measuring this is by comparing the energy we acquire from food in the form of calories with the energy required to cultivate that food in the first place and then ship it to our plates. For example, 97 calories of transport energy in the form of aviation fuel are needed to import 1 calorie of asparagus by plane from Chile to Europe, and 66 calories of energy are consumed when flying 1 calorie of carrot energy from South Africa. If a head of iceberg lettuce is shipped to Europe from the US by plane, 127 calories of energy are needed to transport every calorie of lettuce. These figures do not even include the energy consumed while growing these vegetables (which is considerable), or in their packaging, cooling and distribution. Nor does it include the energy we expend in terms of motor fuel by getting into the car and driving to an out-of-town supermarket to buy them. Most of us, I think, would accept that this isn't really a sustainable way of conducting ourselves in the longterm and that, at some point, we are going to realise the error of our ways and go back to sourcing food locally.

While the environmental consequences of shipping food around the globe rather than producing it locally are, no doubt, very, very serious (our food chain really does tread far too heavily on our planet), I'm inclined to think that there's another aspect of the food-miles issue that is even more pressing: when they ship a vegetable half-way around the world, how on earth do they keep it fresh? Say something is grown in South America or Asia for sale in Western Europe, imagine how many modes of transport that vegetable gets to 'enjoy' before it arrives on your plate! Imagine how many borders it crosses and customs it has to clear! Imagine all the ferry ports or airports it takes in and how much time it spends in distribution centres and storage! Imagine how many hours it spends rattling along in the back of an articulated lorry!

Researchers at the Swedish Institute for Food and Biotechnology carried out an interesting analysis of the food mileage of tomato ketchup and discovered that the cultivation, processing, packaging, storage, distribution and retail of the final product involved more than fifty-two individual transport and process stages. The commonly quoted statistic on these things is that the average distance travelled by your food before it hits your plate is three thousand miles. How should we feel about the fact that the vegetables on our plate are better travelled than we are? Full of admiration? Jealous?

After all that travelling, how on earth do the suppliers get these vegetables to look so remarkably fresh on the supermarket shelf? I don't know about you, but I would look pretty jaded if I undertook a two-month haul from Peru to Europe in the back of a container lorry. The answer, of course, is that food suppliers have tricks up their sleeves to make the vegetables *appear* fresh. They pick them when they are unripe (and therefore not nutritionally complete) and spray them with preservatives so that they can survive the journey relatively unscathed. It doesn't matter that when you bring them home they will almost immediately turn to mush, because, of course, the shop will already have your money by then. So, yes, it's worth giving some thought to whether it's a good idea to buy food that has done a few laps of the globe. And, yes, it is just pure lunacy to buy vegetables that have been produced on the other side of the world when they could just as easily be produced here. It's even more important, however, to think about the impact that all this travelling has on the flavour and nutritional value of your food.

Here's an experiment that you could try. Try growing some carrots this year. Get a deep container, fill it with compost and then buy a packet of carrot seeds and sprinkle them into it. I promise you that you will be blown away by their colour, crunchiness and incredibly sweet flavour. While you are enjoying your harvest of carrots, go out and buy a packet of carrots in the shop – this is what I like to call 'death by comparison'. Once you have directly compared the taste, appearance and texture of the two in this way, you will find it very hard to go back to shop-bought carrots. And that's the point – it's the same with almost every other morsel of food that you will grow or rear on your Home Farm. It will always, ALWAYS, be of higher quality, and taste better than the shop-bought alternative. So what are we to do? Should we stop eating carrots when our own carrots are used up and we can't get our hands on any local, and preferably organic, alternatives? Well, yeah – probably. Seasonality truly is a double-edged sword. The painful side is that you can't eat every vegetable all year round. But the flipside? Well, the modern food chain has deprived us of the *joys* of seasonality, and these are considerable. The great moments of the growing year for any Home Farmer are the moments in which a favourite vegetable starts to harvest. The first crop of purple sprouting broccoli in March, the first new potato in June, the first tomato in July. These are payback moments that make all the hard work worthwhile.

Nature tells such a wonderful story with the bounty that she delivers during the year and we need to re-learn to trust that the food she produces is the best food for us *at that particular time of the year*. Think about it this way: in the summertime, she makes available succulent fruits like melons and tomatoes that have a high water content to help us to re-hydrate in warmer weather; in the autumn, the hedgerows are laden with berries that provide a boost to the immune system before the winter. These are only a couple of examples of the vast bank of wisdom that we need to get ourselves attuned to. Amazingly, the food we harvest in each season seems to fit the mood of that season. A coincidence? I think not. In the melancholic winter, we have an abundance of root crops to go into stews and stocks to warm the heart, and nature equips those hardy vegetables with the tough skins they need to survive at this time of the year. In the spring, full of excitement and anticipation, we see shoots of recovery and get the first greens of the year in the form of peas and beans. In the summer, the garden is resplendent and we have our first strawberries, tomatoes and wonderful salad crops that we can eat while we enjoy long, lazy garden evenings. In the autumn, there is a pause in the grower's year as we take time to enjoy the fruits of our labour during the abundant harvest – we enjoy those really ripe (not just *pretending* to be ripe) apples as well as squashes and pumpkins. In the context of this joyous culinary romp through the seasons, where exactly is the fun in being able to get any bland vegetable you like at any time of the year?

Our food chain, though highly advanced and efficient (arguably), churns out some really poor-quality product. Why? Because the focus of commercial food production is almost totally on yield, output, uniformity and profit. Taste, flavour, nutrition, variety – these things are scarcely given a thought. Tonnes and tonnes of the same vegetables are produced year-in, year-out on the same jaded patches of land (developments in agri-chemical technology mean that a single acre of land can produce 110,000 heads of lettuce in a single season). The soil becomes tired and emotional, and the vegetables produced become progressively less nutritious and flavoursome as time goes on. Fertilisers are required just to keep the whole show on the road. Diseases and pests build up in the soil and so the farmers have to use pesticides to keep them under control. It's a vicious circle of chemical dependency, with you and me sitting just outside the circle with our knives and forks at the ready. Scientists are already starting to worry that pests and diseases are building up resistance to the arsenal of insecticides, pesticides and fungicides that are blithely considered the saviours of modern agriculture – for example, the fungicides that were once effective in controlling the wheat disease, *Septoria tritici*, are now virtually useless and scientists have nothing in their back pockets to keep the more aggressive forms of the disease from destroying crops. It goes to show that the idea of working against nature and trying to suppress her desire to express herself is the ultimate folly.

And then there is the trust issue. I don't know about you, but I have no trust left whatsoever when it comes to commercial food producers (or if the truth be told, commercial entities of any kind) and this translates into an almost obsessive scepticism about the food that I buy. This is either completely OTT or just plain sensible, depending on your point of view. I reckon it's the latter, especially when you consider that scams, hustles, tricks and deceptions are endemic in our food chain. Every time you pick up produce in the supermarket you need to think really carefully about what exactly it is you are buying. We can never assume that producers are just nice guys who have our best interests at heart. They don't. They have profit in mind. And so they have been busy little bees, dreaming up increasingly elaborate ways to fool us into buying things – making things look or smell nicer than they really are and making things last longer than they really should.

In her book, *Not on the Label,* the *Guardian*'s consumer affairs correspondent, Felicity Lawrence, talks about 'formed' ham. As you know, a pig has just two hams – it's basically the top of its back legs – and it is by far the most coveted cut of the animal. According to Lawrence, a lot of the supermarket and deli-counter ham does not, in fact, come from this part of the pig, but is 'formed' from other, cheaper parts – for example, muscle meat from the leg bones. These cheap cuts of meat are then put into a giant machine, rather like a cement mixer, which contains a solution of water, sugars, preservatives, flavourings and other additives. This process dissolves an amino acid, called myosin, in the muscle fibres, so the meat becomes sticky and can then be put into ham-shaped moulds – it comes out of these moulds looking like a single piece of meat. Sometimes the producers even go to the trouble of sticking on a layer of fat around the edge to make it look authentic. You really couldn't make this stuff up, could you?

A friend of mine told me that he visited an apple farm in the UK one time and he climbed up on a large truck filled with apples, just to have a look; he was about to grab an apple to taste it when this guy started running towards him, gesticulating wildly. My friend was pretty annoyed – after all, he had paid to get in and here was this guy giving out to him for taking a single apple! But the guy wasn't interested in petty apple theft at all – he was actually trying to prevent my friend from poisoning himself. The apples were about to leave the farm bound for a very well-known multinational supermarket chain and they had just been sprayed with a chemical, presumably one that would help prolong their shelf-life. 'I wear a mask when we're spraying them,' he told my friend. 'So it's probably not a good idea to eat them just yet.'

If you've grown a crop of apples yourself (or anything else, for that matter), you will know that storage is a difficult proposition. Apples have the annoying tendency to rot and they start to lose nutritional value as soon as you pick them. It's the same with most fruit and vegetables. To counteract this problem, producers and retailers use chemicals like 1-methylcyclopropene (known as 1-MCP) to block the naturally occurring ripening gases that fruit and vegetables produce, which causes them to soften and ultimately rot. This, then, is how we have apples on our supermarket shelves all year round – chemicals like 1-MCP can keep an apple 'fresh' for up to a year.

Scientists have come up with another neat trick to prolong the life of perishable produce – they pack it in a specially designed bag or pillow called Modified Atmosphere Packaging (or MAP) which creates a rarefied atmosphere in which the produce is stored. Oxygen levels within the bag are reduced to just 3 percent (regular 'air' contains 21 percent oxygen) and CO^2 levels are raised correspondingly – the overall affect is to retard the level of deterioration and discolouration of the produce. A perhaps unintended side-effect, however, is that the process strips the fruit and vegetables of their nutrition. The *British Journal of Nutrition* found that packaging vegetables this way strips produce of vitamin C, vitamin E and other micro-nutrients. The consumer rights magazine *Which?* found that sliced, chilled runner beans stored in MAPs contain nearly 90 percent less vitamin C than fresh runner beans.

I don't know about you, but I don't want to eat 'formed' ham; I want to eat proper ham. I don't want to eat fruit and vegetables that have been stored in a specially designed oxygen-free 'tent' so that they last longer. I don't want to eat an apple that's a year old but pretending to be younger. I don't know what's in 1-MCP and what impact it could have on my health, but I would prefer to forego the nutritional value of an apple-a-day all year round rather than eat an apple sprayed with chemicals. I don't want to eat produce that has been boiled, irradiated, sprayed with additives and preservatives, or washed in chlorine to destroy bacteria. I don't want to eat eggs from chickens that have had stuff added to their feed to make the yolks yellow. And, most of all, I would really, really like it if the supermarket had the good grace to inform me if an apple they are selling has been sprayed with chemicals, or that the ham in my sandwich is not ham at all, but reprocessed leg meat, or that the chicken breasts have been injected with water and animal proteins to make them look bigger than they really are. This all comes back to the trust issue – these examples of shady dealings and crooked practices are just the things we know about. *What else are they up to?*

Amidst all this bad news, there is, thankfully, some *great* news. The problems with our food chain are enormous and highly complex.

But, unlike many other enormous and highly complex global problems, there is a very simple fix. GROW THE FOOD YOURSELF. Home-grown produce addresses all of the problems mentioned in the last few pages – every single one of them. Home-grown produce will not be sprayed or messed with, and since you have control over every facet of its production, you can trust the grub a hundred percent. If you practise some very simple crop rotation (more on this topic in Chapter 5) you won't need any pesticides or fertilisers, and the resulting produce will be the tastiest, most nutritious food you or your family have ever eaten. There won't be any wasteful packaging to throw away into landfill and, if you grow it yourself, there probably won't be any wastage, full stop – many vegetables such as carrots, leeks, spinach and parsnips can be left in the ground until you're ready to eat them and, in any case, after nurturing a vegetable plant from seed, you are not likely to want to waste a single morsel. Home Farming comes with genuine, in-built, pre-loaded seasonality – the food you eat from your own garden will always be seasonal, so you know you are eating the vegetables and fruit that nature intends at that time of the year. And food miles? Well, our vegetable plot is about thirty paces from the kitchen, so I guess that's pretty much as close to zero food miles as you can get. Every time you tuck into a plate of your own, home-grown chow, you can congratulate yourself on your impeccably low carbon footprint.

That's the beauty of turning your garden into a Home Farm – it is such an utterly *proactive* thing to do. It's easy to feel overwhelmed and powerless about the world's problems – climate change, global warming, health scares, terrorism, economic woes – because there's practically nothing that any of us can do about these issues. The leaders of the world's most powerful countries come together once or twice a year, closeted behind security fences to keep the baying mobs out, and they decide on policy that can make our lives a misery or a pleasure, depending on their mood. There's precious little we can do about it. But, thankfully, there *is* something we can do about food security and food quality. We can do it right now, or later today, or tomorrow – stick a seed in the ground and watch it grow. Growing your own is not the preserve of any one social class. It's not the pre-serve of country people or city people. It's accessible to anyone with the motivation and access to even the smallest patch of ground. You would probably be amazed if I told you that most experts agree that a vegetable plot of 150 square metres (that's 15m x 10m) would pro-duce enough food to feed an entire family, all of the time. In Chapter 11 you will meet some *urban* farmers – people growing in small, and sometimes tiny, urban gardens who are, in many cases, more self-sufficient than we are here on our rural acre. So go on, take back control of the food that is going into your body. Become truly inde-pendent and take a rebellious step back from a food system that is inherently unstable, unhealthy and immoral.

One of the questions I am frequently asked is whether growing your own food is time-consuming. It's tempting just to say, 'Of course it is', and leave it at that. It takes time to plan a vegetable garden and, initially at any rate, it takes time to execute it. Some of the work can be back-breaking, laborious, even tedious. Growing vegetables is not something that you do once – it is a year-round, year-in and year-out affair. I have been asked in interviews to try and quantify exactly

how many minutes or hours a week we spend growing vegetables –
and it's always a question I try to dodge if I can because, of course, if
I say 'five hours a week' or 'four days a month', or something like
that, then at least some of the people listening are going to think, *Well
now, I don't have time for that! Don't you know how busy I am?*
Whether my answer to the time question is palatable or not depends
entirely on the person listening. If I say that we spend ten minutes a
week at it, and you hate spending time with a spade, then you are
likely to think it is too much. If I say that we spend four hours a week
at it, and you love your spade so much you would happily take it to
bed with you at night, well then, you might think that is way too little.

Suffice to say that some times of the year are busier than others.
There are usually a few large projects to get done over the year,
which might take a weekend (like a major bout of sowing, weeding,
harvesting or manuring, for example) and after that you're really just
spending time each day or every other day keeping the whole thing
ticking over. For us, the growing year kicks off in earnest in February
with the first sowings, and is in full swing until at least November.
You could quite happily find things to do in the depths of winter too,
if you're so inclined, but we tend to take a bit of a breather from
growing during December and January.

There are loads of ways for the savvy Home Farmer to reduce the
chore quotient. Raised beds, for example (see Chapter 10) are increasingly popular because you don't have vast tracts of open land getting
overrun with weeds (weeding really is one of those necessary evil
chores in the veggie plot that is almost never fun). We have gravel
paths in between our raised beds, which keeps the whole thing looking
neat and tidy, but, most importantly, weed-free t. Psychologically, it

just seems less upsetting to have to weed one raised bed as opposed to an area of open ground. In any case, digging is a lot less in favour these days. It used to be that you had the dig the living daylights out of your veggie patch every year – and a stooped back was like a badge of honour among vegetable growers – but most growers that I know now prefer the 'no-dig' approach. The no-dig movement is made up of a rather unlikely coalition of really lazy growers, like me, and cutting-edge science, which suggests that walking on soil when you dig it compacts the soil and makes it impossible to grow stuff in. Therefore, the advice of the no-dig gospel is that you shouldn't dig at all – yippee! – instead, pile on lots of rotted organic matter in the winter, which will then be dragged down by unwitting earthworms who are essentially doing the digging for you (only really slowly, one mouthful at a time). With raised beds, you don't walk on the soil at all (just turn the soil over with a fork each year), which means it never gets compacted and an additional benefit is that it doesn't matter what type of soil you have in your garden, because you basically get to bring in whatever soil you like from outside. Our house is basically built in a bog and our soil is terribly wet and spongy – but we have built about ten raised beds and brought in tonnes of topsoil, which we have then enriched over time by adding manure and compost annually.

We also do a lot of mulching (putting a compost or a manure 'dressing' around the base of plants) throughout the year, which has the twin benefits of reducing the amount of watering we have to do as it reduces surface evaporation, but also the amount of weeding, since it deprives weeds of the sunlight they need to take off. The mulch gradually rots down and incorporates into the soil, further enhancing its quality. There is still work to do, of course – like everything else in life, anything that's worth having takes a little bit of time and effort. At the very least, you have to take the seed from the packet and place it in the soil; then you will need to look after it and water it (though lack of water hasn't been a problem round these parts for a long time) and, of course, you have to pull it from the ground when it's ready. But nature does most of the hard work – all you are really doing is loading up the arrow in your bow and pointing it in the right direction. This, then, is why I always find that question about how time-consuming (or not) vegetable growing is, to be so perplexing. To compartmentalise things this way is such a typically depressing, modern approach. Growing your own food is not something that you can break down into a chunk of time per week like that. It is not a chore that you can schedule in on your BlackBerry or shoe-horn in between the time you allot to watching your favourite TV soap and doing the ironing. It's a way of life, and if you love doing it, it is no chore at all. There's an old saying about work which is apt here – if you find a job that you love, you will never work a day in your life. The same applies to growing your own vegetables. If you hate it (don't worry, you won't), you will resent every minute you have to spend doing it. But if you love it, then you will happily spend a day up to your neck in muck getting a bed ready for planting – and you will rue the time you have to spend away from your beloved patch.

Looking back on the past growing year, there's one thing that strikes me as particularly interesting. At the start of the year it was just the two of us, armed only with our enthusiasm and gamely battling against our own lack of expertise. But gradually, over the course of the twelve months, we ended up quite by chance (or was it by design?) surrounding ourselves with fellow Home Farmers. I don't know whether this is because there are more people interested in the whole idea than there were twelve months ago (I suspect there are), or whether we're getting more sociable in our advancing years. Perhaps it's a bit of both. It started in July with the courses we started to run here in our garden for people interested in keeping some hens, and we began to realise just how wonderful and useful it was to talk to like-minded folk about their food-production experiences. Later in the year, we got together with other growers in GIY Waterford (you can read about it in Chapter 9), which basically replicates the camaraderie that you get on allotment sites. We meet once a month with other enthusiastic amateur growers like ourselves and talk about growing and rearing things. We exchange ideas and swap produce. We listen to and learn from each other. We make friends. The GIY network has helped to take the 'self' out of our 'self-sufficiency' and our isolation has slowly ebbed away. We are starting to get to know more and more people in the area (and beyond) who are growing their own food and we are discovering that there are lots and lots of us. By the end of the year, we had almost totally emerged from our splendid isolation and in the chapter on December (Chapter 12) you can read about *meitheals* (pronounced 'meh-hills'), an Irish word for 'working gangs' – in this context, groups of us going around to each others' gardens to help out on big vegetable-growing projects.

The amount that we have learned from our fellow growers is astonishing. We now know people whom we can call up or visit if we have a question, and so the projects we have taken on in the Home

Farm this year have seemed far less scary – there is always someone who knows someone who has done it all before. Above all, we have made friends with people who share our interests and our passions – who don't look at us strangely when we rave about a particular variety of potato or the unparalleled flavour of our tomatoes. They seem to understand. Maybe we all sought each other out to prove to ourselves that there are other people out there pursuing this lifestyle too and that we're not alone (or mad). In these rather depressing times, there's something very, very comforting about the idea of a *meitheal*, and of all the things that have happened this past year, that was by far and away the most exciting. So, without further ado, let's get going on a journey through the Home Farmer's year. I hope you find it interesting and enjoyable and that this book will be a good thing in your life.

Michael Kelly
Dunmore East, Co. Waterford
spring 2009

A NOTE ON THE SEASONS

One of the most exhilarating things about Home Farming is that you hitch your wagon, so to speak, to the venerable rhythm of the seasons – from the barrenness of winter to the hope and renewal of spring, the lushness and colour of summer, the abundance of autumn, and finally back to the slumber of winter again. You have a choice about how you feel about this relentless cycle of life: you can choose to be terrified, or you can take immense comfort from it. Personally, I love the fact that the seasons are so *all-encompassing*. They are quite obviously happening 'out there' in your veggie patch, but their moods are also reflected 'in here' – in your heart, your mind and your soul.

It is, of course, nature herself who ultimately decides *when* those seasons transition from one to the next, but down through the ages mankind has gamely tried to apply chunks of time (in the form of calendar months) to the task of defining when a season begins and ends. 'In month X, it shall be season Y,' we proclaim, attempting to be lord of all we survey. Mother Nature smiles to herself and thinks: *We shall see.*

There is little consensus among the denizens of the northern hemisphere about when the seasons start. Many countries use what are called the 'meteorological' seasons, where spring begins on 1 March, summer on 1 June, autumn on 1 September and winter on 1 December. The 'astronomical' seasons are broadly similar, but are based on the dates of the equinoxes and solstices: so, spring begins on 20 March (vernal equinox), summer on 21 June (summer solstice), autumn on 22 September (autumn equinox) and winter on 21 December (winter solstice).

Just because we enjoy a bit of divilment, the Irish calendar (which is based on the seasons of the ancient Celts), ploughs a lonely furrow, with a completely different system that is a month earlier than those above. And so, in Ireland spring traditionally begins not in March, but on 1 February, with Lá Feabhra (February Day), also known as St Brigid's Day; summer begins with Lá Bealtaine (May Day); autumn begins on 1 August with Lá Lúnasa; while winter arrives in November with Lá Samhna (November Day).

From a Home Farmer's perspective, there are arguments for and against using each of the different systems as your guide: for example, September seems to me to be the natural month to begin autumn, whereas in the Celtic system autumn begins in August, which just seems plain weird – I always think of August as high summer. On the other hand, there is a strong argument that February should be seen as spring, as in the Irish system, since it is a month when things start to happen in the garden, the first seeds are sown and activity levels start to ramp up. So it doesn't really feel like winter.

In the debate over which system to use to lay out the chapters of this book, my heart ultimately ruled my head (no surprise there, really, it usually does) and I opted to go with the Celt's way of doing things. I reckon it would be just plain rude (never mind potentially bad karma) to ignore the ancient wisdom laid down by our ancestors. I suppose, in the end, it doesn't really matter what system you use – the cycle of the seasons advances in its own sweet time, anyway. If you decide, on the basis of a seasonal calendar, that it's spring in February and therefore time to plant out all your little seedlings, nature will probably decide to humble you a little by sending a few nights of frost. So the best advice is to maintain some flexibility on the issue and be guided by your senses. If it feels too cold to be spring, then it's probably still winter. The chapters are laid out as follows:

CHAPTER 1 – LATE WINTER, JANUARY

CHAPTER 2 – EARLY SPRING, FEBRUARY

CHAPTER 3 – MID-SPRING, MARCH

CHAPTER 4 – LATE SPRING, APRIL

CHAPTER 5 – EARLY SUMMER, MAY

CHAPTER 6 – MID-SUMMER, JUNE

CHAPTER 7 – LATE SUMMER, JULY

CHAPTER 8 – EARLY AUTUMN, AUGUST

CHAPTER 9 – MID-AUTUMN, SEPTEMBER

CHAPTER 10 – LATE AUTUMN, OCTOBER

CHAPTER 11 – EARLY WINTER, NOVEMBER

CHAPTER 12 – MID-WINTER, DECEMBER

This book was written in 2009 and based, largely, on our experiences in 2008, but it is meant to represent any typical year on the Home Farm. I stole in a few stories from 2009 where I felt they were appropriate or necessary (it's my book, so I can do what I like!).

1

THE ATTENTION-
GRABBING OPENER

LATE WINTER: JANUARY

the hungry gap – spinach and chard – springsumautwin – kohlrabi

If you want to blame someone for the fact that this book opens with the month when there is practically nothing happening in the garden, blame Mother Nature. Not the publisher, and certainly not the author. It was Mother Nature who inserted this fundamental flaw into the design of the grower's year, not I. This book completely abandons the rules of sensible, profitable book writing, which typically dictates that you start with an attention-grabbing opener and end with a thrilling finale. Instead, this is a book that starts and finishes with months when there is very little of interest happening and has its exciting denouement (if harvesting can be considered an exciting denouement) taking place somewhere near the middle. Dear, oh dear. Let's hope, for all our sakes (okay, mainly for my sake), that it's not like one of those movies you watch that presents the stunning climax and then inexplicably drags on for another twenty unnecessary minutes, wrapping up various minor plot lines.

Sure, the grower's calendar in this and other books will tell you that there's plenty that you can be doing to busy yourself at this time of the year – and if you are a certain type of person there assuredly is. But most, if not all, of them will be ridiculous things that sensible people never really bother with, like sharpening or cleaning their tools, getting the muck off their wheelbarrow wheels, hosing down paths or putting their seed packets in alphabetical order (okay, I have done the last one). These are, I confess, at best, preparatory tasks and, at worst, just a way to pass the time until the real work starts next month. Cleaning your spade has its uses, of course – it will almost certainly make your spade last a little longer, for starters, but it won't put food on the table in any direct sense. (And if you're like me you will probably have a whole garageful of broken, rusting spades in varying states of disrepair, so you're unlikely to be the type of person who will go to the bother of cleaning your spades in winter anyway.)

It doesn't take much for me to dump myself into a bout of self-doubt at the best of times, but at this time of the year, in particular, I always find myself questioning my abilities as a Home Farmer. On the face of it, I know that the lack of bounty from the garden is not my fault – we've already agreed that we are blaming Mother Nature for that – but still, I am a tortured, introspective soul, and so in January I can be found wandering listlessly around my garden, poking at my kale plants with a stick and feeling mightily depressed that there's nothing much worth eating. And, of course, wondering: Is there more I could have done? Are there things I could be growing if only I knew a little more? Should I give it all up and find another hobby, like model aeroplane-making or collecting paperclips or philately? I find that it helps at this time of the year to visit other gardens, especially the professional ones, just to remind myself that other people's gardens are idle at this time of the year too. Though it's not nice to take comfort from other people's misfortune (and that is, after all, what an empty vegetable bed is – a terrible, terrible misfortune), it always cheers me up immensely to discover that I'm not alone.

From this juncture – the miserable affair that is January, with its depressingly short days and insipid, watery sun – it seems like a long time since the fecundity of summer and autumn, when a month could pass without a trip to the dastardly supermarket (and even then it was just to buy the basics, like olive oil, butter and flour). Back then, in those gloriously abundant days, because of the bounty from the Home Farm, we were spending almost nothing on vegetables, fruit or meat. Fast forward just a couple of months and we are officially on the dregs of last year's harvest and full of resentment at being reliant on the supermarket again. In times past, they had a lovely expression to describe the interminable length of time between the end of last year's produce and the onset of this year's harvest – it was called 'the hungry gap' and it was so called because, of course, back then people actually went hungry unless they were sufficiently skilled in growing and storing to make sure the previous year's harvest lasted until the start of the following year's. (Incidentally, there's a variety of kale that's actually called Hungry Gap, such is the ability of this unsung hero to produce harvest at the time of the year when nothing else seems to be bothered.)

I always think that the phrase 'hungry gap' is a great reminder of just how fragile life once was on this planet, and still is in some places. March is generally considered to be the hungry gap month, but our hungry gap tends to come earlier and last for longer because we aren't all that good at storing our produce *or* getting our crops going early enough – *or* growing things, for that matter! The idea of a hungry gap seems like a quaint concept now, of course, to us affluent (relatively speaking) westerners. At worst, the Home Farm's lack of produce in late winter is an inconvenience but very little else, and we should be thankful for that. But it means we have to go to the supermarket more than we would like to and we moan and grumble about the quality of vegetables on offer and wish that we had more skills in the garden to make our hungry gap shorter. But in the context of an *actual* hungry gap, these seem like incredibly whingy, comfortable concerns.

Aside from a quickly diminishing store of root vegetables, onions and the occasional rather uninspiring green vegetable like cabbage and that stalwart of the winter garden, perpetual spinach, we have almost no fresh vegetables left. Normally we would have at least some garlic hanging in braids somewhere, but our garlic crop failed miserably last year (I think because we planted it in soil that was too damp and most of it rotted), so we are faced with the ignominy of having to buy garlic, which readers of my first book may recall was the reason we got into this whole growing malarkey in the first place.

With all those doomed New Year's resolutions, scary credit-card bills and the fact that we are probably still carrying some excess Christmas weight around the midriff area (they call it frontal obesity now, the gits), January truly is the most miserable of months and I always think that it's a time for plenty of warming stews and casseroles. Thankfully, the vegetable plot will usually pitch in with some leftover root vegetables; the Danes call this *hygge* cooking, by the way – the word 'hygge' does not have a direct equivalent in English, but it hints at a warmth and comfort that we derive from these one-pot, slow-cooked winter meals. We have a large container filled with sand in our garage in which we stored the remains of our root crops back in November, and in January we take great solace from being able to pluck an odd carrot or a nice beetroot from the sand. It's not quite the same as plucking a vegetable from the soil, but it's a damn fine substitute. I love that ritual of carefully rummaging in the container to see what you can uncover (there's no great mystery since it's almost always a carrot, but you catch my drift) – it's almost like dunking for apples at Halloween, only not as wet or silly. Having selected three or four nice carrots I rush them back inside and rinse them under the tap. I get all excited seeing the glow of bright orange gradually appearing as the sand washes down the sink – far more excited than I should, but hey, it's January and with so little happening in the garden, even the most subtle events are cause for celebration. Unfortunately, we used up all of our pumpkins before Christmas, but there are some winter squashes, such as butternut, left on a shelf in the utility room and these too are a rare treat at this time of the year, their beautiful orange flesh revealed after hacking off the tough outer skin.

The freezer provides occasional items of interest too. We still have a good stock of meat from last year's pigs and chickens and it is at this time of the year that any fruit and vegetable processing work carried out last harvest pays off in spades. We blanched and froze quite an amount of celery, chilli-peppers, peppers, peas and beans back in late summer and early autumn, and we also made up individual portions of tomato sauce and froze them too. All of that was a complete chore at the time, of course, but it was done in the knowledge that leaner months would surely come and we are mighty glad of it now. If you're not feeling in a *hygge* sort of mood and can put up with some Mediterranean type fare in mid-January, then a pasta dish made with a tomato sauce, chilli-peppers and broad beans will brighten up your day immensely. Eating a broad bean in January that you can recall shelling last autumn (not the *individual* broad bean, of course) is like a little culinary time machine that transports you back to the heady days of high summer.

The cupboard in which we keep our chutneys, preserves, jams and pickles is becoming more and more empty too. During the autumn, there is a constant competitiveness to our chutney-making. Mrs Kelly makes a fine green tomato chutney with tomatoes that didn't ripen or that fell to the ground. I make a more standard chutney, which uses up gluts of courgettes. Because the crop of unripened tomatoes is very small, her chutney is like a product made from a rare consignment of truffles – being reliant as it is on an entirely finite core ingredient, it is always much sought after. I like to think that my chutney has its moments too, but it's difficult to get too excited about something that is made from abundant, half-metre long courgettes that would otherwise be fed to the pigs. Mrs Kelly is unbearable about how wonderful her chutney is and she is spurred on by family members who each year put in a request for a jar as a Christmas present, as if it were some sort of rare culinary wonder. Anyway, in this context, it is perhaps not surprising that the green tomato chutney is now but a distant memory and all we are left with is my courgette chutney – it may lack a little in taste, but it is, at least, prodigious.

We are on to shop-bought marmalades and jams by now (not a terrible sin, I guess, since you can buy wonderful artisan and homemade varieties in the shops), but it won't be long till the Seville oranges are available and I can make a balls of making marmalade, as I do each year. Pickled cucumber might not be everyone's cup of tea, but I like the old-fashioned simplicity of pickling and it was a great way to use up excess cucumbers back during the height of summer. We spent some time in Germany when we were young and interesting, and perhaps we picked up a penchant for pickled cucumber there – either way, we're pretty much alone in thinking that it tastes nice, so there are quite a few jars of the stuff left. Incidentally, I was stunned to see a small tub of organic pickled cucumber in a shop recently for €4, which gave me a different impression of the giant unopened jars of it sitting unused in the back of our cupboard. Do the maths on this one – €4 will get you a packet of cucumber seeds, and each packet contains four or five seeds; since each plant might produce up to thirty cucumbers you would have a total yield from your €4 of 150 cucumbers!

You can get round the hungry gap in this day and age by shopping, of course, but it's not a satisfying thing to do when you are used to eating your own vegetables. When I pluck the last carrot from the sand and revert to buying carrots in the supermarket, I am neither grateful that they are available nor impressed with their taste – invariably I just feel disgusted with myself for not growing enough. That's the bind that we Home Farmers find ourselves in. Growing your own food is highly addictive because you end up sowing more and more each year to reduce the length of the hungry gap – once you've tasted your own tomatoes, if you have to go back to buying the Dutch ones you will only do so with a heavy heart and an unrequited palate. So, rather than an all-out re-embracing of the commercial food chain, we continually look for ways to get around the hungry gap instead.

For example, we have tried to change our attitude towards some vegetables to which we have had a lifelong aversion. They say that when you sit down to plan what you are going to grow in your garden, you should always steer clear of vegetables that you don't like to eat. The argument goes that if you hate cauliflower, for example, you are unlikely to enjoy the home-grown variety any more than the shop-bought. There's a certain amount of logic to this, of course, but it's not a hundred percent foolproof advice. Some vegetables are just easier to grow than others and sometimes, sod's law, the ones that are easiest to grow are likely to be the ones you don't really like to eat. If that happens, it's only right and proper to give them another try. If they are easy to grow, it would be foolish to ignore them. On the other side of this hard-luck story lies the fact that some of the most difficult vegetables to grow may well be the ones that you most like to eat. We've had all manner of hassle growing parsnips, for example, which is a huge pity because the parsnip is arguably one of the tastiest and most useful vegetables going and has suffered considerably from the rigours of mass production and mono-cropping.

Ease of growing has forced me to take another look at some vegetables that, frankly, I've never had much time for, which, I guess, is a triumph of practicality over fussy taste-buds. Thankfully, some of them have proved quite surprising in the kitchen and I've found that the traditional method of cooking has been the problem all along, and not the vegetables themselves. Cabbage and spinach are good cases in point. When I was a kid I had a friend who used to eat boiled cabbage all the time and the smell of his house stayed with me all my life – the guy himself actually smelt of cabbage, come to think of it, though maybe I am imagining that. Then in school in my teens, cabbage was a regular feature on the refectory menu – great, big, steaming, smelly piles of it alongside the 'dog food' that they euphemistically called shepherd's pie. Cabbage does smell awful, but only if you boil the arse out of it, which was the only way it was cooked. Finely sliced and then briefly fried or steamed with some garlic and butter (and perhaps some chopped nuts thrown in, for good measure), it's another dish entirely. You're unlikely ever to really relish it if you've hated it all your life, but you may well be able to convince yourself to just get on with it and appreciate the fact that it's *still in season* when very little else is.

Perpetual spinach is bountiful all year round too – which, I guess, is why it's called perpetual and not occasional – and we've become quite fond of spinach in our house, especially when we use the baby leaves for salads or omelettes and give larger leaves an Asian feel with the addition of a splash of sesame oil or soya sauce. You can also use the stalks from larger leaves in a stir-fry. Some people reckon that regular spinach has a better flavour than perpetual spinach – I can't say that I really notice much of a difference and perpetual spinach has the advantage of being much easier to grow since it's less inclined to bolt (where a plant spoils your intentions for it by going to seed). We had a bit of a disaster some years back with a crop of regular spinach that we planted too early and the whole lot went to seed, producing lots of lovely flowers, but absolutely nothing worth eating. Perpetual spinach is also one of those unfussy vegetables with regard to soil – it's a doughty survivor and will do well pretty much anywhere. Because it's harvestable pretty much all year round, it provides you with those all important greens in the winter and spring when the larder and garden are depressingly empty and you might be tempted to head for your local retailing behemoth to buy some out-of-season vegetables that have been flown half-way round the world.

Interestingly (well, I think so), perpetual spinach and its sister

vegetable, Swiss chard, are related to the beetroot, which explains why they are sometimes collectively called 'leaf beet' – a source of confusion for some (okay, me). We ordered chard seeds a few years ago and when I received them, I called the supplier because it said 'leaf beet' on the packet. I said, in a haughty manner, 'Kind Sir, I will be returning this product to you, for it is incorrect!' Calmly and with considerable patience, the man informed me that leaf beet and rainbow chard are, in fact, one in the same thing. Ouch. To add to the confusion, chard is sometimes known as 'seakale beet' and perpetual spinach is often called 'perpetual beet' – I know, it's ridiculous. Anyway, though they are related, leaf beet and beetroot obviously differ in one very fundamental way – the beetroot is essentially harvested for its root, while the leaf beet is harvested for its leaves.

Though the naming convention may well be complex, growing them, mercifully, is not. Very little can go wrong with either chard or spinach and you can basically treat them as one vegetable with the same growing regime. The things that can really tend to annoy you about growing other vegetables (eg diseases, stubbornness, seasonality) just won't be an issue here. They are also 'cut-and-come-again' crops – a wonderful treat, which means that you can harvest away on them as you need to and they will produce new leaves to replace the ones you have taken away. Chard is undoubtedly the more beautiful of the two (perpetual spinach is not the most attractive-looking plant, it must be said), producing beautiful red, yellow or even purple stalks. It is, in fact, so eye-catching that lots of people grow it in pots as a sort of edible ornament. A large pot containing a mixture of spinach and chard, sown in the summer, will provide a good crop of winter greens. I have to admit that I'm not a huge fan of chard leaves when they get too big; they are, however, handy for adding to pasta sauces and so on, disappearing down to practically nothing and improving the flavour of the sauce immeasurably. You can freeze chard leaves raw, incidentally, and then use them for this purpose as you need them. Baby chard leaves are nice and tender and they taste good raw – they also look really cool in salads.

Spinach is more conventional looking, but is lent a considerable *cachet* by the fact that it made Popeye's muscles bulge. I'm always sceptical about the lofty claims made about so-called 'superfoods', and spinach has had more lofty claims made on its behalf than most. It is accredited with everything from decreasing your chances of cardiovascular disease to causing outbreaks of peace in wartorn regions of the world. I was thinking of writing a book called *Spinach – the Food that Made Me Rich*, just to see would it sell. I bet it would. Anyway, when any publication tells me that a food will change my life, I always take it with a large grain of salt (the spurious claim, not the food). As you will see from Paula Mee's nutritional information below, however, spinach *is* a nutritional powerhouse. It is also incredibly prolific – a 3 metre row of perpetual spinach plants will churn out a whopping 3kg of leaves. The most important time to sow it is in July and August so that it will keep you in greens over winter and into spring the following year. We don't see it as being hugely important to have either spinach or chard cropping in the summer months because, quite frankly, there are far nicer things to eat then. Both plants are so hardy and robust, they don't even get upset with us for relying on them so heavily when there's very little else growing and then dropping them like hot cakes as soon as some nicer produce comes along.

PAULA MEE'S NUTRITION BITES: SPINACH AND CHARD

Popeye was right about spinach being good for you and there's little doubt that his robust immune system must have helped him sock it to Sea Hag and Bruto! Mind you, I couldn't recommend eating it from a tin and it's not particularly good for muscular forearms either! It is, however, high in vitamins A and C, and in folate, a water-soluble B vitamin; it is also a source of vitamin E and the minerals calcium, iron and magnesium.

Leafy vegetables, such as spinach, are also rich in lutein and zeaxanthin, which are two antioxidants called carotenoids. High intakes of these protective phytochemicals may reduce the risk of age-related macular degeneration, the leading cause of blindness in people aged over fifty.

Chard is like two vegetables for the price of one – the stalks can be cooked like asparagus spears and the dark leaves can be steamed or stir-fried. It is high in vitamin C, folate and beta-carotene. Both vitamin A and beta-carotene are important nutrients for healthy eyes and vision. Beta-carotene has also been the subject of extensive research regarding its cancer-fighting properties and its potential to prevent oxygen-based damage to cells and tissues. Beta-carotene may help to protect against certain forms of cancer since it belongs to the family of phytonutrients known as carotenoids.

Nutrition per Portion (80g):

Vegetable	Calories	Fat (g)	Salt (g)	Saturated Fat (g)
Spinach	20	0.6	0.28	0.1
Chard	15	0.2	0.43	0

As for most vegetables, we sow the little seeds for spinach and chard in modules or pots and then transplant them when they are big enough to handle, spacing them about 15cm–20cm apart. Leaf beets don't mind a little bit of shade but will appreciate some well rotted manure being put in the ground before you plant them. ('Well-rotted manure' is one of those maddeningly subjective phrases that vegeta-ble-growing books are usually littered with, but in this case it's vague for good reason: how long it takes for manure to rot down depends very much on where you store it, ambient temperature and how much of it you have; the more you have, the quicker it will rot. Six months is probably a good rule of thumb, but if there are wood shavings mixed in with the manure, it can take up to a year. Perhaps a better way to judge it is to use your senses: if it smells of anything more than 'earthi-ness', it's not ready; if you can see straw or hay in it, it's not ready. To help the rotting process, pile the manure into a loose heap and cover it with old carpet to keep the worst of the weather off it.)

We usually do a sowing of leaf beets in the polytunnel as well as outside, which gives us a bit of variation in terms of harvest time. Per-petual spinach doesn't seem to mind the oppressive heat and dryness of the summer tunnel as much as true spinach would, and the resulting winter leaves are more tender than the ones growing outside.

Though it takes some time to get going, the leaves will be ready to start eating after about two months and you will be harvesting from a single plant for a year or longer. Once it has taken off, you can cut the leaves as you need them – because it's a cut-and-come-again vegeta-ble, there's usually a handy array of leaves at different levels of maturity so you can pop down to the plot and grab a few leaves for a salad or bigger ones for cooking. It doesn't store well, so it's easiest just to cut as much as you need for that particular meal.

It's important with spinach not to pull too hard when you are har-vesting – we have found the best way is to hold a bunch of the leaves in your hand and cut the stems with a knife or secateurs, leaving some of the stem behind so that it will re-grow. It's a good idea to start taking the leaves from the outside first and work your way into the centre of the plant (though, to be really honest, we usually just grab the leaves that look the tastiest, paying little attention to where they are being taken from). I could probably write a bit about how to look after leaf beet while it's growing, but it would be entirely disingenuous of me to do so since we don't look after the plants at all (apart from watering them) and they seem to do fine. Three cheers for leaf beet!

Spinach and Lentil Soup

Spinach and lentil soup may sound yuck, but it tastes great and I defy you not to feel glowing with health after eating it. Whenever I hear the word 'lentil' my inner meat eater panics, sensing that vegetarianism is being foisted upon me. It immediately sends a rush of blood to my cheeks – to make me blush and look ridiculous – and serves as a reminder of who's wearing the pants in our relationship! After some delicate negotiations, we have agreed that I will have lentils once or twice a month, and this is one of the recipes signed off on. This recipe, from my friend Eunice Power, hails from Lebanon, where it is typically eaten in the winter months and particularly during the holy month of Ramadan. The lemon juice gives it a lovely fresh, zesty taste.

Ingredients:

    250g/8oz green lentils (don't tell your inner meat eater)
    1.5 litres / 2.5 pints veg stock
    1 onion, finely chopped
    250g/8oz potatoes – peeled and chopped into cubes
    250g/8oz spinach – roughly chopped
    1 tbsp olive oil
    4 cloves of garlic, finely chopped

1 tsp ground cumin

5 tbsp lemon juice

salt, pepper

Put the lentils and stock in a large saucepan and bring to the boil. Add the onion, potato, spinach and oil. Simmer for 15 mins. Then add the garlic, cumin and about half the lemon juice. Cover and simmer slowly for 20 minutes. Add the remaining lemon juice and season to taste (go easy on salt – if you have used a good quality stock cube, it will be salty enough). Thin the soup with some water if you need to. Ladle into warm bowls and serve with brown or focaccia bread.

If you want to serve spinach as an accompanying vegetable to meat, here's a way to turn it from 'worthy yet dull' to spectacular. Boil 200g of spinach per person for literally a few seconds only. This is really important – do not be tempted to go down the Irish mammy route and let it boil for ten days. Drain and set aside. Grind ¼ cup of sesame seeds with a pestle and mortar. To the ground seeds, add 2 tablespoons of soy sauce, 2 tablespoons of water and 2 teaspoons of sugar. Mix them well. Pour this mixture over little bundles of spinach and sprinkle with sesame seeds.

The format of this book – the gentle progression from month to month as a metaphor for the joys of seasonality – belies the fact that since we started the Home Farm, Ireland hasn't really had a standard four-season climate at all. Instead, we've had a mono-season, which I suggest we call 'springsumautwin'. Springsumautwin (it's actually surprisingly easy to say when you practise it a little) is characterised by mild and wet conditions and lasts for twelve whole months. It's mild and wet in the season we once called winter, and it's mild and wet in the season we once called summer too. It has the upside of being entirely predictable, but the downside of being utterly miserable, all of the time. From a growing perspective it has its ups and downs too – the lack of frost is a good thing early in the season when you are trying to get seeds moving and, of course, the abundance of water falling from the sky in warmer months means that you don't have to bother watering things (a considerable time-saver it must be said). But the disadvantages outweigh the advantages, to my mind – it's just so profoundly depressing.

All of which explains why it is so exciting when we get any bit (however small) of frost, ice or snow. It feels almost rebellious since it is in defiance of global warming and in strict contravention of the meteorological rules laid down by springsumautwin. Snow, ice, frost and generally cold conditions are both friend and foe to the Home Farmer. They are 'friend' so long as they come at the right time – you want them to arrive in the winter months of November, December, January as they help to break down the soil (which means it has a nice, crumbly texture, perfect for spring sowing) and cleanse it of any nasty infections that may be residing in it. There are even some vegetables, like garlic, for example, that love a good frost. But frosts are

no friend of yours if they arrive later in spring when you are about to get started with sowing things outside. A bad frost at the wrong time will play havoc with those pioneering spring vegetables, like your early spuds, peas and beans.

This morning I awoke to find a covering of, wait for it, actual snow on the ground. About 8cm of the stuff. Trapped in the unremittingly tight grasp of springsumautwin, snow is not something that we have seen much of round these parts, so it was an exciting development. I was out walking with the dogs in the fields and the snow was blowing into my face, stinging my cheeks. Though the conditions were, indeed, inclement, I found myself not miserable, but euphoric. Most people who know me will tell you that I am not a naturally chirpy person, but I found myself quite unexpectedly bursting into song.

I don't know why a light dusting of snow would make me so happy, it's just that there was something so unnatural about the long years of springsumautwin that we endured, and this appropriately seasonal weather just makes me feel that God is in his heavens again. Hurrah for that!

Every year we have our fair share of disasters in the veggie plot, mostly due to our chronic lack of gardening knowledge. We try not to let this bother us too much – if you did, you would never grow anything at all. I had a conversation with an 'old hand' one time and was telling him that I had spent the weekend planting onions; horrified, he told me that it wasn't the right time to sow onions and that they would all surely be dead the next time I checked them. He seemed annoyed that I was so relaxed about this sorry outcome, but what he didn't understand was this: while I would definitely lament the death of my onions, I would not regret having spent a whole day planting them. Half the joy of growing things is the time that you spend putting the things in the ground. The other half is eating them, of course, which clearly I wouldn't get to do with the onions if they died. But 50 percent of joy is still a whole lot of joy – and actually, they didn't all die in the end. My point is, though, that you shouldn't worry too much about not knowing all there is to know about growing. I gave a talk to a gardening club recently on the subject of vegetable growing and on my final slide I had written the following:

The Good News – vegetables want to grow and they will do so despite your best efforts to prevent them doing so.

I always delight in seeing the smiles wash over people's faces when I put up that slide. Over tea after the meeting (the great thing about giving a talk at a gardening club is that there's always tea after the meeting) a guy told me that that one sentiment was like a happy release for him – he always felt under pressure when it came to vegetable growing because his knowledge just couldn't keep up with his ambition. Knowledge, as they say, is no burden, but while you are acquiring it you shouldn't forget that this growing thing is meant to be fun. Or if not fun, then at least enjoyable. Don't be worried about the list of mini-catastrophes that the growing year will surely send you – embrace them. Be proud of them. Usually they will teach you more than your successes. Sometimes they won't teach you a thing – you will sow or plant something and it won't grow at all and you won't have the slightest idea why. That's the beauty of it. Home

Farm growing is not an exact science, despite what your shelf-load of gardening books will try to tell you. Every year we have an array of failures in the vegetable plot (and elsewhere on the Home Farm) which have us pulling our hair out and thanking God that we are not totally reliant on the produce from our garden: things sown at the wrong time of year (like those onions!); rocket going to seed; rust on our celery and blight on our potatoes; birds getting to our soft-fruit crop before we do; an entire crop of purple kale lost to the lowly garden slug; garlic rotting in the ground; rabbits burrowing in our 'rabbit proof' raised beds; and, most harrowing of all, a never-ending glut of blindingly hot and practically inedible giant red mustard leaf.

Undeterred, we continue to stumble along with blind enthusiasm for the project. Thankfully, there are always successes too to keep us interested, none more so than finding a hardy vegetable that is a cinch to grow, looks great and tastes magnificent: Ladies and Jellyspoons, I give you the majestic kohlrabi. The name might sound a little odd – it comes from the German word for cabbage (*kohl*) and turnip (*rube*), which very effectively describes what the vegetable is about: it is a member of the cabbage family but it looks more like a turnip. Okay, so neither of those things makes it sound particularly promising, taste-wise. However, it is far milder than a turnip, perhaps closer to the taste of broccoli. And unlike turnip (which has kind of ugly foliage above ground), it looks amazing while growing – the 'root' (more accurately, a swollen stem) grows above the ground and is an exotic, deep purple colour, almost alien-like. Visitors to our garden are mightily impressed when they see them and assume we are expert growers. We do nothing to deprive them of their delusion.

KOHLRABI

Kohrabi grows well in most soils and fast-growing varieties will be ready in just six weeks (though more traditional varieties will take three to four months). They are ready to eat when they are about the size of a large orange. As always, we have got the highest success rate from sowing them in pots or modules and then transplanting when big enough to handle (about 5cm high).

Kohlrabi is a good vegetable to sow if you are looking for a quick win to get you started in the new year as you can harvest it after just six weeks. I love harvesting kohlrabi – plucking them from the soil and rushing it inside like I'm Indiana Jones carrying a rare treasure. There are recipes that do this fine root more justice (see below), but I just peel, finely dice and *sauté* it in butter with some fresh marjoram; it is absolutely spectacular. We also use some of the baby leaves, with their attractive pink veins, in salads (if the rabbits don't get them first).

Kohlrabi with Walnuts

I got an email from a German lady called Petra, who has been living in Ireland for years – and when she came here first she was stunned to discover that no one in this country seemed to have heard of kohlrabi. She sent me this wonderful recipe for a quick and light-ish main course. This is even better tasting and higher in smugness quotient if you grow your own shallots.

3-4 young kohlrabi

3-4 shallots

1 tbsp butter or walnut oil

150 ml cream

2-3 tbsp roughly chopped walnuts

a handful of chervil (optional)

good quality vegetable stock cube (or homemade stock)

freshly ground white pepper

nutmeg to taste

Clean, peel and cut the kohlrabi into cubes. Gently heat butter or oil in a pan. Add finely chopped shallots and fry until soft, but not brown. Add the kohlrabi and toss until evenly coated. Pour in the cream, then add pepper, nutmeg and vegetable stock. Bring to the boil, then reduce heat, cover and simmer for 5-8 minutes. Serve with potatoes or brown jasmine rice and scatter the walnuts and finely chopped herbs, such as chervil (or any other early-season herb), on top. (This is also nice as an accompaniment to lamb or pork chops).

JANUARY GROWER'S CALENDAR

Prep Work

- Clean and sharpen your spade – Ha-Ha.
- Okay, seriously – if you haven't already done so, you could still spread some manure or compost on your vegetable and fruit beds and cover them down with black polythene to start warming them up. Make sure you use well-rotted manure, however, and be careful not to spread manure in beds that will take root vegetables in the spring (they don't like or need it).
- If you don't have a compost heap, this is a good time of the year to get one started. For many Home Farmers, a standard plastic compost bin does not produce anywhere near enough compost, nor can it cope with all garden waste in the summer. In our case, we use a plastic bin for composting kitchen scraps (though our hens and pigs devour the vast majority of those), but we also have a homemade 'compost enclosure', made from timber, for composting animal manure and garden waste (grass cuttings, plant and vegetable material etc). A compost enclosure has several waist-high 'bays', about 1m sq each, that are enclosed on three sides with timber boards. To build each bay, you put four wooden posts in the ground and attach timber planks on three of the sides, leaving generous gaps between the planks to allow air to circulate. Cover with a sheet of timber or some old carpet to keep the rain off. The idea is that you fill one bay and then leave it alone to 'cook' for a few months while you concentrate on filling the next bay and so on. You know your compost is ready when the pile has shrunk to about one third of its original size and your compost is dark and crumbly – this takes about six months in our experience.
- Consider a compost trench for the bed in which you will sow legumes (peas,

beans etc) later this year. Dig a trench about 30cm deep and roughly half-fill it with compostable materials like vegetable-garden thinnings and kitchen scraps. Fill the trench back in with soil. A compost trench has a number of benefits: it requires no turning; it gives your vegetable plants nutrition where they need it, ie at the roots; and it is also very quick (materials degrade in as little as a couple of months). If you get this trench done now, the ground will be turbo-charged for planting later in spring.

- Get organised and start collecting old plastic bottles and containers to function as cloches and slug traps.

To-do List

- If you have any root vegetables left in the soil, it's probably a good idea to get them out of there now as January to March are months when you can get very heavy frosts and inclement weather. So lift everything such as parsnips, carrots and celeriac. We normally have our beds pretty much cleared before Christmas.
- If I was a betting man, I would put my money on rhubarb being the first fresh crop of the spring, particularly if you 'force' it now by covering it to exclude any light. Rhubarb was celebrated in times past exactly because it started to harvest just as the last of last season's apples were being eaten. Put a layer of straw on top of the dormant plants and then cover with an upturned pot. Tender little stems should be ready to eat in March. January is also a good month to split the rhubarb plants if you want to propagate them.
- Since there's so little 'real' work to do, January is a good month to sit down and work out what you are going to grow this year and order your seeds. Most garden centres stock a large variety of good-quality seeds now – buy organic seeds if you can. There are also several specialist online seed retailers who will post seeds out to you, but you need to order early in the year or they will be sold out. Now is also a good time to order your seed potatoes and onion/shallot sets because all the good varieties will be gone in a month or two and you will be left with commercially produced rubbish. Do some research on tried and trusted varieties and read the section on spuds in Chapter 3.

Sowing Seeds

- There's almost nothing worth sowing at this time of year – we could all try sowing the seeds of love, perhaps? But be patient. It won't be long.

GRUB'S UP – WHAT'S IN SEASON?

January will be a lean month in your first few years of growing and it requires particular foresight the previous spring or summer to ensure that you have things worth eating at this time of the year.

Perpetual spinach, leeks and kale are the most likely candidates, all of which are very good to eat. You may also have some winter cabbage, cauliflowers and some brussels sprouts left in the ground if you didn't eat them all during Chrimbo.

Depending on how successful your growing and storage regime was last year, you may also still be tucking into celeriac, carrots, parsnips, onions, cauliflower, jerusalem artichokes and winter squash. It's possible to have winter salads like land cress, corn salad and mizuna at this time of the year, particularly in a polytunnel or greenhouse.

2

LIVING IN EGGSTASY

EARLY SPRING: FEBRUARY

hens – beetroot – learning new skills

We gratefully put January behind us and slip into spring. Though it may well still feel like winter, there are signs here and there that we can cast off its oppressive yoke. As we move further and further from the winter solstice, we gain about five minutes of daylight at either end of the day and comparable dollops of optimism. The opportunities for doing things in the garden are limited when it's dark at four o'clock, so the stretch in the day is much appreciated. We progress into the second month of the year and carry with us the faint wisps of food-producing commitments, resolutions and intentions made in January.

The good news is that with the lengthening days, our hens have started laying again after a few weeks when we weren't getting any eggs at all. We've been keeping hens on the Home Farm for about four years, now, and it continues to be a love–hate relationship: we hate the amount of pooh they leave around the place and the scratching they do in our lawn and flower beds, but because they contribute so much to the kitchen, we forgive them. It amazes me just how fascinated we still are with the whole hen thing. Though it probably makes us sound unbelievably nerdy, counting eggs is still a daily pastime in the Kelly household: How many eggs did you collect today? one or other of us will ask. We shake our heads collectively in disgust on days when we get fewer eggs than we should – or worse, when we suspect they are, in fact, laying, but we can't find the eggs. And we still thrill on days when we get five or six fresh eggs on the straw in the nesting box, or even better again if we discover a clutch of fresh eggs in a ditch somewhere around the garden. It really is amazing just how easily pleased we are.

Keeping hens in a garden (yes, even in small, urban gardens) as pets and/or food producers is an increasingly popular pastime, spurred on, I think, by the fact that people are starting to realise what thoroughly useful animals they are to have around. Hens are incredibly independent and therefore easy to keep. Unlike your favourite pooch, your hens don't need to be walked or pandered to, and you don't need to buy them ridiculous toys or cutesy outfits. Once you give hens their daily ration of feed, plenty of water and do them the honour of occasionally cleaning out their house, they will thrive in your garden and repay you in wonderful eggs. Unlike your pooch, which will always be a nett draw on your resources, your hens actually pay their way by providing a high-protein foodstuff for the table. For three or four years after you get her, a hen will lay the tastiest, most nutritious egg imaginable almost every day. In exchange for your kitchen scraps, a hen will also provide you with a prodigious amount of good-quality manure, which you can use to help return nutrients to your soil and make your vegetables grow big and strong – which ultimately makes you and your family healthier. Hens are, therefore, a vital part of the overall health of the Home Farm's eco-system. Above all, though, we just love having hens around the place because they lift the spirits and occasionally the blood pressure. They bring a bit of colour to any garden, particularly at this time of the year when colour is in such short supply.

The taste of a real egg is one of those forgotten thrills that the modern food chain has deprived us of, but the great news is that nature herself hasn't forgotten. Give a small flock of hens lots of space and grass to roam on and they will produce incredible eggs – the more greens they eat, the yellower (if that's a word) the yolk will be. Put too many hens together in a small space in an unnatural environment where they are bored and un-stimulated, and they won't. It really is that simple. I promise you that your own eggs will taste better than the shop-bought variety – even the expensive free-range or organic ones.

TALES FROM THE HOME FARM

GO TO WORK ON AN EGG

Egg consumption rates vary widely across the European Union. In Ireland we eat just 143 eggs each per year on average, compared to the French, who eat 253 per year. Part of the problem is a common misconception about the impact of egg consumption on blood cholesterol levels. For years, we were told that eating an egg a day was bad for our cholesterol and our tickers. Now we are told that an egg a day really is okay. Whom do we believe? Well, my feeling on it is that if you are steering clear of eggs because of concerns about cholesterol, but you still continue to eat biscuits, chocolate bars and all manner of other processed junk, then you are really barking up the wrong tree. Recent scientific studies have found no evidence to show that eating eggs as part of a balanced diet raises blood cholesterol levels – in fact, eggs can play an important role in achieving a healthy, nutritious diet. Two thirds of the fat in eggs is the healthy unsaturated kind, which can actually lower cholesterol.

An egg really is one of nature's most amazing feats and has a phenomenal level of nutrients wrapped up in a low-calorie package. They are made up of 70 percent water, 10 percent protein, 10 percent fat, and 10 percent minerals. An egg contains all eight amino acids as well as vitamins A, B, D and E. They are one of only a small number of foods that can provide us with vitamin D, which we normally get from sunlight. They are also a good source of iron, zinc and selenium. Each egg contains just 75 calories and a standard portion (ie two eggs) provides between one third and one quarter of our daily protein requirement.

For most Home Farmers, keeping some hens for laying eggs, or indeed a few chickens for the table, is probably the only 'rearing' project that they will have the space for. The good news is that as long as you are willing to put up with some scratching in your lawn, even the smallest urban garden will happily support a couple of laying hens. We started with four laying hens about four years ago, but the size and make-up of our flock continually changes – it currently stands at five different breeds, consisting of seven hens and one cockerel, though that will, no doubt, change as the year progresses. This state of flux is partly the result of my short attention span, and partly because we just got hooked on the fascinating world of poultry and are keen to try out lots of different types of bird.

There's a sense of ancientness about keeping hens that appeals to us too. Most families, certainly in rural areas at any rate, up until very recently kept a few in the garden, but in the seventies and eighties all that stopped – inexplicably, people started associating growing vegetables or rearing animals for food with poverty. If you had to grow things or keep some hens in the garden, then you were showing your neighbours that times were tough. The logic behind this might seem strange to us now, particularly given the fact that producing your own food has become incredibly trendy in recent times. The reality is that these ancient skills never go out of fashion for long and common sense ultimately prevails. Frugality does not necessarily need to be of the scratching, grinding kind, it can be wonderfully life-enhancing if approached in the right way. As I said in the Preface, we choose to grow our own food and keep hens and pigs and ducks because we want to live a life that's more straightforward and more connected. Do people look at us and think: Oh God, look at the poor Kellys, they have to keep their own pigs; they must be on the breadline. Of course they don't. And even if they did, well that would be their problem, not ours.

Believe it or not, the ancestors of modern hens are thought to be

Red Jungle Fowl (known as *Gallus gallus* – so good they named it twice) from south-east Asia, dating back as far as 5000 BC. Interestingly, it is thought that they were originally domesticated not for their eggs or meat, but for cock fighting, perhaps as early as 3000 BC. The first domesticated chickens arrived in Europe from about AD700, usually kept by monks or nuns in monasteries so that they could fire the eggs at each other when they got bored (no, not really). Over the centuries, the western world has become infatuated with chickens as a source of meat and eggs and the increased demand has led us inexorably towards the stolid commercialisation that we see today where hens are turned into egg-laying machines.

It would be nice to say that hens are fiercely intelligent creatures who deserve to be treated better, but they are not fiercely intelligent at all, they are incredibly dumb – or they seem to be. For example, we once moved our hen house from point A in the garden to point B, and come bedtime that evening the hens are all gathered around at point A, wandering around in circles and clucking miserably as if bemoaning their bad luck that someone has stolen their house. Even if they do wander over to point B and spot the house, it doesn't seem to occur to these poor, dim-witted creatures that it is the *same* house. Still, I guess nature has built a certain form of intelligence into them – they may not have logic as we would define it, but they must have a strong homing instinct all the same. In any case, the way we humans treat them shouldn't be linked to whether they are intelligent or not. They are beautiful creatures and having watched them for four years I can tell you that they have their own set of pretty complex needs – they have a well-defined routine and social order, and they love roaming around the garden and scratching in the grass for worms and grubs.

Alas, the modern commercial hen rarely gets to enjoy such pleasures. Before we start talking about commercialised egg-laying, it's worth bearing in mind that in ancient times hens laid roughly twenty eggs a year, usually in the spring or summer and purely for reproductive purposes (ie there was a mate around and the eggs hatched into chicks). But hens have an interesting hereditary inheritance which dictates that they want to produce eggs even when there is no male around for them to mate with. Mankind has essentially exploited this quirk of nature and through selective breeding has been able to rear hens that lay upwards of three hundred eggs a year.

There are about two million laying hens in Ireland and up to 60 percent of those are estimated to be 'battery' or 'cage' reared. In the UK, twenty million hens are reared in cages. Cage rearing of hens is still legal in Europe, and will be until 2012 when a new 'enriched' cage system will be introduced. At present, a battery hen shed sometimes contains upwards of seven thousand birds with five birds to each cage. The minimum legal space requirement per hen is about the size of an A4 sheet of paper. Now, we have a pretty big garden and I reckon our hens cover ever square centimetre of it each day as they roam around all day long, foraging and scratching. Imagine confining an animal that loves to wander so much to a space the size of an A4 sheet of paper? By necessity, caged hens are de-beaked to prevent fighting and the lights are kept on up to seventeen hours a day to promote laying (hens lay based on how many hours of light there is per day, which explains why most breeds either stop laying in the winter or at least lay fewer eggs). Hens roaming free on grass are usually exceptionally healthy – we've never had problems with diseases in any of our birds – but hens kept in unnaturally confined quarters and deprived of sunlight have chronically poor immune systems and are therefore prone to disease; as a result, commercial producers put anti-biotics into their feed and/or water to prevent them getting sick. The poultry industry uses three families of antibiotics – macrolides, iono-phores and polypeptides – to control disease and to improve egg-laying performance. The yolk of an egg from your own hen will be a wonderfully vibrant orange colour, thanks to the variety of food that it gets to eat – kitchen scraps, grass, worms and feed. A commer-cial hen doesn't get that variety and so the yolks are typically listless in colour; but producers get around this by adding a colourant called canthaxanthin to their feed. Of course, it stands to reason that what-ever you put into a hen's feed ends up eventually in its eggs, and finally flowing around your body. It makes no sense whatsoever to assume that our bodies can absorb the good healthy stuff like vita-mins and minerals from eggs, but somehow won't absorb the antibi-otics, hormones, yolk-colourings and whatever other chemicals have been introduced to their feed.

Amazingly, a hen is born with all the eggs that she will produce in her life in the form of egg cells in her ovaries, so the number of eggs she produces is an entirely finite, preordained affair, though it varies from breed to breed. She will start laying at about sixteen to twenty weeks old (the hens are called point-of-lay pullets at that stage) and will lay the majority of her eggs in the first season. After that, she will moult her feathers, during which time she stops laying, and then she will recommence laying. Things carry on like this for five or six years with the number of eggs being produced reducing each season, until finally she will stop laying altogether. Some hens will still lay an occasional egg when they are ten years of age, but it will only ever be an incidental affair at that stage, like a reminder of a long-forgotten skill. The most productive time for any hen, therefore, is when she is between four months and twenty months old. I always smile to myself when people say to me that they put light in their hen house in the winter to encourage the hens to lay, as if they have some-how cheated nature to get a hen to produce more eggs than normal – they haven't! The hen may well produce more eggs over winter, but she will ultimately stop laying sooner than she might otherwise have.

In the commercial world, it's considered uneconomical to allow a hen to approach post-lay status naturally like this. The commercial hen is therefore forced to lay as many eggs as possible in her first season (using artificial lighting) and she is then slaughtered, with her various body parts ending up as meat exports, pet food, or stock cubes. Don't get me wrong, I'm not at all squeamish about a hen ending up in a pot – and as far as I'm concerned it is a fitting tribute for the hen's lifetime of service. But the commercial process is just such an unnecessary and brutal thing to put a hen through before they reach that point – to force them into a miserable, unnatural life and then to end that life long before they have reached obsolescence. Some of our hens here on the Home Farm have more or less passed their sell-by date when it comes to laying. They do lay the odd egg (usually a giant of a thing) but their contribution to the kitchen is nothing worth writing home about. I've killed chickens for meat and am happy to dispatch our pigs for the slaughter too, but I usually leave our post-lay hens to their own devices; perhaps because they've been around for so long and given so much, you do ulti-mately get kind of attached to them. And so we have an ever-increasing number of well-fed, contented freeloaders around the place. If they are reading this – *I know who you are.*

When you have a rooster around the place as we do, all the eggs you get are likely to be fertilised – and all the neighbours are sure to dislike you very much indeed (a cock crows around twenty minutes before first light all year around). If he's doing the job that he's paid for, the cock will be mating with each hen several times a day, which, no doubt, contributes to his rather stressed temperament. You will not notice any difference between a fertilised and unfertilised egg in the taste department. A hen will occasionally go 'broody' (usually in the spring), which means that her maternal instinct kicks in and she will sit on eggs if she can to try and hatch them to chicks. She may do this anyway, even if there is no cockerel around and there's absolutely no chance of anything hatching out of them (like I said, not the brightest of animals). We have found hatching chicks to be an entirely random affair – readers of my first book may recall that at one point we had six or seven eggs under a broody hen and twenty-one days later got just two chicks – we duly fattened them up over a period of a hundred days or so, but because they were a laying breed rather than a meat breed, they were hardly worth eating. Still, it's an exciting thing, indeed, to see nature take its course like this, and, of course, the little chicks are unbearably cute for the first week or so. I highly recommend you try it at least once in your lifetime, if you can.

It's traditional for hens to start laying again on Valentine's Day, which is either appropriate or perverse, depending on your point of view. Like everything else in life, you get used to the wonderful eggs that they provide and perhaps an annual enforced abstinence isn't such a bad thing because it makes you appreciate them all the more. We reverted to buying eggs (free range, usually, and, when we could get them, organic) and what a misery it was – eggs with pallid grey-yellow yolks and almost total absence of flavour, which, for some reason, seemed to sort of disintegrate when you cracked them into water to poach them. You can't imagine how excited I was when we got our first egg earlier this month after what seemed like such an interminable winter – it was almost as exciting as the very first egg we got all those years ago.

With our hens back to their wonderful egg-laying selves, we are back into the routine of trying to get them to lay in nesting boxes and not out around in the ditches. We also have to guard against magpies, who wait menacingly in the trees and bushes around the garden so they can swoop in and steal the eggs. For us, the old saying about magpies becomes 'one for sorrow, two for sorrow, three for sorrow ...' Hens like a dark little cubbyhole in which to lay their egg and some-times they seem to prefer the privacy of a ditch or hedge rather than the (splendid) DIY nesting boxes that I have laid on for them. At various times over the years, our hens have been completely confined in the coop (to try and force them to lay in the box); then we tried confining them in the morning (to lay) and letting them out in the afternoon, and finally we let them go completely 'free range', with unfettered access to the whole garden. None of these options is entirely foolproof in terms of ensuring they will lay where you want them to lay. Occasionally, we go through a month or two where they are all laying in the nesting box and we are completely inundated with eggs (friends and family gratefully snap up the excess) and we think we have it cracked (as it were), and then, inexplicably, one or two of them start to lay out and about again. We try hunting around for eggs, sometimes with success, but more often not. Sometimes the dogs might find a little stash for us and if we can get to them before the dogs eat the whole lot, it's quite a find. Eggs you buy in the shop are often several months old, so your own eggs are always impeccably fresh by comparison, even if they have spent a few days hiding in a hedge! Incidentally, you can test an egg for freshness by dunking it in a bowl of water – if it floats, throw it out.

In order to minimise the amount of vegetables that you need to buy in (and at this time of the year the vast majority of supermarket produce is unseasonal anyway) it's important for the Home Farmer to have access to really healthy, hardy vegetables that will thrive during the winter months. One useful vegetable which is still technically in season (ie if you've managed to store some from last year) is beetroot. The Romans used beetroot as a treatment for fevers and constipation, amongst other ailments, and Hippocrates, the Greek (him of the oath), recommended the use of beet leaves as a binding for wounds. Researchers in the American Heart Association found a substantial decrease in blood pressure just one hour after drinking 500ml of beetroot juice and we now know that it is a very rich source of B vitamins. Its glorious red pigment comes courtesy of the powerful antioxidant betacyanin, which is thought to have anti-carcinogenic properties while at the same time purifying the blood and increasing oxygen absorption. It is also considered an aphrodisiac – though I have eaten whole plates of them at one sitting and can't say that I felt particularly randy, no more so than usual at any rate.

We managed to store some beetroots at harvest time last year, putting them in a box of sand to over-winter in the garage. We deliberately avoided them while there were other vegetables available fresh from the garden and then, when everything else was gone, we attacked the beets. If you're really on top of things and have grown enough of them successionally, you can, in theory, eat home-grown beets all year round – fresh from the soil from June until late autumn, from storage until March, and in pickled form right up to June again. We have come close this year to achieving that lofty aim, though we have moved on to the pickled variety already and it's only February. Still, not bad going.

Beetroot is another great example of a vegetable that I never had much time for, but I decided to give it another try because it's a cinch to grow once you get it started and will crop pretty much anywhere. We started growing it about two years ago because I read somewhere that the baby leaves are great for salads (which they are – they give a lovely bite and a splash of interesting colour), but, of course, after a few weeks the leaves get big and coarse and are no good to you any-more for salads, and then the root starts to form and in no time at all you're left with a big vegetable that is begging to be eaten. So you have a dilemma: do you give it to the pigs or give it another try? Can you come up with some way of cooking, serving or poshing it up that will make it more acceptable? In my book, excessive boiling of root vegetables is never a good plan – you only have to look at the colour of the water afterwards to know that most of the goodness (and taste) has leached into it. This is especially the case with a vegetable as vibrantly coloured as the beetroot; and it's that magic burgundy colour you need to get inside you, not into the water you will be throwing down the sink.

So, baking the beets in the oven with the skins on is a better option. Beets are best eaten when small, so take a few small beets (or if they are large, cut them into halves or quarters, though there will be some bleeding during cooking this way), twist off the leaves about 5cm from the root and put them in a tinfoil parcel. Cook in a hot oven for about half an hour (much longer for bigger roots) or until they are so tender that they are practically melting. Rub off the skins and the 5cm stem, then put them in a bowl, throw in a few splashes of your best olive oil and vinegar (balsamic is good). Serve them on a bed of salad, and I promise they will be a revelation.

You can sow beetroot in the polytunnel or greenhouse starting now, and from next month outside, if all risk of frost has passed, and continue to sow them in succession until August. Successional sowing is one of the those really vital vegetable grower's skills that requires a measure of discipline, which is often a challenge for us. It means that you sow seeds 'little but often' rather than doing one great big sowing, which carries the risk of everything going wrong and you losing the whole lot, or everything going right and you having a huge glut ready to harvest all at once. Lettuce is a good example of a crop that benefits from successional sowing, as it becomes unappetising and generally unappealing very quickly.

We've found the easiest approach with beetroot, as with most things, is to sow the seeds in seed trays or modules (at a depth of about 2cm–3cm) rather than sowing them directly outside – beetroot seeds are a little slow when it comes to germination (it can take up to two weeks) so I think they do better in the controlled environment of a seed tray. You can move them outside and plant them in the soil when the roots are bursting out of the base of the module and the little plants are about 5cm tall – at that stage they should be hardy enough to survive. You can, of course, sow seeds directly outside if you want, but we found that we lost more seeds that way than we did when starting them off under cover. Once in the soil outside, they will need to be spaced about 15cm apart in rows about 30cm away from each other. They don't need a huge amount of manuring, or even watering unless it's really dry, because too much water will encourage leaf growth as opposed to root growth, which is what we're after. Sorry to say, you will need to keep the bed where they are sown relatively weed free – this will be a lot easier in a raised bed (more on this anon).

It's best to harvest beetroot when young (the beets that is, not you) but we had some big old roots last year which tasted okay, so don't worry about it too much if they are large. You should start harvesting by pulling every second beet in the row, which gives the ones that you leave behind more space to grow. It's a hardy vegetable, so they will do fine left in the soil for the winter (unless there is a really severe frost), but if you want to store them, put them in boxes of sand. If you have a good supply for the winter, congratulate yourself – you can throw away that multivitamin pill, and while your friends will be pale and uninteresting-looking for the winter, you will have an eerie red glow …

PAULA MEE'S NUTRITION BITES: BEETROOT

Beetroot is high in folate, a vitamin that is essential for a healthy nervous system and the proper functioning of the brain. Beetroot has long been used for medicinal purposes, primarily for disorders of the liver, given its stimulating effects on the liver's detoxification process.

Nutrition per Portion (80g):

Calories	Fat (g)	Salt (g)	Saturated Fat (g)
29	0.1	0.13	0

I love the idea of using the 'gentle pause' in the winter garden as a time to re-skill for the growing year ahead, so for the past few years I have taken myself off in January or February to do courses. It doesn't have to be a particularly long course (a day or half-day will do) and the subject matter doesn't particularly matter either, so long as it's related to food production. No matter what level of experience you have – complete novice or old hand – and no matter where your interests lie, there will be a course somewhere to suit you. You could, for example, do a very general course on organic vegetable growing, or if you have a polytunnel or greenhouse you might learn about growing in the micro-climate they provide; you could find out about forgotten skills, like keeping bees or hens in your garden, or about using seaweed as a source of food and fertiliser. You could learn all about basket-making, making a willow hedge, permaculture or dry-stone wall construction; if you have a decent amount of land you could learn about using horses to work the land, or if you have a very tiny garden you could learn about which vegetables to grow in a small space. At the end of the day, the subject matter is not hugely important – what's important is that you get up off your winter-weary backside and go learn something.

The benefit of it, apart from learning some things you didn't know before (always a good idea, I find, when there's so much to learn), is that it usually puts a considerable pep in your step at a very important juncture in the year – just as you are facing into a mountain of work in the months ahead. I did a course last year on butchering a pig, and while I haven't managed to put what I learned into practice yet, I do have about twenty pages of notes that I glance at occasionally and wonder: *would I really be able to butcher our pigs myself sometime?* I did a course on beer making once and I did put that into practice, with occasionally questionable results. This year, I did a course on home dairying – all the things that you can do with milk, like making butter, yoghurt and cheese. I was most certainly the only person on the course who didn't own a cow – but never mind, it was a complete and utter eye-opener. Who knew that these things were so simple? Have yoghurt-makers and cheese-makers been pretending that theirs is some sort of dark art so that we will keep buying their products rather than making them ourselves? I kind of already knew that butter-making was relatively straightforward because I was whipping cream once in the food mixer and I got sidetracked and went off and did something else (as you do), and when I came back I discovered that I had inadvertently made butter. That's really all there is to butter making – if you whip cream beyond the 'stiff peaks' stage and then keep whipping, eventually you are left with butter sitting in a lake of buttermilk (which you can then use to make some bread).

But I never knew that to make a ruddy big tub of delicious natural yoghurt, all you have to do is boil up a big pot of full-cream milk, add in a small amount of shop-bought natural yoghurt, and then let it sit overnight, wrapped in a few warm towels in your hot press. All the little bacteria from the added yoghurt go completely ape in the warmth of the hot press overnight and colonise the milk, turning it into a colossal quantity of your very own home-made yoghurt. There's a considerable thrill to be had from unwrapping your little bundle of joy the next morning in the hot press and finding that your yoghurt has set and is ready for eating. You can make huge batches of yoghurt at a time because it keeps for about ten days in the fridge (try making yourself some nice smoothies for breakfast each morning with a bit of added milk and some fresh fruit – yum). Why didn't anyone tell me before that something this tasty and thrifty was so easy? Or that you can make a very reasonable soft cottage cheese by boiling some milk and adding a few drops of rennet or some lemon juice, which separates the milk into thick creamy curds of cheese and a watery yellow liquid called whey (which, by the way, can then be fed to the pigs or hens if you have them – our pigs absolutely love it and will ignore the food in their trough and concentrate on sucking up the whey first). I know I am making terribly light of the incredible art of cheesemaking (blessed *are* the cheese-makers), and, I mean, you can't really compare our amateurish efforts with those incredibly complex, wonderful artisan cheeses, but goddammit, it's one hell of a start.

The only drawback of my new-found dairy knowledge is that, once again, the modern food chain lets me down badly when it comes to sourcing the main ingredient – milk. As I said, we don't have a cow on the Home Farm and, unfortunately, it's pretty unlikely that we ever will, due to space limitations. But I still cling to the romantic notion that at some point in the future we will be graced with the presence of a docile Daisy, whom I will milk each morning and evening. She will provide us with enough milk for ourselves and our pigs, with enough left over to make butter and cheese. She will also provide us with a calf each year for meat and as much manure as we can handle to keep the Home Farm productive, and, of course, she will be my friend and I can discuss my problems with her while milking ... Now, I know what you're thinking: he will get fed up of milking Daisy after about a week and since she will produce about five million litres of milk a year, he will probably end up throwing most of the milk down the sink; and you're probably right, but romantic notions do not have space for such realism. In John Seymour's smallholding bible, he talks about the cow as being central to the self-sufficiency project. I love this characteristically no-nonsense quote about a cow's largesse:

> *If you and your children have ample, good, fresh, unpasteurized, unadulterated milk, butter, buttermilk, soft cheese, hard cheese, yoghurt, sour milk and whey, you will simply be a healthy family, and that is the end of it.*
>
> *John Seymour, The New Complete Book of Self-Sufficiency.*

If you are my age or younger, chances are you have never got to enjoy the taste of unadulterated milk; in the interest of 'safety', durability and uniformity, the commercial food chain has whole-heartedly embraced the idea that we are not to be allowed anywhere near the milk from a cow until it has been processed beyond all recognition, using pasteurisation and homogenisation. We read these terms on our milk cartons without really bothering to consider what they mean, why they are necessary or what would happen if we just drank milk in its natural state. Most of us probably have a vague awareness of what we *think* pasteurisation is for – that it makes milk safe to drink, which, of course, implies that milk is inherently unsafe to drink in the first place. This couldn't be further from the truth. In his hugely impressive book *The Untold Story of Milk* (New Trends Publishing 2003), Ron Schmid talks about how pasteurisation – the process invented by Louis Pasteur, where milk is boiled at a temperature below boiling (71.7°C) to reduce the number of pathogens – was first applied to milk at the turn of the last century. It was seen as a temporary way to clean highly unsafe milk that was being produced in so-called 'distillery dairies' in the US where cows were fed slops from whisky distilleries. This stop-gap solution became a permanent fixture, particularly when human tuberculosis was originally believed to have been contracted from bovine TB. Over decades, people started to accept that raw milk was essentially unfit for human consumption, when, in fact, the problems with the milk were largely man-made.

Pasteurisation was not so much a response to safety issues in milk itself, but a response to the hazards and contamination issues that resulted from the early years of the 'industrialised' dairy industry. It's a compromise, and, unfortunately, not a particularly good one. If you boil milk, you kill any bacteria that are in it, but you also significantly affect the taste and nutritional value of the milk. If you have ever had the misfortune to drink UHT milk (those tiny little cartons you get with your coffee on a plane or on a train) you will know just how much the pasteurisation process affects milk. UHT milk is milk that is pasteurised at ultra high temperatures (hence UHT), which completely sterilises the product – it has the advantage for suppliers of being storable for months on end instead of just days, but it has the disadvantage of tasting horrible and having no nutritional value whatsoever.

That milk pasteurisation remains compulsory is a scandal. Of course, you will get sick from unpasteurised milk which is produced in unsanitary conditions, just as you will get sick from any food that is contaminated. You can catch salmonella from a lettuce leaf, but we don't make pasteurisation of lettuce compulsory, do we? Not yet, at any rate. Raw milk from clean, healthy, grass-fed cows is not only healthy, it has astonishing nutritional properties that have been celebrated for millennia – it is replete with fat-soluble nutrients, essential enzymes, calcium and other minerals that are, by and large, in short supply in the modern diet. Come to think of it, if raw milk is so deadly, how come we are even here to have this discussion – our ancient ancestors were drinking raw milk for thousands of years before pasteurisation was even invented (in 1862), and they seem to have done okay. As consumers, we should at least have *the option* of buying unpasteurised product from farmers we trust to produce top-quality milk in a safe and hygienic way.

Homogenisation of milk was essentially an attempt to make sure that the first litre that came from the milk tank was the same as the last. Milk is basically water with fat globules – it has almost 90 percent water content and the balance is made up of fat (between 3 and 4 percent), protein and sugar. If left to itself – God, why can't we just leave it to itself?– the fat in milk (cream) will separate out from the water and rise to the top. Readers of a certain age will, no doubt, recall bottles of milk being left outside their front door by the milk-man (remember him?) and the cream rising to the top – if you're my age you probably won't recall that at all.

Homogenisation breaks the fat globules into smaller sizes by forcing the milk at high pressure through tiny holes – the result is that the milk no longer separates and the fat molecules are evenly dispersed throughout. Sounds harmless enough? Well, perhaps, but it's not without its detractors. When you drink non-homogenised milk, your body can digest the cream and use the fat for energy. But opponents of homogenisation argue that your body cannot digest the cream in this unnatural state and the fat gets absorbed into your stomach lining and goes straight into your bloodstream. There is a growing body of (admittedly controversial) evidence that connects homogenisation of milk with all sorts of illnesses – including lactose intolerance, high cholesterol, heart disease and even cancer. Interestingly, many people who have adverse reactions to standard dairy, can fully tolerate the raw stuff.

Some scientists believe that pasteurisation and homogenisation are delivering a double whammy of health implications to humans who drink milk. First of all, pasteurisation deprives us of essential micro-organisms that protect the gut, while homogenisation allows an excess of proteins to survive human digestion with resulting health implications. On the former point, it's worth pointing out the lunacy of the situation where we drink pasteurised milk and then spend more money buying yoghurts and other 'one-a-day' products that have live cultures added to them. Cows that spend their time grazing on grass produce milk that contains an array of important enzymes and antibodies, which make raw milk digestible for humans – these organisms do not survive the hammering that commercial dairy processing metes out to milk. Anecdotal evidence is no evidence at all, of course, but Mrs Kelly's parents accredit their healthy constitution, and particularly the fact that they never seem to get stomach bugs, to the drinking of raw milk. Mrs Kelly herself always drank raw milk as a child and she seems to have turned out okay (!). In terms of taste, the difference between regular milk and the milk we get when we are down with the in-laws is simply staggering – as the American author Annie Proulx once said, it's like the difference between a plastic flamingo and the real bird.

What I find really strange about all this is that the dairy industry seems to have instigated an all-out war on its own product, claiming that the best way to drink it is to redistribute the fat (by homogenisation) or remove it almost entirely (low-fat or skim milk). Why would they do this? Well, you could argue that the heavily-funded, obsessive marketing of low-fat and skim milk as a healthier alternative to 'full-fat' milk has an ulterior motive. Modern dairy herds (which are predominantly based around the Holstein cow) are bred to produce ever-increasing quantities of milk – so successful has the breeding regime been, in fact, that the latter-day cow produces almost three times as much milk as traditional breeds. But, as is always the case when quantity is the focus, quality is sacrificed – the resulting milk is increasingly low in fat. At the turn of last century, milk contained about 4 percent butterfat; that figure is now less than 3 percent. What's astonishing about this is that the dairy industry has somehow managed to convince us that this is a good thing. In fact, the evidence points to the contrary: the butter fat in real milk contains vitamins A and D, which we need for the absorption of calcium and protein. So, in other words, without that fat we can't properly use the nutrients that are in the milk. Think about it another way: milk processors can clearly make more profit if they can strip the remaining fat from milk to convert it into other dairy products, like butter, cream and cheese. But in order to do so, they have to get us poor unwitting sods to drink the low-fat watery stuff that's left. What better way to do so than to convince us that low-fat milk is healthy?

Pasteurisation and homogenisation create a unique set of problems in the kitchen. It is impossible to make good butter, yoghurt and cheese from milk that has been processed in this way. Making butter from homogenised milk, for example, is complicated by the fact that it's impossible to separate the cream out from the milk (as explained earlier). You could buy cream to make your own butter, of course, but it would be the most expensive butter in the history of butterdom. The same problem applies to making cheese and yoghurt. To make a good cheese you need good-quality milk – you need its fat, you need its cultures. All of which means that if you are really interested in making your own butter, cheese or yoghurt, you really need a source of unpasteurised, unhomogenised milk. The latter you can get in most supermarkets, but the former is nigh on impossible to get unless you know a friendly farmer (he won't sell it to you, though, because that would be illegal). We are relatively lucky in that we know one who will occasionally donate a bucket of milk straight from the tank if we need it!

One problem with my annual forays into the world of education is that I get way too enthusiastic about the subject and this usually means that I end up spending money on lots and lots of equipment, which is used once and then cast aside. After my beer-making course, for example, I bought all the kit you could ever need and then just threw it there when my confidence took a hammering following one particular batch of undrinkable hogwash. This year, after my dairy-processing course, I got so worked up about the whole thing I vowed never to drink commercial milk again, a pretty silly thing to promise when you don't have a cow. But I was dogged – I was going to start drinking only unpasteurised and unhomogenised milk and eating butter, yoghurt and cheese only when homemade. These are the kind of entirely impractical promises I make to myself on a regular basis. A casual search for dairy-making equipment on eBay one day turned up a diamond in the rough – a 1920s milk separator which was used in 'the old days' to separate cream from milk, and which had been mentioned on the course, in passing, as an invaluable, and elusive, piece of kit. You can buy electric milk separators, of course, but they are not nearly as much fun as a ninety-year-old vintage model, which is a piece of history. The only snag was that this particular little beauty was located in New South Wales in Australia, and so, even if I won the bidding war, it would cost about as much again to ship it to Ireland.

Unfortunately, it was my first time buying something on eBay and I got a little carried away by the romance of the whole thing. The bidding started at about AU$7 (about €4, hence my initial interest), but it increased quickly and dramatically, spurred on by an annoyingly persistent Melbournian chap who seemed particularly anxious to own it and trumped me every time I put in a bid. Common sense prevailed when our bidding war reached AU$200 (€114) and, with a heavy heart, I bowed out gracefully. Then one morning, about a week later, I decided to check had it been sold, and, as luck would have it, there were only twenty minutes remaining to the close of bids, and the top bid now stood at AU$245 (€139). Amazingly, I took this as a sign from the universe that I was meant to own this milk separator and decided to put in a bid of AU$250 (about €142). Since all the bidders were Australian (I mean, who else would be stupid enough to buy something like this from a seller on another continent) they were probably in bed instead of at their computers, and I watched with delight as the twenty minutes elapsed with no further hassle from the chap in Melbourne. And then it was all over and my bid was 'successful', if that's the right word to describe paying AU$250 for an old piece of dairy junk. 'Congratulations, the item is yours,' enthused the eBay people in an email a few minutes later. I felt mighty pleased with myself for about twenty seconds and then I realised what I had done and broke into a cold sweat. I went to find Mrs Kelly to sit her down to tell her the good news.

After the euphoria died down, I waited for my parcel to arrive. Our postman always beeps his horn when he has a parcel for me, and over the next few weeks, each time I heard a beep I would run out with great excitement – but, alas, it was always some other far less interesting parcel. Weeks went past and there was no sign. After about six weeks, I started to get concerned and exchanged civil emails with the seller to enquire as to why it was taking so long. After another few weeks the emails turned increasingly tense and then downright hostile – particularly when I realised that you can only get your money back on your credit card insurance if you claim within forty-five days, a period of time that had since elapsed. The seller emailed me a consignment note in an attachment that showed the package leaving New South Wales over two months previously, which seemed to put him in the clear, but the Irish postal service could find no record of it arriving. I was disconsolate. Not only had I been a complete fool to spend so much on this flight of fancy in the first place, now it seemed I wasn't going to get anything at all for my money (and, of course, at this stage my ardour for home dairying had inevitably cooled somewhat).

Then one glorious day, well over two months after it left Australia there was a beep of the postman's horn and when I went out to him, he had an enormous package with an Australian postmark in the back of the van for me. Mercifully, he didn't ask what it was. I rushed inside and unwrapped it carefully. On first inspection, it seemed in good working order and, of course, I immediately felt guilty about the hostile exchange of emails. It's a strange-looking contraption that uses centrifugal force to separate the cream from the skim milk. In all, it's about 70cm or 80cm high. There's a large metal bowl, sitting on top of a heavy base, into which you pour your milk; the milk then flows down into a sort of cone, which has fifteen individual plates in it that spin at a ferocious speed, separating the milk into skim milk and cream – the cream rises higher and flows out one spout which comes out of the middle of the unit, while the milk flows out a second, lower spout.

I have to say that I found the whole thing strangely compelling – before we started using it at all, we had to spend an entire evening removing any rust from each individual component (there are about thirty separate parts) with steel wool. Rather than find this tedious, I found myself daydreaming about the people who had first bought the separator nearly ninety years ago and the hours they must have spent scrubbing it after separating batches of milk in it. Who were they? What were their circumstances? Did the tips of their fingers hurt as much as mine did from trying to get into little crevices with steel wool? Finally, when we had the whole unit sterilised, we cranked it up, turning the wheel to get the gears moving, and then gently letting the milk into the cone from the top. And then, like magic, it started to separate out and the milk flowed out one funnel and the thick cream came out the other, and before you knew it, it was all over and we wanted to go again as if we were two kids on a merry-go-round – only we had no milk left. It's an amazingly efficient contraption, particularly when you consider that these devices first appeared on the market in 1896, well over a century ago. A well adjusted cream separator leaves less than one percent of the cream behind in the skim milk. Incidentally, I had a taste of the milk afterwards and it tasted to me just like the milk you buy in the shops, which I think probably says it all about how much of the fat (and flavour) is extracted from milk before it's given to us. But, of course, separating the cream out of the milk is only the start, because then you have to wash and dry the thirty component parts again, and *then* you have to actually make the butter. So we stuck the cream in the blender to break it down into butter and buttermilk; then we had to wash the butter to get all the liquid out of it, and then pat it into neat little rectangles. And before we knew it, it was midnight and we'd been at it for three or four hours.

Now, you're probably wondering (and you would be right), why bother with all this hassle? Butter is cheap and plentiful – why put yourself to such expense and such heartache? It's a good question and I am not sure I can give you a worthwhile answer. You could argue that it was a total waste of money, but in some ways it was the best €140 I ever spent. To see a ninety-year-old dairy machine being given a new lease of life, to see it become useful again – ah well, now, that was just incredibly heartening. We live in a throwaway society that places no value whatsoever on durability – because, of course, if you manufacture a widget to be durable then the widget lasts for ages and the consumer doesn't need to buy another widget for a long time. Far more profitable, then, to actually build obsolescence into the product so that it expires quickly and we can keep the whole cycle of buy-and-discard going. In a drawer in our kitchen, for example, there are three or four discarded mobile phones – some of them are broken, but some of them are not and were put aside only because a newer model became available with a sleeker look, or better features. We made no effort to get the broken ones repaired – why would we, when the mobile phone operator is willing to give us an 'upgrade' free of charge? Most people would look on a mobile phone as being a far more advanced piece of kit than a big old dairy separator, so how come the former seems to have no value to us whatsoever while the latter ends up on eBay nearly a century later? I like the idea of finding uses for lovely things and loving things that are used.

Depending on how you view these things, making butter from scratch by separating the cream from full-fat raw milk by hand is either enormously fulfilling or a total waste of valuable time. It goes without saying that the resulting produce is more than just butter – it's a spectacular labour of love. And perhaps that is how it always was for my Australian friends back in the 1920s – perhaps every bit of butter they ever made was invested with their love, their effort, their time. And surely the butter they made was savoured all the more as a result? With as much perspective as anyone who has spent three or four hours making a product can muster, I can tell you that our own butter tasted far superior to the commercial alternative – presumably the raw milk helps, but there's a depth of flavour there that you just don't seem to get with normal butter. But perhaps it just tasted nicer because of the two-month journey that we went through to make it. As always with these things, it's also a timely and useful reminder of just how convenient modern society has become and how tough life must have been fifty or a hundred years ago. But you also get a glimpse of how much people must have appreciated the good things in life too. Incidentally, while we took the cream and just threw it in the blender to make the butter, the first people to use my 1920s separator had to churn the butter themselves by hand – so we should be thankful that at least we didn't have to do that. Hmm. I wonder would I find a churn on eBay?

FEBRUARY GROWER'S CALENDAR

Prep Work

- If you didn't do so earlier in the winter, spread well rotted manure or compost over vegetable beds and cover selected areas with plastic or old carpet to start warming up the soil. The soil in raised beds will warm at least two weeks before open ground, which will make it easier to use later in the spring.
- For those beds that are not covered or for open ground, turn over the soil if the weather is good. To prevent soil compaction, don't stand on the beds – use timber planks for access.
- A 'fine-tilth' bed is one of the great sights in a vegetable garden. It's basically where you have a section of extremely well-prepared soil that has been forked over and then raked so that all 'clumps' of soil are broken up and it is perfectly even and crumbly (all debris and stones removed!). The texture should be like coarse breadcrumbs – not easy to achieve! Having a fine-tilth is not so important for those vegetables being transplanted (having been started off in a propagation module or pot), but it is vital for vegetables where the seeds are to be sown directly in the soil. In regular 'clumpy' soil, seeds (particularly small seeds such as carrot, lettuce) will fall down into little holes and will not germinate. Since next month will see the first outdoor sowings, now's a good time to start preparing seed beds. Make sure, however, that the weather is fine – if the clay sticks to your rake or your boots then it is too wet for raking!
- If you have not already done so, order/buy your seeds, seed potatoes and onion sets (basically baby onions; see Chapter 10). Chit seed potatoes – put them in a container (used egg carton or empty seed tray) and leave them in a bright, warm place (see Chapter 3).

To-do List
- Prune fruit trees and bushes if necessary, to improve their shape and remove winter damage to the bushes (it's best to complete this job before spring when the sap begins to rise). Consider netting the bushes after pruning (fruit netting can be bought in DIY stores and garden centres – it's worth it unless you want your fruit to become a nice treat for local birds) and dress the ground around with a potash feed (or use wood ash), which encourages fruit growth.
- Since different vegetables have different requirements when it comes to soil acidity, it's very important that you know whether your soil is acid or alkaline. Adding manure and compost tends to increase the acidity of your plot over time. You can check this by buying a soil pH testing kit in any garden centre. If your soil is acid, you can add lime at this time of the year (ground limestone – usually about 200g-250g per sq metre of soil, also available in garden centres), but this is typically done only with the area of your veggie patch that will be taking brassicas (cabbage, broccoli etc) as they don't like acid soil. In a standard three-year crop rotation plan, therefore (see Chapter 5), your whole plot is limed every three years.
- Scrub seed trays with hot, soapy water in preparation for sowing – dirty old seed trays can harbour disease.

Sowing Seeds
- Finally, we can sow some seeds.
- *On a sunny window sill indoors or in a heated greenhouse:* celery, globe artichokes, celeriac, leeks, onions, lettuce, tomatoes, peas, aubergines, peppers/chilli-peppers.
- *In polytunnel or greenhouse:* beetroot, brussels sprouts, summer and autumn cabbage, carrots, leeks, lettuce, radish.
- *Outside:* weather permitting, you can try planting out broad beans, spinach, kohlrabi, onion and shallot sets, Jerusalem artichokes, parsnip and early pea varieties.

Planting Out
- Plant new rhubarb if required, or divide existing plants.
- Now is a good time to plant fruit trees and bushes
- It's also a great time to start planning a herb garden – get root cuttings of

perennial herbs: mint, fennel, thyme etc. from friends and acquaintances. Buy seeds for the annual herbs like basil, coriander. (See Chapter 10.)

GRUB'S UP – WHAT'S IN SEASON?

If you're lucky, your root crops (like beetroot, carrots, parsnips) will still be going strong either from the ground or from storage. You could also still be eating last year's main-crop potatoes, winter squash, garlic and onions from storage.

Harvest cabbage and winter cauliflower, the last of the brussels sprouts, spinach and chard, kale and leeks, celeriac, Jerusalem artichokes, purple sprouting broccoli, forced rhubarb.

3

SPRING FORWARD

MID-SPRING: MARCH

sowing seeds – seasonality – potatoes – daylight saving

The biting cold of February is behind us. It's bright until 6.00pm now, which means there's time to get out and about in the garden even after a day's work. When the sun shines, you could be forgiven for thinking that it is already summer. You strip off layers of clothing – then the sun disappears behind the clouds and you quickly realise that there is still no real heat in the air and you should really put your clothes back on (the neighbours are talking). Still, these fleeting occurrences of warmth are enough to encourage nature to begin a veritable frenzy of growing. The farmer who owns the land around our acre has some of his cows out in the fields again now after a long winter indoors – so when standing at the kitchen sink we can see them in the adjacent field and hear the crunching noise as they tear grass from the ground. It is wonderful to see them out again. There are rapidly fattening green buds on the trees and, elsewhere in the surrounding area, there are little lambs frolicking (as only lambs can) in the fields.

All of which hints at *growth*, which is just as well because March is considered the leanest month in the vegetable patch in terms of actual harvesting. In the two months since Christmas, we have been itching to get going on our plans for the growing year, but there's very little actual growing that you can do when nature just won't play ball. Almost immediately after Christmas, seed catalogues arrived uninvited (but terribly welcome) by post from various suppliers we have used over the years – every year we sit at the kitchen table on miserable winter evenings perusing the catalogues and we end up ordering more seeds than we need, forgetting that sage advice about only growing things we like to eat. At this time of the year, seed catalogues hold the promise of unlimited creativity – they are chock-full of potential food production successes and we are far enough removed from the sobering reality of last year's growing blunders for the mists of time to have worked their gentle magic. The year ahead is a clean slate, a blank canvas, crying out to be filled with stunning gardening triumphs. 'This year everything will be perfect!' we enthuse, before once again spending our hard-earned cash on vegetables that we like the sound of but will never grow in a million years. Down at the bottom of our seed box are little reminders of the folly of our vernal enthusiasm: unused seed packets for vegetables with exotic names like okra, chicory witloof or scorzonera (also known as poor man's asparagus). What on earth were we thinking?

The dwindling larder probably explains why we are so keen (anxious even?) to get started on the growing year and in our eagerness we always start this process far too early. But nature stubbornly refuses to be rushed. It is really only now – in mid-spring – that it's worth starting to sow most seeds, but every year we try to get things going in January or early February (usually unsuccessfully).

I just love this time of year. In February and March the spare bedroom under the eaves in the house and a particularly sunny window sill in the study get converted into a temporary plant nursery. We take down the electric warming mat and dust it off. Rows and rows of little pots and seed-trays are filled with compost and little seeds are dropped in carefully. They are checked – with considerable excitement (and often much disappointment) – each day for signs of growth. Heating mats, while useful, cannot address the real issue at this time of the year: lack of light. It is longer hours of sunshine that our seeds need to encourage them to leave the comfort of the soil for the outside world, and sometimes I wonder whether the warming mat only serves to make the 'world out there' even less appealing for the little seeds. But eventually, after watching brown soil for days and days on end, a little bit of green appears and a shoot finally pushes itself out into the world. Is there anything in this world more darn hopeful than the sight of a germinated seed?

We get out our notes from last year and try to plan where and what we are going to grow in the season ahead. It feels good to be working on this after the grim emptiness of winter, but it's a complex task, nonetheless, for me at any rate. I suppose, like most men, I have a prehistoric, entirely limited, problem-solving type of brain that has a need to understand all facets of a subject before embarking on any project. For each vegetable that we are going to grow, I like to know when I need to sow, transplant and harvest it; where I am going to grow it, what soil it needs, how much water and light etc. Some vegetable gardeners have spent a lifetime working in the vegetable plot and still don't know all this, so you can only imagine how frustrating this is for me and ultimately how doomed to failure my quest is. Still, former IT nerd that I am, I spend a lot of time setting up an overly elaborate spreadsheet on my computer, outlining all the vegetables, fruit and herbs we grow and listing those key pieces of information for each one. Once I have gone through it and momentarily understood the magnitude of the job ahead, I am happy to leave it at that. It doesn't really bother me that I will rarely, if ever, return to the spreadsheet during the year. Once I map out my year's work in print I feel like it's half the battle – which, of course, it most emphatically is not. Mrs Kelly is not at all devoted to such 'time-wasting' matters, and prefers to get on with the actual growing. So I was amazed (and relieved) to discover that Anne Cullen, who helped me with the Grower's Calendars for this book, is equally strange about these things and likes to keep spreadsheets too – we pooled our resources and the result can be seen at the end of the book. I hope that you find it useful.

SEED PACKETS

For years I have been buying seed packets and ripping them open across the top, such is my enthusiasm to get growing. Unfortunately, by doing so I invariably end up ripping right through the invaluable information on the back of the packet about when to sow and harvest the vegetables inside. So until seed producers realise that it would make more sense to have this information on the bottom of the packet, here's a little tip: to open your seed packet rip across the bottom of the packet, not the top! You still get at the seeds and you leave all that vital information intact!

There is simply nothing in this world more satisfying that sowing seeds. In my opinion, it is the greatest way to soothe a furrowed brow or chase away worries and stresses. To spend a day outside, working your way methodically through a pile of seed packets and getting a whole raft of sowing done will leave you feeling immensely pleased with yourself and gratified at the thought that in days or weeks you will start to see little shoots emerging from the soil, and in weeks or months you will be tucking into home-grown vegetables. Sowing is, without question, my favourite part of the process of growing vegetables.

Nature has equipped seeds with all the potential they need to produce plants, so all we really need to do as growers is to create the conditions that they need in order to grow. When you *really* think about it, we are not growers at all, but facilitators. In our experience, sowing seeds in seed trays, modules or pots, then transplanting them outdoors when they are ready, is the most successful way of doing things. It is, no doubt, a slightly more expensive approach, since you have to buy potting compost, but, as far as I'm concerned, sowing direct is just way too random. I am somewhat a control freak and I know if I sow seeds directly into a bed I might get an occasional seed germinating here and there, but rarely, if ever, do I get the 100 per-cent success I crave. I have this suspicion that when I sow seeds in the soil, I am merely providing a tasty snack for slugs, rabbits, mice and God knows what other little critters who regard our vegetable plot as their meal ticket. There are also some seeds that are absolutely tiny (take celery as an example) and when a seed is practically microscopic you would really need to have a bed raked to within an inch of its life to make sure that the seed doesn't fall down into a little crevice in the soil where it will most assuredly die from lack of light. Raking things to within an inch of their lives – well now, that just isn't really us.

As well as that, a common problem for novice growers is that we just aren't good at thinning out vegetables – we sow a row of seeds, forget to thin them out and then all the vegetables suffer because they are too cramped. Expert gardeners will sow a row of seeds outdoors, then, when the seeds start to progress, will implement an unmerciful cull, ruthlessly picking out the weakest seedlings to give the required space to the stronger ones. Sowing seeds in modules indoors elimi-nates the need for thinning out because you are transplanting the cor-rect number of seedlings into the bed – there is no surplus to cull. Again, this suits us down to the ground. There *are* vegetables that don't really like being 'transplanted'. Root crops, like carrots and parsnips, for example, apparently do not like to be moved on like this, but we have grown both of these vegetables that way with con-siderable success and, conversely, we have sown both direct in the ground and not had a single germination. So I think that pretty much every vegetable will benefit from spending some time getting hardy in a module or tray before going out into the big, bad world. The only thing that you have to be really careful with is to take care when transplanting – some vegetables suffer badly from having their roots disturbed. The only exception we make is for potatoes, which are grown from 'seed potatoes' saved from the previous year's crop; onions, which we usually grow from 'sets' (basically, baby onions); and much larger seeds like courgettes, cucumbers and squashes – these take off really quickly, so we sow them outside.

It's a good idea to check the seed packet (or in a book or online) for the temperature a particular seed requires for germination. The average for most vegetables is about 18°C, but some require higher than that (cucumber plants will appreciate temperatures between 20°C–30°C, for example) and some lower (lettuce will germinate in about three days at about 15°C). Some seeds at this time of the year will need even more heat than a sunny window sill can provide and you might need to invest in a heated propagation pad or mat (or make one yourself if you're good with electrics and there's no risk of blowing up your house). In my experience, though, you don't need to be overly fussy, as there can be anything up to a ten-degree variation between the absolute maximum temperature a seed will germinate at and the recommended average – so don't worry too much about it. I couldn't tell you what temperature our study is, for example, which is where we get most of our seeds going – but there's a corner window there that gets good sunshine pretty much all day and it has plenty of window-sill space. From February on, that corner of the house always looks a mess, with trays, pots and modules all competing for space. The vast majority of our seeds germinate here, while the ones that don't need so much heat will go out to the tunnel, and the ones that need more go on the warming mat in the spare bedroom. We don't mind our house becoming a makeshift nursery for the spring – nothing is more conducive to a happy disposition than having little pots of growing things around the place.

Seeds are simple creatures at heart. Apart from having a suitable ambient temperature, they just need access to the right amounts of moisture and light. You need to water them regularly and never let the compost dry out, but you don't want them saturated either. They also need to have access to natural sunlight. Some seeds – celery, for example – need light to germinate, though most seeds germinate without light, then need it to start developing. A common problem at this time of the year is that there is not enough natural daylight and the seedlings start to get 'leggy' because they are basically craning their necks to reach light that's not there. This is why it's almost always inadvisable to try and get seeds going too early in the year. Someone told me once that you should move seed trays around a lot on your window sill, particularly if you notice that the seedlings seem to be all reaching in one particular direction.

Sowing seeds is a cinch and basically requires one of three container types – a small pot into which you can put one or many seeds; a 'tray' in which you scatter seeds; or a 'module', which is basically a tray divided up into little individual compartments. The module is the one we use most. It's far easier to transplant from this because the roots of the seedlings are less likely to get damaged. To remove a seedling from a module, you can usually just squeeze the bottom of it gently and the seedling will pop out into your hand, with the roots and compost in one handy, ready-to-transplant package. Another benefit of modules is that the roots of the seedlings can't mix because they each have their own private living quarters. If you scatter lettuce seeds onto a seed tray, for example, by the time the seedlings are ready to transplant into the soil, the root systems of the tiny plants are likely to be all intermingled, which makes the transplanting process a total nightmare, like being given a big ball of Christmas-tree lights to unravel. If you have just one or a couple of lettuce seeds in each compartment of a module tray, on the other hand, it's much easier to pop them out and put them in the soil. You can buy the professional seed modules trays (called propagation trays) that nurseries and commercial growers use from good garden centres and online retailers. In my opinion, it's worth spending a few bob on these as they will last for years, unlike the cheap, flimsy plastic ones that you will be throwing out after one season. These big commercial trays have up to 150 individual 'cells' in them, so two or three should be more than enough to cope with most of your seed sowing.

BIN RUMMAGING

Your recycling bin can often be a handy source of 'props' for vegetable growing, if you know what to look for. For example, cut clear plastic bottles in half and place over plants for very cheap and very effective 'cloches', which give protection to young plants. Redirect plastic fruit punnets to be used for covering seedlings to aid germination, or, indeed, as seed trays. Wash out your pots of yoghurt after use and they can be used as pots for sowing seeds, while the plastic tray that the pots of yoghurt came in are also very handy for keeping seedling pots together. Cut the big 2 litre plastic milk cartons in half and stick them (top down) in the soil beside your plants, forming a kind of funnel, so that when you are watering, the water goes direct to the roots. Use old gutters for seed sowing, old egg cartons for chitting potatoes, and an old kitchen colander as a dinky hanging basket. The sky's the limit.

Whether it's a tray, module or pot, fill it up with compost and firm it in well with your hand or a small flat stone. If the compost is too loose, the seed will probably slip downwards after you water it and it may well be far too deep in the soil to germinate. You should always water the compost *before* you sow the seeds – as mentioned before, some seeds are so tiny you could actually wash them away if you water them after putting them in the soil. Depending on the instructions on the seed packet, you may need to just rest the seed on the surface of the compost or stick it further down into it. Celeriac seeds, for example, are just sprinkled on the surface, carrot seed is sown down about 1cm, while a pea seed is pushed down about 5cm. We usually put a covering of very fine compost (which we sift using a soil sieve to get a really fine texture) on top of the seeds. Some seeds you will be able to handle individually, like beetroot, for example, while others are so small you just have to sprinkle them as carefully as possible, trying not to get clumps of seed in an individual module. Some people use vermiculite to cover the compost – this is an almost clear granular compound that allows light through to the seeds while retaining loads of moisture to help them germinate. We use it sometimes, when we have a bag handy. Sometimes we cover the modules with a covering of clear plastic – either cling film or old fruit punnets – which prevents the moisture from evaporating off the surface of the compost. But this comes with a caveat – sometimes the consistent moisture seems to cause a mould or fungus on the compost. So keep an eye on it – if it's too wet-looking, take it off. And always remove the cling film when the seeds have germinated.

SEED SWAP

Seeds can get damaged and go out of date, so it's a good idea not to order more than you will need. I know that's easily said – sometimes your enthusiasm will get the better of you and other times you just won't know how many you'll need. Keep the unused seeds in a cool, dry cupboard or, better still, an airtight container. If you have unused seeds that are going to be out of date by next year, why not organise or attend a thrifty seed swap? This way, you can exchange your unneeded seeds for something you may not have tried before.

I'm getting increasingly into the idea of sowing seeds into lengths of old guttering, just because it's so incredibly retro. We replaced the gutters in our house recently and when the old ones came down (lots of different lengths) we spirited them away quickly before they ended up in the bin. They are absolutely superb for growing all manner of seeds – peas, carrots, parsnips and so on. When you need to transplant, you simply wet the compost so that it is easier to handle, then move the seedlings to the edge of the gutter and slip them into a waiting trench in the soil. *Voila!*

You've heard, I'm sure, how it is said that when you buy three bags of groceries in a supermarket you may as well take one of them and fire it out the window of the car (watch out for people on the footpath) because that is roughly the amount of food that rots in the average fridge. I often feel that we do our own weekly shop out of habit more than anything else, and we go from aisle to aisle loading up with stuff because, well, we have come all this way with our little bags. And besides, I absolutely love food shopping.

All of which is incredibly wasteful, of course, and in these leaner times, we could all do with being a little more thrifty. It won't be long before the Home Farm comes into its own and there will be an abundance of fruit and vegetables available at the end of the garden – once again, I will start to fight that weekly urge to hop into the car and head for my favourite supermarket. This is not as easy as it sounds. You would think that when you go to the effort of growing stuff, you would be happy to enjoy the garden's bounty and turn your back on the supermarket. But it calls for a lot of adjustment in the kitchen. When it comes to mealtime, we have to find recipes that will suit what's ready in the garden as opposed to going out to buy produce for a particularly tasty-looking recipe. It also means giving up whimsical cooking of the 'I feel like x' variety. If your broad beans are ready today, thou shall eat broad beans tonight. Them's the rules.

I interviewed a Dutch chef called Martin Kajuiter who is head honcho in the kitchen at the Cliff House hotel in Ardmore, County Waterford. Martin was formerly head chef in a restaurant called De Kas, which is located in a renovated greenhouse in Frankendael Park in Amsterdam. In that kitchen, the importance of ultra-fresh produce is quite literally front and centre – the kitchen and restaurant sit in the middle of a productive nursery where chefs access fresh, seasonal vegetables, fruit and herbs. That same culinary vision followed him to his new enclave in Waterford. The Dutchman has a straightforward and almost completely ego-less food philosophy and – let's be honest – it's not often you can say that about a chef. Growers and food producers, he believes, are the real heroes, and the cook is but a messenger, telling a story about their food. The menus in his restaurant are based around fresh, local and seasonal produce all year round – this sounds fantastic for punters (and it is), but think about the challenge it presents in the kitchen. Kajuiter could talk all day about the lack of creativity in modern kitchens, where chefs are basically churning out the same meals night after night after night, and the main concern, when it comes to the food they buy, is continuity of supply. Not freshness or quality, but continuity.

Let's take this as an example. You're a chef in a restaurant where you have the same five main courses on the menu every night (with one or two specials, when the mood takes you). Say one of those meals is a rack of lamb. You have a major headache on your hands if there is a problem with the supply of lamb, particularly now that you've gone and laminated your menus and all. As long as you keep your supply of lamb constant, however, you're on the pig's back (forgive the mangled metaphor). The problem, of course, is that the supply of lamb, or at least good quality lamb, may not be continuous throughout the year and so chefs are putting up with all sorts of poor alternatives just to maintain the integrity of the menu. According to Kajuiter, this slavish adherence to a set menu is a recipe for disaster because it sucks the creativity and the life out of the kitchen. If chefs have to design the meals around the available produce and not the other way around, it imposes creativity on them – they literally have to come up with new and exciting ways to cook the available produce, as dictated by the seasons.

When he moved to Ireland, Kajuiter took out a map of Waterford, drew a circle of eighty kilometres around the hotel, and went about researching suppliers within the circle. He told me one intriguing story about his honey 'supplier', a local beekeeper who sells honey from the side of the road when he has an excess. Some days (at particular times of the year) the guy is there with his honey and Kajuiter will pull over on his way to work to get some, but more often, he's not. Most chefs would poke themselves in the eye with their sharpest butcher's knife rather than deal with such an 'unreliable' supplier. But to Kajuiter, this is the beauty of cooking and eating – it's about eating what's fresh and in season and challenging yourself when a key ingredient is suddenly unavailable. When it comes to vegetables and herbs, his chefs are encouraged to forage for interesting titbits for that night's menu in the vegetable garden at St Raphael's Centre in Youghal, a sprawling town about twenty minutes' drive from the hotel. St Raphael's is a respite centre for people with special needs, and a 'care garden' was established there some years ago where residents work, growing fruit and vegetables. Kajuiter set up a working partnership with them – they get his expertise, he gives them good money for their produce. All his chefs need to be creative in the kitchen to make this approach work and the result on the dinner plate is an absolute revelation.

There are lessons for us regular kitchen hackers in this model – after my interview with Kajuiter, I started looking at my shopping/cooking regime in a whole new light. It became abundantly clear to me that the way I was doing things was like a triple whammy of absolute stupidity – I was (a) spending a fortune on shopping, (b) buying so much that I ended up throwing some of it out anyway and (c) was letting the produce from the garden go to waste at the same time. We are all guilty of whimsical cooking – picking up a recipe book written by whatever celebrity chef is in vogue that week, and selecting a recipe, often because we are attracted by the accompanying picture. The recipe might have fifteen ingredients in it and we might only have five of those ingredients in our kitchen, so, of course, we get into our car and obediently head for the local supermarket to buy the other ten. Does it matter that one of those ingredients is courgette, which won't be in season for another four months? Of course not! Because your local supermarket will have courgette of some description on the shelf – it may be shipped in from Lima or sprayed with *something* that has mysteriously kept it looking fresh for six months longer than it should, but, goddammit, the recipe says courgette, so courgette it must be. And so we buy an expensive, flavourless, out-of-season courgette that has crossed continents and oceans to satisfy our numbing single-mindedness. When did we become so unimaginative? So uninventive? Produce-led cooking is a far more challenging way to do things, but the results will be infinitely better and it's a lot more fun.

It's easy to see why the spud is considered 'humble' – it quietly goes about its business, being neither much fêted nor heralded, and yet it is, arguably, one of the most useful ingredients we have in the kitchen. Very few dinners (in our house at least) do not contain some portion of potatoes, whether they be boiled, baked, roasted, fried, mashed, chipped, or if we're feeling sassy, *au gratin, duchesse* or *dauphinois*. So the spud is unquestionably a vegetable that is well worth growing. The problem is, however, that they take up a good deal of space and becoming self-sufficient in them is therefore an unlikely proposition for most of us. Though you can get a small crop of spuds growing in a pot on a balcony, if you so wish, if you are serious about having a reliable crop of spuds from June to October and having some for storage over winter, you would need to dedicate a fair patch of land to the project, and we just don't have the space for that (though having said that, if we were hungry enough I guess we would rip up the lawn altogether and do exactly that).

Add to that the fact that the shop-bought alternative is cheap and ubiquitous, and you might be inclined to think it's not worthwhile growing your own potatoes. We are lucky enough here in the south-east of Ireland to have on our doorstep that venerable county of Wexford, which has a fine tradition of spud growing, so we can usually get our hands on some great spuds in the local supermarket or farmer's market. So why bother growing our own? Well, I suppose I would put it this way – like everything else you will grow yourself, your own spuds will taste infinitely better than the shop-bought ones and you will almost certainly get more satisfaction from eating them.

Harvesting the first spuds in May or June is always up there among my favourite growing moments of the year. There's simply nothing better than grabbing a handful of new spuds from the soil, boiling them up (with a handful of fresh mint) and eating them with more butter than is good for the old ticker. Rummaging in the soil underneath a potato plant and finding lots of lovely tubers is a joy that gives opening presents on Christmas morning a run for its money. If there's someone in your life who is wholeheartedly disinterested in growing food, let them dig up one of your potato plants in early summer – it may well prove to be their 'Road to Damascus' moment.

Fundamentally, potatoes are not at all difficult to grow – all you are doing is basically sticking one of last year's spuds in the soil, which sprouts into a plant, which produces lots of other potatoes. Simple as that. They are, therefore, a great vegetable to try out in your first growing year – it's pretty much guaranteed that if you get as far as sticking that first seed potato in the soil in the spring, it will produce some class of a crop three months later and you will be feeling mighty pleased with yourself. In addition, potatoes won't really mind if you have crap soil and, in fact, they will do a good job of helping you to improve it. The process of 'earthing up' spuds (where you draw soil up around the stem to prevent sunlight from making the potatoes go green) does wonders for your soil, as does the fact that potato plants have dense foliage, which means that weeds don't stand a chance at getting established. Sowing spuds is a universally accepted method of helping to turn an unpromisingly poor piece of ground into a thriving vegetable patch.

Of course, in any discussion on growing potatoes, it would be remiss of me not to mention the problems that potato blight can cause. It seems strange that over 160 years after the start of the Famine, which killed so many Irish people, the latterday potato grower is still grappling with the airborne potato blight fungus, *Phytophthora infestans*. This is our own fifth year growing potatoes and, spurred on by the sloshy sloppiness that is the Irish summer, blight has delivered its mealy-mouthed misery on our crop twice – each time it happened, it was a complete pain in the ass, but it also served as a reminder of the privileged abundance that the modern food chain bestows on our society. While the fungus is, essentially, the same as that which devastated all around it in 1845, the consequences of potato blight on the modern grower could not be more different. Last year, when the leaves of our plants curled up and shrivelled and black spots started to appear on the potatoes, we were pretty despondent, because of the colossal waste of time of the whole enterprise as much as anything else. But, of course, we didn't go hungry or anything remotely like that, and though we were annoyed, we were, of course, able to head to the shop to buy spuds to replace our own. And that really was the end of that.

By comparison, in 1845 almost half the population of Ireland was completely and utterly reliant on the spud – it's hard for us to imagine a diet that consists of nothing other than potatoes, but that was pretty much all that people ate. The potato crop failed for four years in a row and as they had nothing else to eat, one million people quite simply starved to death (and another million were forced to emigrate). Perhaps the cruellest thing about it was that the blight got progressively worse year after year – after the first attack in 1845, in which about 50 percent of the crop was hit, people planted a huge quantity of potatoes the following spring, presuming, I guess, that lightning couldn't strike twice – but it did, with a vengeance. It failed almost totally in 1846 and again in 1847, which is often called Black '47 because of the utter catastrophe that three failed harvests brought to the Irish people. I did a walk a few years back in the Maamturk Mountains on the Galway–Mayo border with a local archaeologist and he pointed out the remains of a deserted nineteenth-century village, which, like many others in the region, had been abandoned after the famine. The remains of potato drills that you can still see on the slopes of the mountain are as poignant a snapshot of tragedy as the excavated bodies of Pompeii and show the brutal speed at which the famine wrought its misery.

Cocooned in the warm embrace and relative certainties of the latter-day food chain, we don't spray our spuds (out of principle) and we are too lazy to go online and figure out a recipe for an organic alternative to the nasty chemical sprays that are out there. We prefer, in our innocence, to leave things in the lap of the gods – and the gods have occasionally rewarded the trust we placed in them by plundering our spud crop. Anecdotally at least, it would appear that the only way to deter blight these days is to spray the life out of your spuds every other day, and commercial spud growers do exactly that. In recent years, highly aggressive strains of blight are attacking spuds and making a mockery of attempts to foil them. There have been developments in genetics resulting in so-called blight resistant potatoes (like the Sarpo Mira varieties, for example), but I don't know, that all just seems a bit GMO for my liking – plus, I was talking to a fellow Home Farmer recently who'd got blight on a crop of so-called blight resistant potatoes, so where does that leave you?

Our plan for this year is to focus our energies on early crops of potatoes (planted in the middle of this month and harvested in June, and an 'early-early' crop, planted in the polytunnel in February and harvested in May) that are likely to be out of the ground before blight strikes. You get fewer potatoes from your earlies than your main crop (because they have had less time to develop) but, on the other hand, you are getting a good supply of new potatoes at a time of the year when they tend to be really expensive in the shops. Interestingly, most Home Farmers I spoke to this year about spraying muttered darkly that they don't normally, but that they probably will next year. I can empathise with that.

DEALING WITH POTATO BLIGHT

Blight usually strikes in warm, damp summer and autumn weather and you will know you're affected when the leaves become blotched with yellow and brown marks that look a lot like rust. The potatoes themselves develop similar brown marks and then go to a rotten, slimy mess. Many growers spray their potato crops with copper-based sprays (such as Bordeaux mixture) some of which are certified organic. My feelings on this are: whatever works for you. Being completely organic is a very worthwhile ideal to have, but if you're primarily interested in food production, then losing a crop to blight may be a considerable loss and you may consider spraying a necessary evil. Both points of view are valid, in my opinion.

If blight does strike, the only remedy is to cut the foliage down immediately as soon as you see the tell-tale signs and harvest the crop about three weeks later. Blight doesn't travel through the plant to the potatoes, but it does get washed down from the leaves into the soil, which explains why cutting the foliage helps. We did this quite successfully last year and though our spuds were small, at least we salvaged some of them. Make sure to burn the foliage – potato blight is an airborne fungus, so you don't want rotting piles of infected plants lying around the place.

Okay, so all this sounds bad and may deter you from growing spuds at all. I have to say that, despite all these woes, we still love growing potatoes and we revel in getting stuck into sowing them each spring, mainly because it's the first big vegetable-growing project of the season on the Home Farm. It's worth mentioning that, unlike most other vegetables you may try to grow (with the exception perhaps of onions and garlic), potatoes are rarely, if ever, grown from seed, but instead are grown from other potatoes. A potato plant from which you will get anything from five, ten or fifteen potatoes grows from a single seed potato, which, you must admit, is a marvel of efficiency (and truth be known, unpredictability). We buy bags of seed potatoes in late January and come early March we will usually have been 'chitting' our seed potatoes on a window sill for about four to six weeks. This gives the spuds a head start, so that when you put them in the ground they have a better chance of survival. It's one of those annual routines that we take some solace from and which seems to herald the start of the growing year proper. It means all those Mickey Mouse, time-wasting chores are over and things are about to crank up a notch.

If you have left spuds down the back of your press only to discover they seem to be sprouting from all angles a few weeks later, then, congratulations, you're already a successful chitter. Chitting doesn't involve a whole lot apart from putting the seed potatoes in some old egg cartons (or any shallow container) and leaving them somewhere bright and warm to allow them to develop little shoots. If you leave them in a place that's too warm or dark they develop very long, spindly shoots, which will probably break off when you go to plant them. Allow just two shoots to develop – rub off any other ones – as this allows the spud to put its efforts into just those two shoots rather than spreading its energies too thinly across a larger number of shoots. Some growers swear by keeping some of last year's potato crop as seed potatoes for the following year, but unless you can be guaranteed that your spuds are completely disease free, this isn't advisable. For the same reason, it isn't wise to use the potatoes that you would buy in the shop to eat. When you buy specially produced seed potatoes of any variety they will be certified disease free, so at least you have a clean bill of health to start with.

I also enjoy the fact that growing spuds pays dividends quickly. Okay, so it will be late June before you have your first earlies or new potatoes (and I always eat so many at my first sitting that I get a pain), but in a few weeks' time there will be visible signs of growth. The first little deep-green leafy shoots will appear above ground and then the real work of earthing up and watering will commence. In the warmer months of May, when the Home Farm vegetable beds still look pretty bare, at least the spud bed is resplendent in greenery.

GROWING SPUDS IN A SMALL SPACE

If you don't have much space, you can still grow potatoes quite success-fully in large pots or containers – as to how self-sufficient you can become, that really depends on how many large pots or containers you have! The pots will need to be relatively deep – about 45cm deep so the spuds have the depth of soil they need to grow. Put a layer of compost on the bottom of the pot and place the seed potato on it, then cover it with another layer of compost and water-in. Each time the top of the leaf pops out over the soil cover it over again – you can continue with this until the pot is full. This plays a little trick on the poor potato plant because it has to grow more stem to get out of the soil – more stem growth means more space for the potatoes to grow. The spuds will love a nice bright patio or deck, but bear in mind that the containers may be too heavy to lift once filled with soil.

Alternatively, you could try growing spuds in a compost bag. Buy a bag of compost (it will cost you about €7), open it carefully (don't rip the bag), and empty out the compost. Roll the top of the bag down about half-way. Put a small layer of compost back into the bottom of the bag and put two or three seed potatoes on top (spaced as far apart as possible). **Cover them with another layer of compost. Store the remaining compost – you will need it later for earthing up. Each time you see a shoot appearing above the soil, cover it up with more compost and unroll the bag slightly. Keep adding compost every time a shoot appears until you have used up all the compost and the bag is fully unrolled and full of compost again. You will need to water the plants daily as there is a risk with this type of growing that the compost will dry out – make sure it doesn't. In terms of how long to leave them grow, follow the usual guidelines for potatoes. When the plants are finished flowering, empty the bag carefully and harvest your lovely spuds. You can spread the compost in the vegetable garden (but not where you will be growing spuds next year).**

Appropriately enough, St Patrick's Day is the traditional spud-planting day in Ireland because that is when the risk of frost has more or less passed. We find that a major national holiday also serves as a handy reminder (if such a thing is needed) for us to get our act together and start sowing. You shouldn't be too rigid about getting your potatoes in the soil in March, however – if the weather is too cold, just wait. And if you do put them in the ground in March, keep an eye on the weather forecast, and cover the soil with fleece or plastic if you have to. There are loads of ways to plant spuds, and old-hand potato growers will bend the ear right off you, if you let them, on which is the best way. There's a sinfully easy lazy bed way, where you sow potatoes on completely unprepared soil – your lawn, for example; you simply drop the spud on the ground and then turn over a sod from each side on top of the spud to start a ridge. Apparently, as the grass on the underside of the sod starts to decay, it provides the spud with the nutrients it needs, and the spud simply grows right through the sod. If you grow them the more traditional way, the best advice I can give, for what it's worth, is to make sure you have well fertilised soil – try and dig loads of manure into the soil the previous autumn or, alternatively, if you have forgotten to do that, add some at the time of planting. After that, you dig a big, long trench and space the seed potatoes along it. Or you might plant individual potatoes in 10cm-deep holes and cover them with soil. We usually do the latter and we put them in different beds each year to try to prevent the build-up of disease in the soil (though it's the disease in the air you really need to be worried about with spuds). The spuds need to be spaced about 25cm apart in the rows, and the rows about 60cm apart. When you place the seed potato in the ground, allow the shoots to face up (face them down and they will die off – doh!) and don't pack it too tightly with soil or you might break the shoot. Traditionally, you draw a mound of soil over the line of spuds to protect them from early frosts – and also to mark the them out so you know where you've sown them. After a few hours spent sowing, it's pretty cool and immensely satisfying to look back on your vegetable patch and see rows of neat furrows. It feels like proper gardening!

When the first leaves appear over the ground and the plants are about 20cm tall, you start to 'earth up' around the base of the plants – this is a job that will you will have to do every two weeks or so as they grow further. The idea behind this is that it encourages the plant to form more stem, which means more lovely spuds for your dinner. In addition, potatoes that are exposed to the light turn green from the presence of a substance called solanine – though it is localised near the skin (and can therefore usually be removed). There is a woeful, bitter taste to potatoes that have greened and, depending on the book you are reading, they are either vaguely toxic or absolutely lethal. So it's best to try and avoid this while you are growing them. If you see a potato peeking through the soil at any point during the growing season, make sure to cover it up well. Apart from that, potatoes are relatively low-maintenance. Thanks to the dense foliage that the plants produce, there is no huge amount of weeding to do in summer, but before the foliage appears you need to keep the furrows weed-free. They will also need a good watering, particularly in dry weather, so make sure you plant them near a water supply! You really don't want to be lugging buckets of water around, particularly if it's hot.

Potatoes are classified based on how long it takes for them to mature – new potatoes or first earlies are harvested first, followed by second earlies and then the main crop. Early crops will be ready after eighty to a hundred days, while main crops will take almost twice that. Start to harvest earlies when the first white flowers appear on the plants, which is usually a sign that there are spuds under the ground (this will happen from June onwards). Main crops will be lifted much later – in autumn, when the foliage has died off.

To be honest, we don't have enough land to grow that many spuds, so we basically just pick them as we need them (rather than harvesting all at once). I like this way of doing things – it means you get to rummage for some spuds as you need them for each meal and also that they continue to grow when left in the ground. Just don't leave them in the ground beyond autumn (they will be at risk from frosts) or if the soil is too wet, as they will start to rot. Clamping was an old way to store spuds outdoors where they were basically put on the ground, covered in straw and then a layer of muck to create a relatively impermeable mound – I love the idea of this, but we never have enough spuds to get this far. Either we are growing too few or eating way too many.

PAULA MEE'S NUTRITION BITES: POTATOES

Spuds fill you up, not out! Let's smash the myth that potatoes are fattening, once and for all – it's the portion size we eat and how we cook them that can cause weight gain. I like to think of potatoes as 'power on a plate' – they are rich in carbohydrates and therefore a fantastic fuel for our bodies. Unadulterated and unprocessed, they are probably the best source of starchy energy in our diets, and in a world where many carbohydrates are so processed that they are devoid of essential nutrients, the potato stands head and shoulders above the rest. Potatoes also contain some protein, little or no fat and have almost twice the amount of fibre as the same amount of brown rice. They are a good source of potassium, important for healthy blood pressure, and contribute a significant amount of vitamin C, a powerful antioxidant and important for immune health.

Nutrition per Portion (80g):

Vegetable	Calories	Fat (g)	Salt (g)	Saturated Fat (g)
New Spuds	56	0.2	0.02	0.1
Old Spuds	60	0.2	0.02	0

The other major event that occurs in March, which I have thus far neglected to mention, is daylight saving. It is such an inherent part of life now, it's easy to forget that it is a comparatively recent invention. Depending on who you believe, it was invented either by an entomologist from New Zealand called George Vernon Hudson in 1895 or an English builder named William Willet in 1907. Either way, it would appear it was Willet's suggestion that led to the widespread introduction of daylight saving in Europe. Willet was an early riser, and he was riding his horse in Kent very early one summer's morning when he happened to notice that most of the houses in his locality had shutters down to exclude the light. It occurred to him that for nearly six months of the year the sun shines upon the land for several hours each day while we are asleep, while artificial light is required to light up homes at the other end of the day. This struck Willet as a colossal waste of money, and, busybody that he was, he came up with a proposal to move the clocks forward by twenty minutes on each of the four Sundays in April, and then move them back by the same amount on four Sundays in September. His idea was widely ridiculed at the time, until World War I came along and the UK authorities started to see that it would help them to save fuel. Daylight saving can be confusing even now, but imagine how befuddled people were about it then! We do *what* with our clocks?

Willet believed that his proposal would improve the health and happiness of the populace and, you know what, I think he was right. I certainly feel all the better for the extra hours of daylight in the evening time. Daylight saving seems to usher in the spring as surely as any buds growing on the trees, particularly if you are lucky enough to enjoy a nice bright day the day after the clocks roll forward. The hour going forward is a huge milestone in the Home Farmer's year because, of course, it means that from here on in, there are sufficient hours of daylight to get some work done in the veggie plot in the evening, even after a full day's work. If you always struggle to remember which directions the clocks should go in spring and autumn, remember this mnemonic: Spring forward, fall back.

MARCH GROWER'S CALENDAR

Prep Work

- March is a key month in the food grower's garden and the first of three exceptionally busy months for the Home Farmer.
- Continue to prepare ground – there is still time to prepare a plot or make a raised bed to grow vegetables this summer.
- Remove the plastic from covered beds that will need to be used for planting in March. Fork or rake over the soil and break up large clods of earth. Avoid treading on the soil.
- In mild weather you can start to harden off hardier seedlings by moving them outside during the day. Don't forget to bring them back in at night. Don't be fooled by the slight warmth in the air! March can still bring occasional frosts which will cause havoc for some seedlings and plants, such as potato plants. Keep an eye on the weather forecast and cover new seeds with fleece if you think a frost is due.

To-do List

- Once you sow seeds you need to protect them from your nemesis, the slug. Start your nightly slug patrol!
- Don't let new-season weeds take over your plot – now's the time to get on top of them by hoeing. Weed little and often.
- Last chance to prune apple trees and perennial herb plants like thyme and mint. A good clipping in spring (which is the main growing season for them) will prevent herbs degenerating into an unruly summer mess. Pruning makes sure that the plants remain compact, rather than leggy – which should mean better produce. Don't be afraid to prune hard; with thyme plants, for example, you

can take half the length of each stem. Be particularly vicious with weak and lanky stems.

- Top dress over-wintered crops such as onions, spring cabbage. Use good quality compost or well rotted chicken manure – this will give the crops a good spring boost.

Sowing Seeds

- Always check the individual details on seed packets – more often than not, the information on the back of a seed packet will tell you the vast majority of information you need to know about growing that particular vegetable: when to sow, when to harvest, type of soil, spacing and so on.

- *Sow indoors on a sunny window sill or heated greenhouse*: lettuce, aubergines, peppers, chilli-peppers, cucumbers, celery, celeriac, fennel, sweet corn, basil, leeks, summer cabbage, cauliflower, brussels sprouts, parsley, courgettes, French beans.

- *Sow outdoors or under cover*: broad beans, red cabbage, carrots, cauliflower, spinach, kale, brussels sprouts, onions, leeks, turnips, peas, radishes, early lettuce, asparagus.

- I've never been a huge fan of plants and flowers that you can't eat (all that work and for what?) but I think it's worth growing the following flowers on the Home Farm because of the benefits they bring to your veggies: calendula (marigold), centaurea (cornflower) and nasturtium. These pretty annuals will help deter aphids and whitefly while attracting beneficial lacewings and ladybirds.

- Take the pain out of springtime sowing: consider a seed-growing group with friends. For example, five people form a group; one person takes responsibility for sowing tomatoes and sows twenty-five tomato plants. They give five plants each to the other four in the group and retain five for themselves. Someone else does the same with courgettes, peas, beans etc, and then you all get together to swap. This is a great way to lighten the load of sowing and to experience new varieties.

Planting Out

- Have you been chitting your spuds? Plant your first early seed potatoes as soon as weather conditions allow. Paddy's Day traditionally, but wait until the soil is warm and weather has improved.

- Plant asparagus crowns and globe artichokes.
- Plant Jerusalem Artichoke tubers (although not to everyone's taste, they are very good for soups and stews and they are also very handy for feeding pigs – a plot can be planted and when the artichokes mature (December – February) can be left in the ground for the pigs to root out themselves.

GRUB'S UP – WHAT'S IN SEASON?

March was called the hungry gap because of the dearth of fresh vegetables. The efficient Home Farmer thumbs his nose at the notion of a hungry gap and this month is enjoying (from the ground or from storage) onions, leeks, parsnips, potatoes, mint, sprouting broccoli, kale, perpetual spinach, rhubarb, chard, the first of the spring cauliflowers and cabbage.

Under cover in the polytunnel or greenhouse, you could also be harvesting lettuce, radishes, rocket, and carrots (ready now from late autumn planting).

4

LET THEM EAT CAKE

LATE SPRING: APRIL

*loving spring – the pork crisis – keeping pigs – traditional breeds –
broad beans – pigs' arrival*

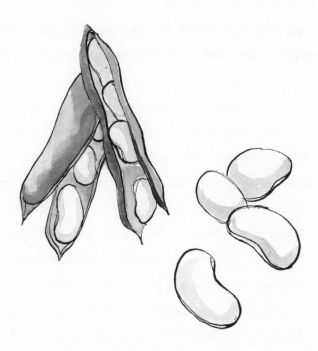

Did you know that the number one April Fool's prank of all time, as voted by the Museum of Hoaxes, involved duping an entire nation about pasta growing on trees? The year was 1957 and the respected BBC news show, *Panorama*, announced to a grateful nation that thanks to a mild winter and the virtual elimination of the dreaded 'spaghetti weevil', Swiss farmers were enjoying a bumper spaghetti crop. This wonderful news was accompanied by footage of Swiss peasants pulling bountiful strands of spaghetti down from trees. Huge numbers of viewers were, apparently, taken in by the idea and many called the BBC wanting to know how they could grow their own spaghetti tree. The advice offered was to 'place a sprig of spaghetti in a tin of tomato sauce and hope for the best.'

Ah yes. You really would want to be very miserable indeed not to love the inane foolishness of April. There is new warmth in the air, increased length in the days and the soil is starting to warm up. There may not be a huge amount of new-season vegetables worth eating just yet (though, if you are lucky enough to have planted asparagus and purple sprouting broccoli last year, you will be savouring them round about now). Our vegetable plot is starting to take shape and by the middle of this month the vast majority of our new-season seed sowing is more or less complete. The black plastic we used to cover down our raised beds for the winter has now been removed and put away for the year, and the beautiful soil beneath turned over to aerate it. So the vegetable plot looks ready for action. After a good spell of rain over the past few days, there are signs of growth and reasons to be cheerful pretty much everywhere you look.

In the hedges around our house we see the first signs of beautiful snow-white flowers on the blackthorn tree. The flowers will look magnificent for just a few weeks and will be followed by dull green leaves and then by incredibly sour blackish-purple sloes in the autumn. We made an interesting concoction called sloe gin a few years back – we still have some of it left, come to think of it, which I think probably says something about how successful it was. But it's great to have it all the same.

SLOE GIN

It's enormously satisfying to make an alcoholic beverage yourself, particularly if it contains freshly picked free fruit from a hedge. In the autumn, pick about 900g of sloes in a colander and bring them inside to give them a rinse. You then have to prick each sloe a couple of times, which is incredibly time consuming – the only way to approach this task is to sit down with friends or family and divide the sloes between you. The task will turn into a convivial, companionable affair if you have a good gossip at the same time. Sterilise a large preserving jar that has a tight-fitting lid and pop each sloe into it as you go. Add 250g of white sugar and then 1.2 litres of good gin. Mix it well and then put it away in a dark place for four months, giving it a good shake every few days or whenever you think of it. The liquid will gradually turn a wonderful purple colour. It will be ready just in time to get your guests well and truly hammered on Christmas day. If you can't get sloes, you can use damsons, and if you don't like gin, you can use vodka.

Over the next month the mighty gorse or furze bushes dotted around the countryside in these parts will produce an explosion of beautiful golden-yellow flowers and every year I vow to make gorse-flower wine, which I am told is quite the brew. Of course, I never get around to it, and on my walks around the fields with the dogs I dolefully notice the yellow fading to off-white and I know my chance has passed for another year. Still, even if you never get to pick a batch of gorse flowers for brewing, it's worth stopping occasionally to pick a flower and breathe in its extraordinary coconut smell. Gorse has flowers on it most of the year, but it's only in spring that they are really worth looking at. The old saying goes, 'When gorse is out of blossom, kissing's out of fashion' – in other words, kissing is in all year round. Thank goodness for that.

Speaking of randy behaviour, the dawn chorus is in full swing these mornings. Ireland's domestic birds are joined by migrants from all over the world around the middle of this month and these overseas invaders turn the volume control on the dawn chorus up several notches – the young males are singing to attract mates and, it seems, the louder they sing, the more chance they have. I like to wake up a bit earlier than usual and open up the window – the songs of these tiny Romeos set me up for the day.

We have started to harvest our rhubarb already and the other fruit bushes, plants and trees are starting to show signs of life – strawberry plants, raspberry canes, gooseberries, blackcurrants are all on the move after a long lay-off, and, of course, the apple and pear trees are starting to blossom. After being hardened off for a week or so, our little pea and broad bean plants went out into the legume bed over the weekend, with a chicken-wire fence for them to grow up and protective netting overhead to give them cover from birds (and hens) – they look so tiny and fragile and we fretted a little when the weather turned inclement on the Monday, but they seem to be bearing up fine and the bit of greenery in the outdoor beds (finally) looks great. All of our potatoes are in the ground by now, as are our onions and garlic. We sow an early crop of potatoes in the polytunnel and these are already pushing up those wonderful luscious, deep green leaves – they need regular 'earthing up' already.

The polytunnel is looking increasingly busy – we transplanted some tiny lettuce seedlings and French breakfast radishes (a beautiful, elongated radish with a red body and white tip) from module trays into the open ground last week, so our night-time slug patrols take on a new urgency. Lengths of old guttering are filled with sowings of early carrots and are being watched eagerly for signs of growth. There are also (in various stages of development) beetroot, calabrese (regular broccoli), brussels sprouts, summer cabbage and successional sowings of peas and beans. Rocket is starting to take off again and the perennial herbs and perpetual spinach, which were growing sheepishly for a few months, are taking on new signs of life. Purple sprouting broccoli for next year (imagine that) has been sown in modules already – such a long growing season and yet you just know it's worth it because it will bring considerable cheer to the kitchen next March. There are also lots of plants in pots, modules and trays getting the full five-star hotel treatment inside on the window sill in the study. Tiny, stringy little leeks are just starting to push themselves out above the compost, while other plants, like courgettes, aubergines, tomatoes and peppers, are all coming along well.

Spring is a very busy time for the Home Farmer, although the main bulk of the work is in the seed sowing – and to my mind that's not really work at all. There's not a lot of watering to be done yet, apart from occasional hosing of thirsty plants in the polytunnel on warm days, but it is an important time of the year to do some weeding; if you can stay on top of the young weeds that are starting to germinate right about now, you will have less weeds to deal with for the rest of the year. It's like the old maxim about eating an elephant one mouthful at a time – pull a weed any time you spot one. We also try and do a bit of a spring clean in the garden, as is fitting for this time of the year. Things inevitably become a little untidy over the winter, so a day spent clearing and cleaning will make things easier on the eye. The Home Farm should always look neat and tidy, I reckon, because while there is a good, noble and productive enterprise under way, it is also a place where we will spend a serious amount of time over the next eight months, so you want it to look nice too. By the way, if you haven't sown any seeds yet, don't worry – there is still time and seeds sown around now will usually catch up pretty quickly. Worst case scenario, you can always cheat and buy some plants from your local garden centre. We've been known to do this over the years if we are just too lazy, or if we forget to sow something, or if seeds occasionally fail to germinate – it happens. Though it is obviously more expensive to do things this way, it's still a hell of a lot cheaper (and far more satisfying) than buying the end product in a supermarket.

You might recall that Ireland experienced a very significant food crisis in December 2008 when a sample of Irish pork was found to contain unacceptably high levels of toxins. The problem originated with a feed manufacturer who was converting the leftovers of human food – chocolate, stale bread, out-of-date biscuits, crisps, old dough etc – into a high-energy feed for farm animals, known in the industry, rather quaintly, as 'cake'. The cake is used by some farmers as an alternative to barley, the price of which has gone through the roof over the past few years. So far, so thrifty, you might think. Well, yes – to a point. But the company was using low-grade oil from electricity transformers to heat the feed and, somehow, tainted fumes containing PCBs (*polychlorinated biphenyls*) were absorbed by the cake and entered the food chain. At first, it seemed like it was no big deal – first of all, the feed manufacturer was supplying only seven of the country's four hundred pig farms, and secondly, everyone involved was keen to stress that the risk to human health was very small (even though the pork tested had dioxin levels literally off the charts – over two hundred times higher than 'safe' levels).

But there was a snag. Pig meat is the most processed of all meats – beef, lamb and chicken usually show up on your plate relatively unadulterated, but think about all the pig-meat products that have to be processed first: bacon, rashers, sausages, chorizo, salamis and so on. As a result of all this processing, the Department of Agriculture and Food's much-vaunted tracing system, where every pig herd in the country has a unique herd number, was found to be severely wanting. A sausage, for example, may contain meat not only from different pigs, but also different herds and different farms. In this context, traceability is possible only to the *processing plant*, but not to the farm, and, as a result, the government had no way of telling which products had the toxic meat in them. It was therefore forced into an embarrassing, complete recall of all pig-meat products, as well as telling people to dispose of any meat they had in their fridge or freezer. The result was the almost apocalyptic vision of empty meat shelves in the supermarkets. More than 130,000 pigs and over 2,000 cattle (cows eat cake too) had to be slaughtered and the crisis cost Irish taxpayers over €180 million in 'compensation' to processors and producers. It also did incalculable damage to Ireland's reputation as a food exporter and, in particular, to the pig industry, which exports nearly €370 million worth of product each year to over twenty-five of our European neighbours. Ouch.

There were a few things that struck me about the whole thing. First of all, we were feeling mighty smug that we had our own pork and bacon in the freezer and that we didn't need to worry about its safety. After I got over feeling smug, I felt pretty angry about all the hoops that we are forced to jump through to comply with the department's tracing system with our own two piggies – and you really had to wonder what the bloody point of it all was when it clearly only works up to the door of the processing plant. On a more general level, I was also struck by just how complex the food chain has become and how vulnerable our food security is to the shenanigans of the unscrupulous and the hopelessly inept. The more levels we introduce between the act of producing food and the act of eating it, the more unstable and vulnerable the whole thing becomes. Just one little link in the chain, one feed producer supplying just seven pig farmers, could bring the whole house of cards falling down and had Europe-wide implications. I also had a feeling that the whole thing was terribly unjust – it didn't matter a jot if you were rearing pigs in a free range or organic manner and knew definitively that you weren't feeding them 'cake' – your product was recalled too and effectively tarred with the same brush.

Anyway, if we needed further encouragement to keep going with our pig rearing here on the Home Farm, then the pork crisis surely supplied it, or at least validated our continued efforts. We fatten two little pigs over a five- or six-month period between spring and autumn each year, with a view to stocking up the freezer with almost a year's supply of pork and bacon. April, therefore, is usually the month in which our piggies arrive and is always a time of huge excitement here. Pigs really are one of the most useful animals that you can have around. They eat almost any food you give them, converting all manner of garden and kitchen waste into delicious food, while at the same time fertilising your land with their manure. The fact that you get top-quality, free-range pork and bacon into the bargain at a time when such things are simply impossible to get your hands on, means that you have an animal that is literally worth its weight in gold.

We are usually quite happy to take a break from pig rearing over the winter months because it is, quite frankly, a lot of hard work. When the pigs leave our garden, bound for the abattoir in August, they are huge creatures and we are happy enough to see the back of them. Well, okay, maybe that's a little harsh; we're not exactly *happy*, but we are certainly relieved – you see, in their final weeks here you literally can't keep up with how much feed they need, and there's a huge amount of very unpleasant 'mucking-out' to do in the pigsty. But when they arrive here first – ah well, now that's a different matter entirely. A pig that has just been weaned from its mother is about the size of a little puppy and just as cute, so there is always great excitement when they arrive and invariably lots of curious visitors.

Keeping a few weanlings (young piglets of about eight to twelve weeks, just weaned off their mother's milk) each year is the fastest and easiest way to raise pigs if you don't have much land. If you do have a lot of land you could get yourself a sow and start breeding them yourself; if you do this, you will have progressed further than I have and I'm afraid I can no longer offer you much advice. Typically, young pigs (up to about five months) are kept for fresh meat, ie pork. The meat from slightly older pigs (about nine months to a year) would be a little too tough to eat as pork and it is therefore processed in some way (dry-cured or wet-cured, smoked etc) to make bacon. In our case, however, we send our two pigs to the slaughter at the same time, usually when they are about six months old and we use one for pork and the other for bacon (though we love pork, we think bacon is just as useful and delicious).

The basics of keeping a few piglets is essentially as follows: have a bit of ground and appropriate shelter for them; grow or buy grain to feed them; make sure they get fresh water every day; toss a few bales of straw into their house to keep them warm; watch them grow over a few months and then take the finished pigs to the slaughter. Oh yeah, and then eat them.

The beauty of keeping pigs yourself is that you can try out traditional and rare breeds, of which there are many varieties. An old breed of pig reared outdoors will be a revelation in the kitchen for three reasons – first of all, it will have far more fat on it (particularly back fat) than the meat from a commercial pig that is reared to be lean. All of us, as consumers, are guilty of driving the demand for lean meat because we somehow feel it's healthier and that we are getting more value for our money. But lean meat is, unfortunately, flavourless meat. The more fat you have in your meat, the more flavour it will have. If we are worried about our health (which, of course, we should be) we would be far better off, in my opinion, eating smaller quantities of proper meat with the normal amounts of fat, rather than eating larger quantities of freakishly lean meat. We have found the meat from our pigs to be an absolute revelation – divinely juicy dark pork, exquisite ham, and sausages and bacon that taste like they used to taste.

A Home Farm pig will generally have a longer life than its commercial cousin; because it's out and about, getting some exercise, it takes about a third longer to get to killing weight, and, let's be honest, if you do grow a little more attached to it than you should (always a danger), you won't be in any real hurry to kill it. It stands to reason that a pig that can be killed sooner is a more profitable proposition for a pig farmer, and commercial breeds can be finished in sixteen to eighteen weeks, but on the Home Farm it will take from six to ten months. This less frenetic pace of life means that the pig has time to build up the fat, muscles and tissue that contribute the 'marbling' effect to the meat and makes it taste all the nicer. And because the animal will spend its short life rooting in the soil for nutrients, it will be a healthier pig, all round. A happy, healthy pig, reared in the outdoors in a stimulating environment, will *in all cases* produce better quality meat than a miserable pig reared indoors, deprived of stimulation and its natural way of life. Here are four things that a commercially reared pig never gets to appreciate in its lifetime: sunlight, straw, fresh air, soil. Even after just a few years of rearing pigs, I can tell you that these animals greatly appreciate all of those things. Our pigs are like sun-worshipping holiday-makers – they love to lie out in the sun; when you provide them with straw for bedding, they bury deep down inside it for warmth and comfort; they just love being out in the fresh air; and, as for rooting in the soil, well, I'll come back to that in a moment, but suffice to say that a pig's life just would not be complete without rooting.

The vast majority of pork and bacon that most of us have consumed throughout our lives comes from pigs reared indoors and usually from a single breed (or a variant thereof), for example, the Large White. Cross-breeding of pigs to get them to grow quicker and produce leaner meat has not been without consequences for the pig – it has created a lean, muscular hybrid pig that is only suited to an indoor life. It is generally hairless, for one thing, which means it would freeze to death if left outside in cold weather, and it is also pink-skinned, which, as Western Europeans will know only too well, leaves the skin vulnerable to sunburn. Even if the pig industry suddenly decided to embrace free-range systems (believe me, they won't), the pigs they currently have at their disposal would be wholly unsuitable for the job. In any case, the pig industry simply does not have the land it needs to rear enough pigs outdoors to keep up with our insatiable appetite for pork and bacon.

Around 1.3 *billion* pigs are slaughtered worldwide each year for meat. A company called Smithfield, the world's largest and most profitable pork processor, killed – wait for it – 27 million pigs last year and produced 2.7 billion kg of packaged pork. That's just *one* North American company. In an area in the Netherlands known as De Peel, which is more densely populated with pigs than any other area of the planet, they kill 20 million pigs a year and use multi-storey sheds, called pig-flats, to maximise space. Even in a small country like Ireland, we kill almost one pig for every person each year.

These numbers are astonishing in their own right, but it is the conditions in which these poor animals are kept that should really give us pause for thought on so many levels: animal welfare, environmental impact, meat quality, even human health. Commercial pig-rearing systems deprive pigs of everything that makes their lives worth living and, worse than that, they are inherently cruel. Jon Henley reported in *The Guardian* in 2009 that *the norm* in the European pig industry is: pigs kept on slatted, concrete floors; pregnant sows kept in cages so small they can't move; piglets castrated without pain relief and tails routinely docked to prevent animals attacking each other. Life is absolute hell for the commercial pig, which is not natural and it's not right. It stands to reason that pigs reared in these abysmally cramped, poisonous and cruel conditions would be very sick indeed if they were left to their own devices. But, of course, they're not.

According to the National Academy of Sciences in the US, a whopping 70 percent of the antibiotics produced in that country are given, not to humans, but to farm animals to promote growth and prevent disease. The problem is that many of the most common bacteria, like salmonella, campylobacter, and E. coli, have already developed a resistance to these drugs, so the meat industry has no choice but to react by inoculating even more. In the rush to put on our facemasks at the start of the recent Mexican swine fever outbreak, very few people stopped to consider what caused such a deadly virus in the first place. The problem is thought to have originated at a giant pig farm in the Perote Valley that rears almost a million pigs a year. According to the environmental organisation GRAIN, locals had long complained of a fearsome stench and appalling conditions at the farm and in December 2008 a serious respiratory illness sickened 60 percent of the local community.

The problem is that pigs are notorious 'mixing bowls' for inter-species infections, and many swine 'flu viruses have long contained the genetic components of human influenza. Scientists have worried for years that crowded indoor pig factories, which rely heavily on vaccinations and antibiotics to keep down disease, are breeding grounds for aggressive new pathogens that could easily infect humans and then spread out rapidly into the general population. Pigs don't fly, but people who come in contact with infected pig-factory workers do – which is why we quickly had cases of swine 'flu in the

US, Canada, Asia, Australasia and Europe.

And what about the environmental cost? *Rolling Stone* did a major exposé on the US pork industry in 2006, which made for difficult reading. It found that the 500,000 pigs reared at a single factory in Utah generate more faecal matter each year than the 1.5 million inhabitants of Manhattan. Most of this waste, according to the writer of the piece, runs out of the barns, where it sits in the open and gets pulled down into the groundwater and river systems by gravity (or, if that doesn't work, they resort to spraying it onto neighbouring farmland). The same article reported that most of this effluent is highly toxic because of the amount of antibiotics and vaccines that the pigs are injected with.

Pig farmers and processors are not the only villains of this rather gruesome piece, however. Supermarkets share a lot of the blame through aggressive discounting, which forces the price of meat down so low that pig farmers can scarcely make a profit on the meat they sell; the only way they can do so is to sell more, and in order to do that they have to find ways to produce even more pigs in the same space, using fewer resources. And, of course, driving this 'growth' in the industry are the lines and lines of hungry consumers like you and me, queuing up for those '2-for-1' offers that we are so wild about. It is our continuing demand for cheaper food that drives the whole process. It might make you feel uncomfortable or even upset to be held responsible for the way the system is set up, but if you are a meat eater, then, I'm afraid you are. We all are – each and every time we vote with our wallets instead of searching out local farmers and retailers and supporting them. We complain about the price of free-range and organic meat, hiding behind the 'I have a family to feed' argument at every turn, ignoring the profound health and moral implications of our choices. The irony is that it is exactly *because we have a family to feed* that we should be seeking out the highest quality meat we can find, regardless of what it costs. Why is it that we are happy to shell out top dollar for the best clothes, the best toys and the most expensive games consoles for our children, but we are often not willing to pay for top quality food to keep them healthy? Cheap meat comes at a cost – a cost to the environment, to the animals involved, but, above all, to our own health and the health of our families. We are not helpless in these things. We can all find a reputable free-range producer and buy their meat – and pay what they ask for it. It is our dosh that can force changes. I firmly believe that there are better, healthier ways to make savings on the household budget – and, God knows, in these times we all need to do that.

The most wonderful thing about rearing your own pigs, or support-ing organic and free-range producers of pig meat, is that you can choose to promote traditional and, in some cases, endangered breeds, like the Berkshire, Saddleback, Duroc, Tamworth and Gloucester Old Spot. These pigs are tough as old boots and will live quite happily outside the whole year round. (In the summer months, if it is warm, our pigs actually prefer to sleep outside at night.) Plus, if you opt to keep rare-breed pigs, you are playing your part in the survival of the breed.

The first thing to consider, before diving headlong into the mucky world of pig-keeping, is how much space you can give to them. The basic rule is: the more the better. There are basically three systems for keeping pigs, and which of them you adopt really depends on the amount of land you have available. You can keep them in a concrete sty; in a combination of a concrete sty with a 'yard' or run attached; or, best of all, you can let them be completely free range, with a house to which they can return for shelter. Though pigs have been kept successfully in small pigsties for centuries, it is an approach that has generally fallen out of favour with smallholders because (a) it's cruel to the pigs to confine them in this way and (b) it's so close to the commercial approach to fattening, you may as well just buy your pig-meat in the supermarket and be done with it. Pigs, essentially, live by their snouts – one of the most heartening things you will ever see is a weanling left out on open ground for the first time. Though they have never been taught how, they instinctively start to root in the soil immediately. Using their hind legs as leverage, they dig their snouts into the soil and, using a sort of rocking motion, they get to work – you can see by them that they are absolutely LOVING it. It is a basic, inherent part of their being and to deprive them of this by keeping them on concrete for their whole life is really not on. We have also noticed how irritated piglets get when we put them back in the sty after they have been out rooting – once they've tasted life beyond the concrete pen, they are never really satisfied with being confined after that. And pigs are not stoic like cows – they are very vocal when they are annoyed.

TRADITIONAL PIG BREEDS

SADDLEBACK: a big black pig with a white 'belt' around its shoulders. The sow is reputedly an excellent mother, having large litters and milking well. Very suitable for outdoor breeding, as it is very hardy and a good grazer.

LANDRACE: great for lean bacon and high quality pork, the Landrace is a long white pig with big droopy ears and fine hair. The sow makes an excellent mother. Often cross-bred with other traditional breeds to reduce the amount of fat in those pigs.

GLOUCESTER OLD SPOT: white with black spots, the Old Spot is another hardy old pig. Sometimes known as the Orchard Pig because it was traditionally kept in orchards and reared on windfall apples. It is known to be a good forager and grazer, and very docile.

TAMWORTH: though named after the region of Tamworth in Staffordshire, it is thought to have originated in Ireland where it was known as the Irish Grazer – perhaps, appropriately then, it is red, hairy, fast and gregarious. Good dual-purpose breed (pork and bacon) and a highly effective rooter. Hams typically lack the size of other breeds.

BERKSHIRE: thought to be the oldest British pigs, the Berkshire is also one of the smallest breeds and has a reputation for producing top quality pork with excellent texture and flavour. It is a black pig, sometimes with white legs.

OXFORD SANDY & BLACK: Another hardy outdoor pig (it is a natural forager), the Oxford has an excellent temperament and mothering abilities. It produces meat of very high quality (both pork and bacon) and finishes quicker than many traditional breeds. It is also less inclined to run to fat.

Having your pigs free range is the best approach of all, of course, but it is not particularly practical for most of us. If you have the space to dedicate about half an acre of land to your pigs, it would be absolutely perfect – two pigs will completely rotovate that amount of land in the time it takes to fatten them up for the table, and the land will have about seven or eight months to recover from the shock. If you are keeping pigs permanently (ie you have a breeding sow) you will need more land than that. In this situation you would need about three half-acre plots and keep moving the pigs on, say once a year. In this way, they do not return to any piece of land for three years, which prevents a build-up of para-sites or disease in the ground. We don't have anywhere near that much land to dedicate to pigs and we are forced to keep them in the same area down at the end of the garden every year.

Using a combination of sheep-fencing and two strands of electric fencing, we have cordoned off a plot of about 100 sq metres (20m long x 5m wide), which we have divided in two. We have found, unfortunately, that because of the space constraints, this ground has suffered badly and in wet weather can become what is called 'pig sick' – it gets so damaged from their rooting and running around that it goes beyond muddy into a liquid consistency. Pigs don't mind a bit of muck (they love it, in fact, and in the summer they will wallow in mud to keep themselves cool and to prevent sunburn), but when they are up to their shins in a soupy liquid, it's not very pleasant for them. Over one winter, therefore, we put in a walled, concrete pen around their house, about 20 sq metres (5m x 4m). We can keep them in this area if the weather is particularly wet, which is when we get the worst problems with the ground turning soupy. Though confined, they still have a good deal of space to move around in, and we try and keep them occupied as best we can by throwing kitchen leftovers and garden waste into their trough so that they have something interesting to root for. Then, when it's dry, we can let them out to root in the soil. It's not quite free range, but it's the next best thing, I think.

MR ROTOVATOR

Say you have a relatively large area in your garden, or part of a field, in which you are hoping to grow some vegetables, but which is currently overrun with weeds or scutch grass. If you are not in too much of a hurry, why not let a few pigs do the job of preparing the ground for you, rather than spraying it with weed killer? Pigs will successfully root up any type of land, even that which a mechanical plough can't manage, and they do something which even the most technologically advanced modern tractors can't do: they fertilise the land at the same time. And, of course, you can't eat a tractor when it's finished its work.

Using moveable electric fencing (and portable housing, such as a pig ark), divide the space into four or five segments, and then rotate the pigs through the sections, putting them in each section for about a week – as long as it takes them to root it over well but before they start damaging the soil or leaving large holes everywhere. After they leave a section, you could rake in a green manure or fast-growing crops like grass or turnips. By the time you get the pigs back onto the first area, it will be a wonderful treat for them to munch on whatever is growing there and you will also save yourself some money on feed for them. After six to eight months, courtesy of their prolific manuring, you will have incredibly rich soil in which to sow your vegetables.

Housing for your pigs doesn't need to be too fancy, but it does need to be dry and relatively draught-free (so try to have the entrance out of the prevailing winds). Specially made corrugated iron pig arks are probably the best option since they are relatively portable and can therefore be moved around if necessary. An old outhouse, stable or stall would be absolutely ideal too. A few years ago, we built a small concrete-block house for our pigs down at the bottom of the garden – it is about 4 sq metres and 1m high and has a corrugated iron roof on it. It's a perfect size for them, but not terribly practical for cleaning out because it's too low to walk into. Apart from that design flaw, it's pretty decent. Whatever housing you provide for them, it needs, above all, to be strong. Pigs are powerful and gregarious animals and when lolling about in their house they like to test its strength by occasionally giving it a good old puck – bear in mind that a pig for slaughter will weigh anything up to 100kg and a full-size sow will weigh 300kg, with enough strength to move something with her snout that weighs as much as she does.

Our pig palace is big enough to allow two finisher pigs (ready for slaughter) to stand up and turn around inside. By and large, pigs won't usually pooh in their house if they can help it, and they keep it in relatively good order, but we give them fresh straw for bedding every month or so, anyway. A friend of mine told me about a really good trick for keeping their house clean and dry – put some timber pallets on the floor, particularly if the floor is concrete, and put their bedding on top of that. For some reason (I would imagine because of the air circulating beneath the pallets) the straw seems to stay drier and in better condition for longer and the pigs feel pretty good about themselves with their fancy-schmancy floating wooden floor. Pigs produce a lot of pooh and if they are kept confined it seems to highlight that fact. So, if you are keeping pigs confined in a pigsty, you will need to climb in there every other day, muck the place out and maybe add fresh bedding – you may need to remind yourself when doing so that it's really worth it for all that wonderful compost (I would anyway!). It's vital to keep their pen clean – if you allow pig manure to build up around the place, you are providing a breeding ground for worms and other parasites. Cleaning their sty is a job that requires you to wear old clothes, wellies and, most importantly, gloves – the smell of pig manure is insidious and cloying, so you really don't want it on your hands.

The great thing about having pigs around is that they eat pretty much anything, which means that all the food scraps we produce go out to them. When the pigs are not here, we try to compost most of our kitchen scraps, but there are some things we cannot put in the compost bin as they will attract rats – for example, cooked food, or dairy leftovers, like sour milk or butter. I always hate putting out our 'brown bin' for collection because it seems like a double waste to be paying for food in the first place and then paying someone to take it away, a classic disease of over-consumption, if ever there was one. When the pigs are here, most of the food that would have ended up in the brown bin is diverted to them and received gratefully. We have a pig bucket under the sink, into which we plonk pretty much all of our waste food material – the scrapings of the porridge pot, leftover or stale bread, pasta and rice, the remains of cooked vegetables and vegetable peelings, uneaten biscuits, cakes, butter, milk, beer, the dregs from the teapot – the beauty with pigs is that they aren't fussy in the way that your compost bin is fussy. They are also far more efficient than a compost bin – in the process of extracting the nutrients it needs to be healthy, a pig will turn waste vegetable matter into manure within a day. It will take your compost bin weeks or even months to do the same job.

We rinse plates and cups and so on into the pig bucket because this nutrient-rich water is a valuable source of 'food' for the pigs and shouldn't be wasted. The only thing we do not feed them is meat – though pigs are omnivores (like humans), it is generally accepted that feeding them meat brings with it a danger of cross-contamination and the introduction of diseases such as foot-and-mouth and swine fever. Meat, and food that has come in contact with meat, is therefore considered to be 'swill' and should not be fed to pigs. To be honest with you, if we have a leftovers plate that has some meat and vegetables on it, the meat goes to the dogs while the vegetables go to the hogs – officially speaking, I imagine that the vegetables in that case probably shouldn't go to pigs since they have resided next to the meat on the plate, but in the privacy of your own home you can probably cut yourself some slack.

Pigs also love getting their greedy mitts on any excess produce from the vegetable garden when it's available, and from this bounty they get not only nutrition, but also an element of distraction. A spent brussels sprout stalk, for example, will keep a pig happy for an hour or so, chomping away on the leaves and trying to get at the remains of any sprouts that might be left on the stalk. When I cut the grass I usually throw them in some of the grass cuttings, which they seem to appreciate too. We also get lots of food for the pigs from family and neighbours, who contribute a bucket of vegetable scraps when they can or when they think of it. As well as that, our local greengrocer and the chef in one of our favourite local restaurants give us bagfuls of waste vegetables a few times a week, which is a real boon for our pigs – the vegetables are generally in pretty good nick too and we have to fight the inclination to reach in and salvage some of them for ourselves (ah no, not really). When I initially approached the grocer to ask him would it be okay to collect some scraps from him, he mentioned to me that two other Home Farmers do the same on different days of the week – I'm hoping that I bump into one of them some day so that we can discuss *all things pig*.

Even with all these fresh and slightly-less-than-fresh vegetable scraps, pigs need more than leftovers to keep them thriving. For the first two years that we kept pigs, we fed them barley to start, and organic pig nuts (which are special blends of grain) to fatten them up at the end. The woman who sold me the pigs this year reckoned I was stone mad to be using pig nuts at all, given the price of them. Basically, pigs need a mixture of cereal, such as barley or maize, and then a protein supplement of some form to help with fattening. Soya flake will do the trick here – this year, therefore, we are going to buy 40kg bags of rolled barley and soya flake and give them about 80 percent of the former and 20 percent of the latter.

The basic rule is that you give your pigs about 500g of food each per day for each month of age, ie if they are 3 months old, they get 1.5kg a day each; note, however, that is per day, not per feed (we feed the pigs morning and evening). You can continue like this as they get older, but don't ever give them more than about 2kg a day in grain each – anything more than that and they will get too fat, too quickly. Another rule of thumb is to give them enough feed so that they are eating for twenty minutes or so. Pigs are not self-regulating, like hens, when it comes to eating – they will keep on eating if the food is there, and you will end up with ridiculously fatty meat. Having said that, our pig's trough generally contains vegetable scraps they munch on throughout the day. Perhaps the best advice is to keep a close eye on them – if they appear thin or hungry, then feed them more. Of course, a pig will let you know it is hungry with lots of impatient squealing! Pigs also need lots of water and drink a surprising amount of it – though they spill a lot of it too. Given their propensity to have mucky snouts, they will also dirty any water you provide and it's up to you to make sure their water trough is relatively clean and refilled regularly. We soak their feed in water too so they're taking in water that way as well, and this apparently helps them to digest their food.

Keeping pigs would be a far more sensible investment if you had them out in a field, as they would help themselves to whatever pasture was available and you would only have to supplement that with some grain. Buying in bags of grain makes it less economical. But cocooned in the naivety of our enthusiasm for pigs, we still think it's a good investment to keep a few each year, given the amount of meat we get out of it. Once you have your initial fencing and shelter costs sorted out, the annual cost of keeping two pigs is as calculated roughly below. As is always the case when rearing animals, the biggest cost component is the feed – these figures are based on two pigs munching their way through 420kg of grain in the time that they are with us.

COSTS

two piglets	€120
approximate grain costs	€140
slaughter	€100
butchering / processing	€80
total:	€440
cost per pig:	€220

A few comments on these piggynomics. These are very much guideline costs – there can be a good deal of variation in the cost of the initial pig, for starters. I have heard of producers looking for €150 for a piglet, which is absolutely scandalous to my mind – search around for value and get your order in early. Most of the good breeders will have a list of longterm clients to look after and may be sold out early in the season. There is also a good deal of fluctuation in the cost of grain, and the amount that you need could be reduced, depending on the quantity of kitchen scraps you can provide your pigs with. You could also save a good deal of money each year if you opted to butcher the meat yourself (the abattoir does the actual slaughtering – by law – and returns two halves of a pig to you for processing) and doing it that way you would have more flexibility, with the option to process the meat into higher-value cuts as well as making your own sausages, salami, chorizo, parma ham. I haven't done that yet, but, armed with the knowledge from my pig-butchery course, I am gearing up to it one of these years.

So, if it costs €220 to rear each pig, how much meat are you getting? That's a tough one to calculate, given the different options that you have in terms of processing cuts and the wide variation in meat prices. But we estimate that each pig is worth about €350 in meat, which means that on two of them we make a 'profit' of €260, which is a really good return. It is worth bearing in mind, however, that it is virtually impossible to get free-range pork these days, and it's therefore hard to put a value on the fact that our pigs have a nice (though short) life, space to roam around in and we have complete control over what they are fed. Not only is it cheaper than buying pork and bacon at the supermarket, you are also eating a far superior product, and you know exactly what went into making it. It's also worth remembering that you will get a very significant quantity of farmyard manure from your pigs to help return nutrients and fertility to the Home Farm soil. Despite (or perhaps because of) our rudimentary grasp of the economics of the situation, I still think we would keep a few pigs each year even if it was *costing* us money – we just love having them around. They are a charming, wonderful addition to our year.

A final word: if you are thinking about rearing animals, my advice is to tread carefully. Don't just dive right into the muck, tempting and all as that might be. Start small, perhaps with some laying hens, and try and get used to the routine involved with them before moving onto pigs, which are a lot more complex. Read up as much as you can – there are lots of good books out there as well as a huge number of internet sites and forums dedicated to the topic. It's worth noting that keeping any animal is going to tie you down – of course, family and neighbours can usually be called upon to give a dig-out if you want to head away for a weekend, but they will get mighty fed up of that if you call on them too often. Above all, don't even think about keeping pigs, hens, chickens or ducks (or any other animal, for that matter) unless you are happy to get your hands dirty and can put up with some muck and dirt around the place.

Broad beans may not be everyone's favourite vegetable (and scientists tell us that it is not a bean at all, but more closely resembles a plant normally grown as cattle feed), but I absolutely love them, mainly because it's usually the first real harvest of the growing year. You can start sowing broad beans as early as November or December outside and they will start to crop towards the end of this month, which makes them the first of the pulses to visit your plate, well ahead of your peas, which probably won't show up for another month or so. If you do opt to sow them before Christmas, it will be wonderful to see them growing in the winter garden when there's bugger all else going on.

There are other things I love about broad beans too. First of all, I like that they get going quickly, with little of the fuss or nonsense that is often associated with seed sowing. In that sense, they are the ultimate Home Farm hacker's vegetable. It seems like a long time ago now, but those first sowings of broad beans in the winter showed signs of life quickly, which was greatly appreciated at the time. I just hate those vegetables that take ages to germinate, causing us palpitations, before they finally show a shoot above the ground. Broad beans will typically germinate after about a week and you will be starting to pick them approximately fourteen weeks after you sowed them (though it will be a lot longer than that if you sow them in the autumn) – you have to admit that's a pretty impressive turnaround.

Secondly, I just love their packaging. Every time I split open a broad bean pod and take out the five or six kidney-shaped beans inside, I get all wide-eyed at just how incredible nature is. If you have ever seen the inside of a broad bean pod you will know what I am talking about, and if you haven't, well it's worth growing or buying some just to have a look. I promise you that you will feel mighty envious of the humble broad bean once you've seen the bed that it gets to spend its formative weeks in. Never have I seen a more comfortable-looking slumbering environment – it is lined with an incredibly furry white fleece-like material that protects the soft beans inside. And we humans think we have got food packaging down to a fine art – do we heck.

Finally, I really like their flavour. I think there is more complexity to them than peas and they are ultimately more satisfying as a result. Eating broad beans is an early taste of summer for us – you can cook them, of course, as you would a pea (and you can also harvest them really young and cook the pod and all as you would French beans), but I think they taste better raw, either pounded in a pestle and mortar or just thrown into salads. They are also very good in a pasta, thrown in at the end of cooking. Broad bean plants are basically three vegetables in one – you get the beans, but you can also eat the growing tips *and* the upper leaves of the plant – the former are considered a delicacy and the latter can be cooked up as you would spinach. There are loads of vegetables from the garden that we are happy to share with people: courgettes, leeks, cucumbers, for example, that we are practically throwing away by the end of the summer, but we DO NOT share broad beans! Repeat, DO NOT SHARE!

If you sow broad beans once a month from March until the end of May, you will have beans throughout the summer. They keep for about a week in the fridge and if you have a good crop to harvest you can freeze whatever's left over (in our experience they freeze really successfully if you blanch them for a few minutes in boiling water first). They are incredibly good for you too, being full of protein and phosphorous, and rich in vitamins A, C and E. I was lucky in that I don't think I ever tasted broad beans until I grew my own – having fallen in love with them, I subsequently bought some in the shops out of season (I know, I know – I hang my head in shame) and was severely disappointed. First of all, the commercial varieties are almost always left to grow too big, no doubt because they look so damn impressive when the pods are really long. But the bigger the beans get inside the pod, the less flavour they have and they also develop a very tough outer skin which then has to be shelled before eating. A broad bean is at its best immediately after being picked – it's the same with any vegetable, I guess, but it is particularly true with the broad bean because the carbohydrates in the bean turn to sugar after it has been harvested and this starts to impact on the flavour. So, I was lucky to have started with the Rolls Royce version – my own, home-spun broad beans. I reckon if I had started out with the shop-bought ones, I would never have been tempted to grow my own.

Broad beans are not particularly fussy when it comes to soil and they will actually return nitrogen to the ground for you while they are growing, which makes them doubly useful. As I mentioned, you can sow them in November, but be prepared for the fact that you might lose some if the winter is particularly cold – only attempt it if your vegetable plots or raised beds are relatively dry. The second option is to start sowing them from February. Broad beans are relatively hardy, so you can sow them directly into the ground, but we tend to start them off in small pots inside and then transplant them when they are about 12cm–15cm high. There's no particular reason for doing it this way, and I am sure it's a phenomenal waste of time, really, but I just like watching them grow in the house before we plant them out and they always seem to do pretty well that way. Mice, birds and slugs are partial to seeds, so we get more success from transplanting as opposed to sowing direct. The seeds need to be sown about 5cm deep and the seedlings spaced about 45cm apart when you plant them out – the plants will need some support when they grow (they will reach well over 1m eventually) so you will need to put some canes along the row and run some twine or cable between the canes so that you can attach the stems to them. Alternatively, you can use some big old twigs or prunings. Don't sow more than about ten seeds at a time – broad beans are prolific when they get going, so you don't want them harvesting all at once – a good rule of thumb is to sow another batch when the first plants are about 20cm tall.

SPACE SAVER

If you don't have a lot of space, you can grow dwarf varieties of broad beans in containers and pots. These will grow to about 30cm high. The Sutton is a good variety of dwarf bean – it produces lots of pods with five little tender beans inside. Ahhh! Broad beans need plenty of moisture – a good way to make sure they have that is to use plenty of mulch or manure at the base of the plants where they meet the soil. This will also keep down weeds. A good option when planting them out is to dig a trench and line the base of the trench with shredded newspaper, then cover it with well-rotted manure and fill in with soil before planting. This method will also help retain moisture.

Broad beans are a delight to grow because they are so straightforward. Pea plants can get a little unruly when they are at their peak, but broad beans are neat and handsome-looking. As soon as the first flowers begin to fade, the tiny pods begin to grow – at this point you should pinch off the top growing shoot on the plant (don't forget to pop it in a salad, risotto or pasta, it tastes fantastic), which will encourage the plant to put its energy into producing beans rather than growing any taller. When you are growing broad beans it's important to put your ego and all thoughts of a glorious victory in the 'longest pod' category at the local agricultural show to one side. Pick the pods when you can see the beans starting to bulge through, but before they start to get all knobbly-looking. After this point, the beans will get starchy, the skins will be bitter, and they will require shelling (though shelling a pot of broad beans is an immensely satisfying activity if you are in the right frame of mind). Most books advise using a scissors or secateurs to snip off the beans, but to be honest, we just yank them off with a sharp downward twist and that doesn't seem to cause too much damage. You start harvesting from the bottom of the plant first, and, joy of joys, the more you pick, the more pods you get.

Our broad beans have been relatively trouble free in terms of diseases and pests. Last year, towards the end of the summer, we got chocolate spot, which is a lot less fun than it sounds – basically the leaves, stems and pods get brown streaks on them, but, in fairness, Ireland was in the grip of the wettest summer in living memory, and since it didn't have a huge impact on the beans themselves, we just ignored it.

PAULA MEE'S NUTRITION BITES: BROAD BEANS

Broad beans are high in vitamin C and fibre. They also contain levodopa (L-dopa), a chemical the body uses to produce dopamine (the neurotransmitter associated with the brain's reward and motivation system). Runner beans are also a source of vitamin C and have marginally fewer calories.

Nutrition per Portion (80g):

Vegetable	Calories	Fat (g)	Salt (g)	Saturated Fat (g)
Broad Bean	47	0.8	0	0.1
Runner Bean	18	0.3	0	0.1

This year I was a little more organised than normal with regard to the pigs. For the previous two years, it has been tradition for me to inveigle the poor father-in-law to come with me to collect my weanlings in his trailor and to come back later in the year to deliver them to the abattoir. I'd like to say this is me calling in a favour, or some such, but it's a long time since he owed me a favour, and, if the truth be known (but don't tell him), I probably owe him more than a few at this stage. It's a terrible burden on the poor man because he absolutely hates pigs – they had them on his farm when he was a nipper and I suppose the smell and noise of a large quantity of them is something you never forget. To make matters worse, I am his son-in-law, which means he can't really tell me to shag off the way he could his own son. In an effort to stand on my own two feet this year, I convinced the in-laws to 'sell' me a very old calf trailor they had that was rusting away down in their yard – it was really more of a nominal fee that changed hands. I can't tell you how happy it makes me to own a calf trailor. It's highly unlikely that there will ever be a calf in it again, and, truth be known, it will probably only leave the Home Farm a handful of times a year, but I don't care – I love having it in the driveway, just in case. I wonder am I the only person in the known universe who owns a calf trailor and a milk separator, but not a cow?

The brother-in-law and I cleaned it up and put a new set of lights on the back – and, bob's your uncle, I was in business. If you have ever used a trailor, you will know how difficult they are to manoeuvre, especially in reverse. So, when no one was looking, down on the farm, I practised reversing around the yard, but after ten sweaty minutes I decided that she (of course, the calf trailor is a 'she') had a mind of her own and I gave it up as a bad job, hoping that wherever I took it I wouldn't have to do any reversing. We had a nervous trip from the Real Farm to the Home Farm, with me looking in the rear-view mirror every couple of seconds to make sure she was still there and afraid of my life that I would shave a parked car as we were going through towns. When we finally got it home, I tried reversing it into our driveway with Mrs Kelly helpfully shouting directions and instructions at me from the sidelines: 'Lock it hard! Not that way, the other way!' After another ten sweaty minutes, I again gave it up as a bad job and decided to take the trailor off the hitch and turn it around 'manually', terrified that I would lose control of it and it would take off down the driveway and crash through the garage door.

For the past two years we have kept Tamworth pigs, and we were pretty pleased with them and the meat that they provided, though we felt that we probably let them get too fat. A chop, or indeed, some bacon from our pigs could have up to 4cm or 5cm of fat on it – this is great for the flavour of the meat, of course, but not so great for the Kelly family tickers. Anyway, we decided that this year we would try something new and we opted for Saddlebacks.

It's important to point out that if you do decide to get some pigs, it's best to get them relatively locally – the shorter the journey home, the less stressful it will be for the pigs (and you). I set off with Nicky, a friend of mine, in my inaugural outing with the trailer. Nicky and his wife and three children are fellow Home Farmers – in fact, they are basically living the dream, as far as I am concerned. Nicky grows his own vegetables, as well as keeping sheep, pigs, ducks, hens and turkeys, and when we visited his house once he tried to get us drunk on home-brew cider and damson vodka after serving up a meal of home-reared pork, chicken and tripe! He's a mine of information and the first guy I call if I have questions on rearing animals.

Setting off to get pigs is always a very 'hopeful' occasion. Spring is in the air and it's the first big project of the Home Farm year. Before you load them up, however, there's the trauma of having to catch them and put tags on them. When you buy pigs you have to put a tag on each ear – one has the herd number of the person selling and the other has that of the person buying. It's a way for the Department of Agriculture to keep tabs on where pigs are, which makes sense, but it's a terrible trauma for the poor little pigs, who have to be held upside down while basically getting both ears pierced. Pigs don't like being held, never mind being held upside down – and, of course, they *really* don't like having their ears pierced. After much indignant squealing, we got them one by one into the trailor, which I had filled with straw and they both disappeared underneath it, as only pigs can.

Once we had them safely loaded up and the necessary paperwork filled out, I started to fret about how I was going to turn the trailor around – my reversing skills just weren't up to the job yet and the pig woman's (I'm sure she won't like me calling her that) lane was ominously narrow. I explained my predicament to her. 'Oh you don't need to reverse at all,' she says genially. 'Just keep going straight, then turn left and left again and you will get back to the main road.' 'God, that's a relief,' says I, 'because I've just got this trailor and I haven't a clue what I am doing with it.' 'Sure I'm the same myself,' she says with considerable empathy, 'the last thing you want to do is jack-knife it.' Nicky pipes in: 'Well, with the speed he drove down here at, there's precious little fear of that. It was like we were part of a funeral procession.'

The Saddlebacks are a nice change from the Tamworths. We'd grown used to having orangey-red pigs around the place, but, of course, the Saddleback is black with a white stripe. They also seem to me a little tamer than the Tamworths. Within minutes of being dispatched to their pigsty on the Home Farm (more ear-splitting squealing), they were happily roaming around the place, sniffing at the ground and eating the chow in their trough. It's wonderful to have pigs in our world again!

APRIL GROWER'S CALENDAR

Prep Work

- April is the banker month. No, not *those* bankers; what I mean is that if poor weather in March has hampered your outdoor work, then April is the month to catch up.
- Remove the last of the plastic covering from your beds if the weather is relatively dry. Fork over and rake the soil in preparation for the crops.
- If the soil is in good condition, put up canes, wigwams and other supports for climbers such as beans and peas.

To-do List

- Two words: weeds; slugs. You need to stay on top of them both.
- Check your early spuds regularly and 'earth-up' as required.

- Water the plants in your tunnel/greenhouse – things can get pretty warm on a nice sunny April day and seedlings will dry out quickly. As the weather improves, ventilate during the day to harden up those plants that will be transplanted outdoors in the next few weeks.
- Cabbage-root fly attack cabbage/cauliflower and all their brassica cousins by laying eggs at the base of plants. Cut discs of soft material, like carpet underlay, and lay flat around the base of the plant, which means thay can't get at the plants. Depending on the weather, cabbage butterflies will also soon be laying eggs. Check the undersides of leaves and scrape off eggs before they hatch. You will need to keep this vigilance up in the coming months. Collect the caterpillars and feed them to your hens.
- Pick huge bundles of tender young nettles; divert around 140g to the kitchen for a delicious nettle soup and use the rest for an organic fertiliser. Nettles are extremely high in nitrogen, so if you soak a large bucketful in water for a week, you produce a brilliant nitrogen-rich fertiliser, which will be hugely beneficial for any plants which need leafy growth, for example lettuce, cabbage, kale etc. Put a kilo of nettles in a hessian bag and soak in a bucket with about 20 litres of water; leave it to stew for a month or so. It gets pretty stinky, so put a lid on top. Mix one part nettle liquid with ten parts water when applying to plants.

Sowing Seeds

- *Indoors on a sunny window sill or heated greenhouse*: lettuce, tomatoes, peppers, chilli-peppers, cucumbers, celery, celeriac, fennel, basil, leeks, cabbage, cauliflower, brussels sprouts, parsley, courgettes, marrow, globe artichoke.
- *Indoors in small pots for planting outdoors later*: beans (dwarf French and climbing French), runner beans, sweet corn and pumpkin.
- *Outdoors (may require cover in bad weather)*: broad beans, peas, beetroot, cabbage, spinach, brussels sprouts, parsnips, spring onions, leeks, carrots, radishes, broccoli, turnips.

Planting Out

- Hardening off – seeds raised indoors/under cover need to be acclimatised outdoors before planting out. Begin by giving the plants less heat and water and more light and air. Bring them outside during daylight hours on good days for at least a week, but take care they don't dry out or wilt in the wind and sun.

- Spuds – you can now get your second earlies and maincrop spuds into the ground. Last chance to plant onion sets until late autumn (when you can sow over-wintering varieties).
- Plant out cabbage plants when they are 15cm–20cm tall into well prepared soil that has been manured. Water the plants well the day before and lift each plant with as big a root ball as possible. Firm the plants in well and water. Plant out tomatoes into the greenhouse/tunnel soil before the middle of the month.
- If space is at a premium, use plant pots to grow herbs and strawberries.
- Grow asparagus – although it can take years to get a decent crop, it is quite low-maintenance and occupies the same bed for many years. If you sow seed now, the plants will be ready to plant out next spring or, alternatively, buy fresh 'crowns' from a good source.

GRUB'S UP – WHAT'S IN SEASON

Stored fruit and vegetables are likely to be a distant memory at this stage (you might still have some spuds left if you're lucky) and new crops are only starting to trickle in, which makes April a tricky proposition. The middle of this month might see the first asparagus and the first early spring cabbage. The other two star performers this month are sprouting broccoli and rhubarb.

You could also be harvesting leeks, spring cauliflowers, kale, spinach and chard, lettuce, carrots (in polytunnel), radishes, spring onions and wild garlic.

5

THE LUSTY MONTH
OF MAY

EARLY SUMMER: MAY

crop rotation – pure-breed hens – piggy feelings – peas – lamb

Now is the month of maying

when merry lads are playing,

Fa la la la la!

Each with his bonny lass

a-dancing on the grass,

Fa la la la la!

Sir Thomas Morley

If you are looking for an excuse for a party, you need not look very far in May. May Day, the first day of the month, is traditionally a celebration of the beginning of summer. It has marked a time of growth, renewal and fertility across Europe since pre-Christian times and is one of the two great celebrations in the Celtic year (the other one is Halloween, which marks the onset of winter). Ancient May Day customs included decking the outsides of houses with flowers or newly-leafed branches, moving herds to higher pastures, extinguishing all hearths in the community and relighting from a fire rekindled by nine men, making May wreaths, driving cattle between bonfires to ward off evil spirits, walking the circuit of one's property (known as 'beating the bounds' – only takes us a couple of minutes if we walk fast), archery tournaments, processions of chimney sweeps and milkmaids (no, I don't get that one either), and maidens bathing in the dew of a May morning to retain their youthful beauty. Basically, as long as your May Day celebrations involve feasting, drinking, nudity and phallic symbols, you are pretty much on the right track.

There's plenty to celebrate. Every green thing, whether it be your favourite vegetable plant or your most detested weed, is growing at such a dizzying pace, you could see the growth before your very eyes if you took the time to sit down and watch it. Trying to keep on top of things on the Home Farm at this time of the year can be difficult, made all the more so by the fact that you might well be still 'getting up to speed' after the relatively languid spring months. There are many animals to feed and water, as well as an increasing array of 'routine' tasks to attend to, like weeding and watering. There is still quite a bit of sowing to do and (whisper it) even some gentle harvesting. In fact, there's so much to do that it's a good idea occasionally to just slow down and take stock.

I sometimes relax in the hammock and try to take it all in – and be thankful for the stunning abundance of nature. I observe the antics of our ducks or hens ('Look at them, sitting up there at the back door, poohing on the step, sure aren't they just hilarious ...') or I just gaze at the white flowers on a potato plant. These chill-out moments are surely one of the blessings of being a Home Farmer. As that colossal genius GK Chesterton once said: 'Wonder will never be lacking in this world. What is lacking is wonderment.' Deliciously, Chesterton himself was so full of wonder and awe at the world around him, he was invariably late for every appointment he ever had. Good for him. Being on time is really, really overrated.

Crop rotation. Two words guaranteed to strike terror into the beginner Home Farmer, particularly if, like me, you are more *home* than *farmer*, if you catch my drift. On the face of it, I understand the necessity for crop rotation – if you plant the same crops in the same place each year, you can get a build-up of pests and disease, and the soil will eventually become starved of nutrients – but I have to admit to finding it all somewhat of a bother. Our vegetable patch is a mixture of open ground and an array of raised beds that we've put in over the years and I've always thought that the open ground is the appropriate place to grow potatoes. Our potatoes do well(ish) there too (apart from the blight, of course, but that's hardly the ground's fault) and their foliage keeps the ground relatively weed free, so it's a matter of considerable inconvenience to me to have to move them away from there. But if you are going to practise organic growing (and really, if you're not going to at least try to be organic, then what's the point in doing it at all – your local supermarket has plenty of sprayed vegetables that you can buy), then crop rotation is something you really should incorporate into your plans.

Growing any vegetable in the one place year after year is likely to result in a gradual depletion of the nutrients which that particular vegetable needs to thrive. Moving crops around to different areas of the vegetable plot breaks the cycle, so to speak, therefore preventing funguses, pests and disease from getting a toe-hold, and allowing the soil to rediscover its mojo each year. Commercial vegetable cultivation, of course, does not involve crop rotation at all because it is focused on what is called mono-cropping, where the producer specialises in a single crop or a small number of crops and grows nothing else, so there's basically nothing to rotate. When you grow mega-tonnes of carrots every year from the same piece of land, it goes without saying that the piece of land will be in dire straits after a time, as the carrots extract the same nutrients from the soil year after year – this is why modern farming is so reliant on fertilisers and pesticides. It leads to a vicious cycle of increased soil depletion and declining yields, necessitating more fertilisers ...

Worldwide, there is a very serious problem with mineral depletion of soil. Scientists have been able to measure soil mineral levels
for well over a hundred years, and as far back as the 1930s the US
Senate was discussing the problems of severe mineral depletion in
US farmland. Imagine how bad things have got in the eighty years
since then? At the 1992 Earth Summit, scientists reported that compared with a hundred years ago, the average percentage mineral
depletion in North American soil was 85 percent. And before you go
getting all smug and thinking that things aren't as bad in Europe –
well, they are. Compared with a hundred years ago, European soil
has been depleted by 72 percent. The dangers of this are not just that
soil that is so deprived of any life force requires fertilisers to allow
things to grow (though that, in itself, causes problems); far more serious is the fact that this has a direct impact on *our own health*. The
human body predominantly obtains the mineral nutrients that it
needs from the food we eat, and the mineral content of that food is
dependent upon the mineral content of the soil it grows in. When the
minerals are not in the soil, they are not in the vegetable and, by
extension, they are not in the human body. The sad fact is that our
farmland is so depleted it can no longer, on its own, provide the minerals we need to thrive. Dr William Albrecht of the University of
Missouri has said that mankind is extremely vulnerable to pathological
conditions resulting from being fed deficient foods grown in infertile
soils. Fertilisers, he said, were responsible for 'general loss of mental
acuity in the population, leading to degenerative metabolic disease and
early death.' When you add to all this the general increase in pollutants
and toxicity in our environment, it's little wonder that we have such
alarming rates of chronic and degenerative diseases.

The problem with chemical fertilisers is that they return only a handful of minerals to the soil (typically the essential triumvirate of nitrogen, phosphate and potassium known as NPK) which is far short of the sixty minerals scientists now believe human beings need for optimal health. But since that small number of minerals will generally allow a plant to grow, at least, that is considered enough, particularly since modern agriculture is almost totally focused on yield per acre as opposed to the nutritional value of produce. There is an additional problem: most crops are pulled from the soil while still green or unripe so that they can begin their (often) mammoth journey to your plate and be still 'ripe' when they get there. The fact that they are plucked from the ground before they are finished growing means the plant is unable to fully absorb whatever nutrients are available in the soil. Vegetables then spend weeks or months in transit, distribution and storage, resulting in further mineral depletion before finally ending up on a supermarket shelf, far from home. That's where we come in – we pop a nice 'ripe' cucumber into our shopping basket in January, amazed at how the modern food chain allows us to get a cucumber when it's clearly not in season. The terrible irony of this is that when we get home and put the cucumber in the fridge, we congratulate ourselves on being so healthy and making such great progress towards our 'five-a-day'.

It's strange that society's response to mineral depletion in the food we eat is to focus on taking vitamin and mineral supplements rather than to try and address the problem at its root, so to speak, with the depleted soil. The vitamins and minerals we're taking in supplement form should already exist naturally in our food. Why not fix that problem instead of taking them in a form that some scientists aren't even convinced our bodies can actually absorb? Thankfully, the solution to all these problems is something that every Home Farmer can address by growing their own produce and taking some care to regenerate their soil every year. We can address the mineral depletion problem ourselves, in our own little patch, and dramatically increase our nutrient intake.

Feeding your soil so that it will feed your body means adding lots and lots of organic matter every autumn, which rots down and nourishes the soil in preparation for sowing the following spring. Healthy, fertile soil means healthy, productive plants, which ultimately means providing your body with all the nutrients it needs. A vegetable-growing friend of mine (and a particularly wise old head he is) once told me that clay or soil only covers the plant, it's the manure or compost that you add that helps it to grow – I think this is a wonderful way to look at it. Adding compost or manure before and during the growing season transforms your soil and because these are bulky materials they also radically improve the composition, structure and water-retention qualities too. I am always fascinated by the idea that the manure pile in the garden was the pride and joy of every rural family in times past because people understood its miraculous regenerative properties. The fact that the pride and joy of every family these days is their motor car, or some other ostentatious thing, is a good metaphor for just how much our priorities have changed.

Farmyard or stable manures are ideal if you can get your hands on them. Very few of us are lucky enough to have our own supply of cow or horse manure, but usually you can access some if you look hard enough and, in my experience, most people are only too delighted to give this stuff away when they know it's being put to good use. There's a guy down the road from us who keeps some horses, and he is quite happy for us to help ourselves from the manure heap outside the stable. We have transported bags of the stuff in the back of Mrs Kelly's jalopy over the years (much to her chagrin) and it's absolute dynamite for the soil. Our friendly local farmer is also happy to give us a great pile of cow manure each year in return for some bacon from our pigs. And, of course, our own animals on the Home Farm (pigs, ducks and chickens) are prolific manure producers in their own right. If you have absolutely no way of getting your hands on some manure free of charge, you can buy bags of it in your local garden centre these days, though this is the most expensive ways to do things and should really be a last resort. It's good to remember that for roughly the same price as a tub of chicken manure pellets, you can buy a hen that will pooh prodigiously for years – and produce an egg a day for years too!

The second major source of nutrients for your soil is compost, which is decayed plant matter from the garden or kitchen. It's an excellent source of nitrogen, phosphorus and potash. It's probably not fashionable to own up to this, but we've had some problems with compost heaps degenerating into slimy sludge heaps over the years – we're getting better, but I'm inclined to think that making good compost is not as easy as some people let on. I was researching an article that I was writing for a magazine some years back and came across a guy who had a business that involved him going around to the houses of well-heeled people in leafy suburbs to take away 'failed' compost heaps from the bottoms of their gardens. He was sort of like a horticultural version of The Wolf, Harvey Keitel's character in *Pulp Fiction* who is called in to orchestrate a 'clean up' after a murder. While half of me thought the idea of a compost heap removal service was hilarious and ridiculous, another part of me could really empathise with that desire to get a heap taken away so that you can forget about your compost-making failures and start again with a clean slate. It's nice when you see someone on the telly putting their hands into the compost heap and taking out this beautiful, crumbly black compost – but I have to admit that while we've produced some cracking compost over the years, we've never got it *that* good. So it drives me absolutely crazy when I hear people say that producing compost is easy. It's easy *when you know how*.

Anyway, we have a two-bay compost heap made from old wooden pallets into which we pile garden waste – grass clippings, leaves, veggie-patch trimmings, and manure-covered straw from the chicken, duck and pig houses. When the pigs aren't around, kitchen waste goes into a separate, covered, compost bin, because I think putting this stuff in the open heaps would attract rats. I'm definitely no expert, but I find that if you keep to a basic layering system of 'green' (nitrogen sources such as grass clippings, vegetable scraps) and 'brown' (carbon sources like straw, paper, sawdust) and occasionally try to remember to turn it over with a spade to let some air in (which speeds up the composting process), you can't go *too* far wrong. Sometimes our heap appears a little wet, and sometimes we get a sort of white dust on it, which, I think, means it's too dry. Ultimately, what you're hoping to get is that all that waste turns into dark compost that you can put on your soil, feeding the bacteria which, in turn, release the nutrients we so badly need.

Crop rotation schemes (and there are loads of them) are based on grouping together vegetables that are similar and then moving them around en masse each year. This makes it easier, since it means you can divide all the vegetables that you will ever grow into three or four major groups and rotate those groups around the available space. The groupings generally have the same or similar nutrient requirements and keeping them together means that you can more easily provide them with the best growing conditions – for example, brassicas like a slightly alkaline soil and you therefore need to put lime in the bed where they are to be planted to reduce acidity. Having a crop rotation scheme in place also removes the guesswork about where you are going to plant things each year.

We find that having a number of raised beds makes this a whole lot easier because you can have the first group in one bed the first year and then move them on to another bed the following year, and so on. In theory, it should be easy to remember what went where (though really, you should draw a little plan of your garden and write down where you planted things so that you can refer to it the following year – gardeners, as the saying goes, have great plans but poor memories). Some rotation plans are complex and have five or six groups that you work through over five or six years – it's self-evident that the longer your rotation is, the better. I don't know about you, but I am lucky if I can remember the things that I was doing yesterday, never mind five or six years ago. So we find that a three-year, three-group system is more than adequate for our needs.

A SIMPLE 3-YEAR CROP ROTATION

To help us with our Home Farming, Mother Nature has pre-programmed vegetables with the ability to help each other grow. It works like this – some veggies that you grow will actually leave nutrients behind in the soil which the veggies planted the following season will then use to grow and thrive. Other vegetables will grow better because nutrients that are harmful to them have been removed from the soil by the veggies grown the previous year. Magic or what? Crop rotation is therefore about more than just preventing the build-up of disease in the soil – it's also about using this incredible symbiotic relationship to grow vegetables successfully without the need for chemical fertilisers.

This system divides vegetables into three groups which you then rotate around three beds (you could, of course, give more than one bed to each group) in the following order:

Legumes and fruiting vegetables: The former includes peas and beans (broad, runner etc), while the latter is made up of tomatoes, aubergines, peppers, cucumbers and squashes. We lump the onion family – or alliums as they are collectively known – (leeks, onions, shallots, garlic) into this group too. Legumes take nitrogen out of the air and in the course of a growing season fix it into the soil. This is why you will often see it recommended that when your broad beans, for example, have finished cropping, you cut the plant but leave the root in the soil so that its abundance of nitrogen gets left behind.

Brassicas: The usual plan is to grow your brassicas in the area or bed where you grew legumes the previous year because they love the nitrogen that plants like broad beans and peas have 'fixed' in the soil the previous year. I call brassicas the 'Eat your veg!' group in honour of the fact that it contains those vegetables that my mother always told me to eat up as they'd make me big and strong (they didn't!). It includes cabbage, broccoli, turnips, kale, cauliflower, brussels sprouts and the like.

Root Crops: The final group is root vegetables, which do not require a lot of nitrogen and therefore will do well if planted where the brassicas were last year (the brassicas will have taken most of the nitrogen from the soil). Root vegetables include some of the great stockpot vegetables such as carrots, onions, leeks and parsnips. Sometimes you will see potatoes grouped with tomatoes in the fruiting vegetable group, sometimes with root crops. We tend to group them with the roots.

So your three year plan looks like this:

	Year 1	Year 2	Year 3
Bed 1	Brassicas	Root Crops	Legumes
Bed 2	Legumes	Brassicas	Root Crops
Bed 3	Root Crops	Legumes	Brassicas

Our modus operandi to date has been to try and stick roughly to this three-group rotation, but our plans are complicated by the fact that we're really just not as conscientious or well organised as we need to be to pull it off and also the number of raised beds we have is not divisible by three! We also grow certain things from each of these groups in the polytunnel each year and not outside at all. So, in the polytunnel we have four imaginary quadrants (from a planting perspective), and we move things around these quadrants in a rather haphazard manner – no doubt it doesn't help that the quadrants are imaginary. The most important thing we grow in the tunnel each year is tomatoes, so we try to be sure to move them. Our herb and fruit growing sits rebelliously outside of the crop rotation – we grow perennial herbs (those that you don't need to plant every year) like mint, sage, parsley and thyme in the tunnel, and we have a permanent area outside in the vegetable plot where we grow rhubarb and the soft fruits such as raspberries, strawberries, blueberries. Our fruit trees are in a different area of the garden altogether.

Two wonderful Home Farming neighbours of ours, John and

Bridget, who have been growing their own vegetables for thirty years told me about a wonderfully easy way to remember a rotation system that is roughly based on the three-group principle as mentioned above, but keeps onions and potatoes separate. The groups are potatoes, legumes, brassicas, onions and roots (rotated in that order) and the way you remember it is through the mnemonic: **P**eople **L**ove **B**unches **O**f **R**oses. I'm terrible at remembering such things, but even I can remember that one. If you have five beds, you could do a five-year, five-group rotation using that very straightforward system (and maybe have a sixth bed for things that don't need rotation, like asparagus and globe artichokes).

My feeling on crop rotation is that it's something enormously worthwhile for the organic Home Farmer, but that you shouldn't be too worried if it's compromised on occasion. If you feel the whole thing is a bit of a pain, at the very least it's best to try and avoid planting one type of vegetable in the same bed in consecutive years. If a space appears in one of our beds in high summer because we've harvested a particular crop, we don't feel too bad about popping something in there that the crop rotation would normally forbid. There are some vegetables such as lettuce, spinach, squashes and courgettes that I consider relatively 'neutral' and I shove them in anywhere I can find the space. I am hopeful that our loose interpretation of the rules won't come back to bite us any time soon.

The number and type of hens that we keep is a constantly moveable feast, and four new hens joined Kelly's Fancy Fowl Retirement Home recently. We have a mixture of pure-breed and cross-breed birds of all shapes and sizes, which tends to keep things interesting. Most of the commercial and garden hens in Ireland (including ours) are hybrid or cross-breed birds, mainly hybrids based on the ubiquitous Rhode Island Red. They are bred for their ability to pop out eggs like they're going out of fashion, which makes them perfect for the egg-a-day-is-okay Home Farmer. Laying so many eggs is an artificial enterprise for a hen – but they don't seem to mind too much and I'm not complaining. Still, I like the fact that pure-breed hens are stingier with their egg largesse. Perhaps it is that little bit closer to how nature intended it?

Anyway, this month, when it came time to extend our flock (God, I love using that word, 'flock', to refer to our hens), we opted for pure-breeds: a Rhode Island Red and a Buff Sussex, who will each lay about 260 eggs a year; and we were also smitten by the beautiful brown/green/black feathers of a Barnevelder, who will lay a miserly 200 caramel brown eggs a year. The Barnevelder was named after the Dutch town of the same name that was the centre of the egg-laying universe in twentieth-century Holland.

The birds cost me about €15 each, which is roughly double what you will pay for a hybrid, but I reckon their sheer beauty and grace makes up for it. When they arrived here first they were tiny compared to the grisly veterans in our flock, and, at only fourteen weeks old, were still, technically, 'pullets' (a hen before her first egg). It was another three to five weeks before they started to lay their eggs – well, two of them did at any rate.

We had our suspicions from the start that the Buff Sussex was, in fact, a cockerel and not a hen at all – she was bigger than the other two, for one thing, and the comb on top of her head and the wattles (the fleshly lobes that hang down beneath the beak) seemed rather too large for a hen. The other two seemed to be following her around all the time too – not a good sign. Our suspicions were confirmed after a few weeks when 'she' started to crow, pathetically at first, and then more confidently as the days passed. Our chivalrous cockerel Roger's patience is always sorely tested by new arrivals, but another *rooster* on the scene was pushing things way too far! As soon as the Buff Sussex began to crow, Roger went into crowing overdrive. He would climb to the highest point he could find (up on the deck railing or on top of the chicken coop) and crow like mad for about twenty minutes non-stop.

Then, one day, we were away for a few hours and when we came back the Buff Sussex had disappeared. It's unlikely that a fox took him because there was no sign of a disturbance and foxes would normally take more than one bird. So we think that Roger somehow forced or intimidated the poor fellow sufficiently to convince him that his future lay elsewhere (or perhaps he bribed him?). It was a huge pity, because he was a beautiful bird. (Incidentally, it is quite common to be unable to determine the sex of a young chicken. I certainly haven't a clue how to do it, as you may have gathered, but what's alarming is that the breeder clearly didn't know either – I trust him enough to think that he didn't offload the bird on purpose.)

Anyway, whenever we get some new arrivals they have to be kept separate from the main flock – the trick here is to introduce them to their peers gradually so a new pecking order can be established with the minimum of fisticuffs. After the departure of the Buff Sussex, Roger was happy enough to take the Barnevelder and the Rhode Island into his harem, but, of course, the other hens weren't a bit keen and made that clear by pecking the life out of them. Eventually, though, a new pecking order was established and an uneasy calm descended.

We also recently got a beautiful little hen, called Luidín (pronounced Loo-deen, it is the Irish name for the little finger) from my friend Feargal, who is a fellow poultry fancier. Feargal and his son, Oisín, keep a fairly sizeable collection of hens in their garden, but, unfortunately, the hens had been letting them down bigtime on the egg-laying front. In fact, they hadn't had a single egg in months. I'm a sucker for a hard-luck story, so I agreed to swap one of our good layers with him in the probably vain hope that she might bring a bit of egg-laying form to her new flock. We had one particularly persistent layer, who ventured across the garden each morning to lay in her favourite spot in the ditch. At different times over the years, we have confined our hens in behind fencing, only to decide shortly afterwards to give them free rein in the garden – either way, this hen didn't particularly care. If there was a chicken-wire fence to negotiate on her way to the ditch, then negotiate it she would. We agreed that her can-do attitude to laying might be just what Feargal needed to whip his errant hens into shape. In return, Feargal gave us Luidín, a beautiful little white Silkie.

We don't really get into naming our hens (apart from Roger, but he's different), but we've stuck with the name Luidín, and, because she's so small and so beautiful, she stands out from the rest sufficiently for us to be able to tell her apart. I've been relatively successful up to now at keeping our hens at arm's length when it comes to our affections. Partly it is their own fault; I mean, collectively they are fun, but individually hens don't really have much of a personality. Roger, I guess, is the only one that really stands out because he's big and white and has big, long, intimidating spurs sticking out of his legs, and, of course, there's all that manly crowing – but we are kind of reverential towards him rather than affectionate. Luidín is a different story.

None of our hens is particularly friendly and they will scarper if you go near them or try and pick them up. I think this is partly Roger's influence – when there is no cockerel in a flock, the hens respond better to you. Luidín, on the other hand, is a tame little thing, and follows me around the garden and lets me pick her up – I think this is because she's afraid of her life of the other hens and she likes to get off the ground whenever she can. The Silkie hen is named for its lovely plumage (which is, indeed, silky to touch, and feels more like fur than feathers) but they are also known for their calm demeanour and many people keep them as pets. While they make excellent mothers (so much so that they are often used to hatch eggs from other breeds), Silkies are terrible layers, which can't have helped Feargal's quest for eggs. In a good year, a Silkie will lay only about a hundred eggs and more often than not, her propensity to lay eggs will be interrupted by her propensity to go broody. They are not a particularly hardy bird and they don't do well in damp or cold. Whenever it rains, poor Luidín sits under a tree by herself, looking completely and entirely miserable.

Sad to say, Luidín has had a terrible time of it since her arrival. The other hens are enforcing the pecking order with particular viciousness in her case, probably because they sense her all-round vulnerability. It can be hard to watch, but you just have to accept that it's the way they order themselves, and leave it at that. For the first few days, I would go out at night to close them in and find her cowering under the house, afraid to go in with the others. I would take her out and put her on the perch and close the door (I read somewhere that it's a good idea to try and acclimatise new hens to each other at night-time as they are less likely to cause a ruckus when it's dark and they get used to the smell of a new arrival. Apparently you can help this along by spraying all the hens with a vinegar and water mixture to fool them into thinking that they all smell alike, but that sounds like a lot of hard work.) Some irritable clucking would be heard inside and occasionally some outright fisticuffs. In the morning, poor little Luidín would either be first out of the house, literally jumping out as soon as the door was opened, or would be cowering in the corner long after the others had emerged, blinking in the light (do hens blink?). It all seemed so unnecessary – but who are we humans to argue? Our own attempts at social order are not exactly textbook creations either.

Most of the day she would follow the others around the garden at a safe distance, clucking pitifully – every now and then she'd get too close and one or two of the other hens would chase her and peck the living daylights out of her. It was like the initiation rites of a particularly vicious sorority club. Eventually, of course, they relented somewhat and they now *almost* tolerate her. I still have to throw out some food for her on the ground behind the hen house, and, while the rest are pecking at the food bowl, she cowers there behind the house, pecking like mad to try and fill herself up while they aren't watching. I stand guard beside her and if any of the other hens come around to bother her, I shoo them away (I know what you're thinking – he has *way* too much time on his hands). Eventually, I tire of this, of course, and head back up the garden

and as soon as I am gone, the hens converge on the miserable few pellets left on the ground, chasing Luidín away in the process. Hens can
be kind of assholes when they want to be.

She also still can't manage to climb the ladder into the hen house,
so each night, when it gets dark, she now sits in a nesting box we have
left on the ground especially for her. We have to go down after dark
and lift her from her repose there and put her up on the perch with the
rest of the hens. I don't mind this little encumbrance – in fact, if I am
really honest, I sort of like the little bonding sessions we have. I lift her
out of the nesting box and say to her: 'You know something, Luidín?
You really are some pain, do you know that?' but it's said tenderly.
And this, you see, is my problem – I am growing fond of her.

Speaking of growing fond – God, but I *am* getting fond of those two
pigs. It's tough not to, because they have such obvious and distinct
personalities and, of course, in our case, there are only the two of
them. It's different to chickens – with a big batch being fattened for
the table, you never make any sort of a connection with them because
they all look and act the exact same, so you can't tell one from the
other. But our pigs have been here for a few weeks now and today, for
the first time, and after a couple of days of tentative approaches, one
of them just stood there and let me rub her head. There are two interesting points here – firstly, that I would want to rub a pig's head is
perhaps a little strange and probably says something about me. But,
more importantly, isn't it strange that the pig wants its head to be
rubbed? I was standing there rubbing her head and she was grunting
in a way that sounded quite similar to a cat purring, and I was

thinking: hold on a minute, *this pig is enjoying this*. There are some rather disturbing ramifications. First of all, it means that pigs like – perhaps even crave – affection. She was not getting any physical benefit from it – I mean, if I was scratching her I could understand that would be meeting a physical need that she has. But patting her like that was just a sign of affection and she was clearly enjoying it in a way that, for example, a hen would not. And if she is capable of enjoying affection, then, of course, it hints at a complex series of emotions that kind of puts us into dangerous territory. If she enjoys affection, what other emotions does she feel? Joy, pain, sadness? To make matters worse, a pig has disturbingly 'human' eyes that always seem to be sizing you up. Winston Churchill is quoted as saying: 'Always remember, a cat looks down on man, a dog looks up to man, but a pig will look man right in the eye and see his equal.'

The other interesting thing about this little incident was that only one of them (for now) was willing to be rubbed. The second little pig was hanging back, taking it all in. Sizing it up. There's no doubt that she is curious, but she's not willing to commit to it just yet. There will be another few days of coming up to me and sniffing my hand and then recoiling quickly if I move my hand to her head. And then, eventually, she too will give in. Anyway, my point is they have different personalities – though they look pretty similar, we can already tell them apart just because one of them seems slightly more gregarious and the other seems shy (and the gregarious one has a splodge of black beneath her eye). And with that fact, arise opportunities to form some class of a relationship with them because, of course, when they are different, you have occasion for preference. You prefer the shy one. Or you prefer the bold one. And then the affection you have for one or the other grows deeper.

Since we already have 'the outgoing one' and 'the shy one' we really gain no protection from not naming them. The first year we kept pigs, we named them Charlotte and Wilbur, which, by all accounts, was a bad idea, because the names were far too cute – and it's very difficult to kill an animal you have named, particularly if they are named after characters in a children's novel. Everyone I spoke to who had any experience of these things, shook their head and muttered, 'Oh dear, rookie mistake.' So, in the second year, we complied with the conventions in these things and didn't name them at all. This year, I've decided that the whole thing is a complete nonsense – whether we name them or not is not going to make it any worse or any better when we go to kill them. Let's clarify this: for all the reasons that I mentioned above, it's not pleasant when you have to take your pigs away to be killed. But if you're a meat eater and particularly a lover of pork and bacon products, then you get over it. And if you do feel a little sad about it, then who bloody cares – you've reared this animal from tiny little piggy, you've fed it and watered it – and (stupidly) got some pleasure from patting it on the head. So what's wrong with feeling a twang of ... I don't know – remorse, regret, indecision? You'd be bloody inhuman not to because you're basically killing a companion. So I've made a decision that I am on the look-out for appropriate names. Eleanor Pigby? The Duchess of Pork? Piggy Sue? Runty McSnorty? So many options ...

Most books will tell you that the pea has been popular since prehistoric times, but, back then, they were typically dried before being eaten. It was not until the seventeenth century that well-heeled British folk started to eat them fresh. With the advent of canning and freezing, the fresh pea became more and more of a rarity – I mean, apart from mangetout, when's the last time you saw fresh peas in a supermarket? The commercial world has done a pretty stellar job of convincing us that frozen peas are just as good as fresh peas, plucked straight from the pod. They are not. Certain pea producers make their sales pitch around the fact that their peas are frozen within hours of being picked – this is impressive but, I'm sorry, it's just not quick enough. No matter how advanced the food distribution chain becomes, it still can't cope with the fact that as soon as you pick a pod, the sugar content of the peas *immediately* starts to convert to starch (as it does with broad beans). Don't get me wrong, I'm a fan of freezing – we'd be lost without the option of freezing produce – but we've grown so comfortable with it that we tend to assume that it sort of locks produce in a time- and taste-warp. It doesn't. When you freeze something, tiny ice crystals form in the food, which alters the composition, texture, quality and taste of the produce irrevocably. It's great, for example, that we can kill all our chickens at the one time and then freeze them to be used as required – but we would be kidding ourselves to say that the meat is as good as it would be if we were selecting a chicken every weekend, killing it and then eating it the following day. If you want to taste how good a pea can really be, pick some from the garden and immediately take them inside, boil them up for just five or ten minutes (add a sprig of mint to the pot if you like). I never add salt or pepper – I want to taste and savour every delicious mouthful of pea flavour. Or, best of all, I just eat them raw, direct from the pod – they are sensational.

FREEZING

Freezing is generally frowned upon by purists because it allows you to eat food outside of nature's natural cycle. What a load of rubbish – the same purists would not, I presume, have any problem with us clamping our potatoes in straw, or storing carrots in sand, so you have to think that it's the method of storage that's the problem and not the concept of storage itself. There is, of course, a very valid criticism of freezing and that is that it uses electricity and is therefore more expensive and less environmentally friendly than other methods of storage, but I think that we can offset this somewhat by using the freezer efficiently – try not to have a massive chest freezer powered up just to store a few bags of frozen peas (in fact, the more you have in the freezer the more efficient it is), and don't leave the door open for ten minutes while unpacking the shopping bags. When you put meat and vegetables in the freezer first, it's best to put them in the coldest part – the faster they freeze, the smaller the ice crystals will be and the less damage there is to the texture and flavour of the food. Once the food has frozen, it's possible to move it to another part of the freezer if required.

We find freezing to be a vital way to preserve produce, particularly when it comes to meat from our pigs and chickens. It works by temporarily halting the growth of micro-organisms and bacteria that would normally cause food to rot – these little organisms are not killed, however, and recover when the food is thawed out. Interestingly, while the little critters in the food are dormant, regular enzyme action does, in fact, continue, albeit more slowly, and so food will eventually deteriorate in the freezer. Six to twelve months is about the limit of what's sensible. Freezing is quite successful at retaining the quality and nutritive value of food, more so than other methods of preserving, such as drying, canning or pickling. Since it usually involves nothing more than bunging the food in a freezer bag and throwing it into the freezer, it is also far less labour intensive than other methods. Some vegetables (particularly green ones) benefit from blanching first, which means that you boil them for a few minutes, then run them under a cold tap to refresh them, and then freeze them. This will help to prolong the amount of time that you can freeze them because it reduces the amount of enzyme activity in the food.

A very important consideration is what is going to happen to your food if there is a power cut. Trust me, we have some experience with this problem. We keep our large freezer in the garage and we had a disaster once where the freezer was accidentally unplugged and everything in it thawed out. Thankfully, we discovered the problem quickly and we were able to use quite a lot of the produce, but, of course, it couldn't be refrozen and there was plenty that we couldn't use, which was very frustrating. I recall an enormous bag of sausage-meat from our own pigs, for example, waiting for me to get my act together and buy some sausage casings – it thawed out completely and we had to use the whole lot immediately, making meatballs and the like. A terrible waste. So it's best to bear in mind that a prolonged power cut could ruin an entire year's worth of produce. If you are heavily reliant on the freezer for preservation, it might be worthwhile, perhaps, considering a petrol generator as a backup. (I feel I should – any day now...)

Sampling the first peas of the season (usually late next month or early in July) is one of the great delights of any Home Farmer's growing year – in fact, it is one of a triumvirate of great food growing experiences, as far as I am concerned, the other two being the first tomato of the season and the first spud. Splitting open a bursting pea pod and plucking out the seven or eight peas inside, is an absolutely thrilling experience (so much so that it can be a challenge to get to the kitchen without the whole lot being scoffed on the way). In these moments of sheer abundance, I find it's always worth reminding myself of those hopeful days back in March when I stuck a single pea into the soil and waited expectantly for a little shoot to appear. I marvel at how clever nature is that she can equip that tiny pea with all the potential it needs to become a plant that will produce huge quantities of peas. Think about that – it *really* is amazing.

Having a constant supply of fresh peas from May to October requires a pretty complex successional sowing regime and a good deal of space. We don't have the latter and we're way too disorganised to accomplish the former. If you do want to go down this route, it's best to start sowing them from March and keep sowing every four weeks or so until July. Like potatoes, peas are classified by how long it takes them to grow – first earlies will take about 2½ months, second earlies about 3½, while the main crop will take about 3 months. We usually just get two or three sowings done in the three months of spring, spaced about three to four weeks apart – and we're pretty pleased with ourselves if we accomplish that much.

Peas are a little bit fussier to grow than the mighty broad bean. While easy to get going in modules, your crop will be pretty abysmal if you don't put them in good soil, whereas the broad bean will grow pretty much anywhere. We have had bumper crops of peas some years and not so bumper crops other years, without ever really knowing why. They really dislike acid, apparently, preferring neutral to slightly alkaline soils, so some additional ground limestone is probably a good idea if your soil is acid. They also like good soil structure, which means that when you sow or transplant them you need to make sure the ground is good and firm, otherwise they will become displaced. While the soil needs to be good and fertile, you don't need to over-manure – too much nitrogen, in fact, will do them more harm than good. We get a good dose of manure into the beds in the winter and then leave it at that, and that seems to work okay. The ground is nice and fertile, but the manure is not too fresh, and because the worms have done their job and brought the manure down from the surface, the roots of the plants take off in search of this fertile material, which gives them a steady anchor from which to take on the world.

As with our broad beans, we tend to sow our peas in pots before carefully transplanting them, but you can also sow them directly into the soil by making a trench about 5cm deep and 25cm wide and then placing the peas in a zig-zag line along the trench. Leave about 10cm between peas and then cover them over with soil. As you might expect from their delicate form, they don't like too much cold, so don't be tempted to put them in the ground too early, and do protect them from frosts if you have to. You also need to keep the weeds down, but that won't be a problem once the plants take off as their canopy will do that for you.

Peas are incredible-looking plants – as they grow they send out delicate, yet strong, tendrils that wrap around whatever support you have left for them – old branches, netting, trellis – to give the necessary support to the main stem. Scientists don't yet know how the tendrils sense that there is something near them to curl around, it's one of nature's so-far undiscovered little secrets. Those tendrils are currently incredibly trendy in the culinary world, by the way, and fantastic in salads – they taste a lot like a mild spinach, but there is that definite taste of pea there too.

Pea plants do need support – don't be fooled by the cutesy little plants at this time of the year. By the summer they are substantial and will fall over or blow over in the wind if they are not propped up. We put some canes or narrow fencing posts in the ground and attach a length of chicken wire, and then grow the plants on either side of the netting; the tendrils will grasp the chicken wire as they grow. Sometimes we need to tie the main stem to the chicken wire with twine to encourage that process. An alternative is to use 'peasticks' – branches cut from hazel or birch – which look far nicer than chicken wire. Peas really dislike dry weather and letting the plants dry out has a disastrous impact – if the plants are noticeably dry, it's probably too late to save them. So, as with broad beans, it's a good idea to mulch them to try and retain water, but you will also need to check the soil beneath the mulch to ensure that it is still wet enough. In dry weather, give them a good soaking, particularly when they are coming close to flowering and when the pods are fattening up with lovely peas.

PAULA MEE'S NUTRITION BITES: PEAS

For natural sweetness, you can't beat garden-fresh peas. They may look tiny, but they are giants in terms of their nutritional value. Peas are high in vitamin C, vitamin K and iron, and are a source of folate. They are also a source of soluble fibre, which is the type of fibre that can help to lower your cholesterol. Because they have a low glycaemic index, they are very filling and satisfying and will release their energy slowly, keeping you going for longer. Of the myriad nutrients that peas provide, iron is particularly important since it's hard to find it in plant foods. Red meat, which you might have alongside your peas, is a great source of easily-absorbable iron. Yet a portion of peas provides 16 percent of your recommended daily iron intake, which is very good news for vegetarian growers!

Nutrition per Portion (80g):

Calories	Fat (g)	Salt (g)	Saturated Fat (g)
66	1.2	0.003	0.2

Before we leave May behind to move onwards and upwards into high summer, a word about spring lamb. This year, we did a great pork-for-lamb swap with a neighbour who rears his own lambs – in exchange for some of our own pork, sausages and bacon, we got some wonderful lamb chops, a large leg of lamb, a shoulder and some diced lamb. It's a wonderful way for us to get our hands on home-reared meat from animals we will, most likely, never rear ourselves.

It's a strange tradition, indeed, that associates lamb with the Easter dinner, as it is, in fact, far too early to eat lamb, particularly if Easter is early. Officially, a 'lamb' is aged between four to six months (but can be up to a year old, after which it is sold as hogget or mutton). This means that lambs that are ready to eat at Easter were born in the winter and probably spent some time being reared indoors and fed on sheep nuts. Real spring lambs are the ones that were actually *born in the spring* (traditionally, sheep farmers didn't start lambing until March) – they were the ones that you saw running around the fields in the spring months and they are just about to start hitting the butcher's shelf in late May. Incidentally, the lamb that you can get in June and July will most likely be half the price of the so-called spring lambs that were available at Easter, and they will taste far nicer too because they have had the time out in the fields to help them develop muscle, and hence flavour, in their meat.

I had an interesting discussion with my lamb-rearing neighbour about the 'organic' designation of lamb. The lamb that we got from him is not organic, but it's proper spring lamb as the animals were reared outside on grass their whole lives. They were born in the fields and got to feed from their mothers until they were ready to start grazing – they are completely and utterly free-range, in the proper sense of that word. So, what does the organic designation on spring lamb achieve? Very little, in my opinion. In fact, I would far prefer to eat non-organic, grass-reared spring lamb in May or June than organic lamb in March or April as the latter probably had some concentrated grain in its diet. The grain may have been organic, but it's still not a normal part of a lamb's diet. In my humble opinion, we need to be really careful about slavishly following the organic designation. I am all for buying organic chicken (as you will see in Chapter 7) and I would be all for buying organic pork, if I could get it, as these animals are almost always reared indoors in a completely artificial environment. With beef and lamb, on the other hand, the animals will almost certainly have been reared outdoors and fed grass more or less exclusively. Here's something to ponder about in the context of the organic designation on food: if you catch a salmon in the wilds of the Atlantic Ocean, it cannot be labelled organic because, of course, nobody can stand over what a wild salmon has eaten during its 15,000-mile migration to its spawning ground. If you farm salmon artificially in a cage somewhere off the Irish coast, and give them organic feed every day, then it can be labelled organic. Which salmon would you prefer to eat?

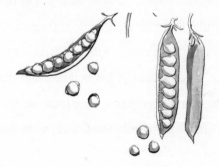

MAY GROWER'S CALENDAR

Prep Work

- May brings the first of the year's new fruit and vegetables – little wonder then that May Day was such cause for celebration. It's the last chance to catch up on your seed sowing.
- Our 'planting out' really steps up a gear in May – early May is the time to get those outdoor beds ready for early summer transplanting. Fork-over and rake. Don't tread!

To-do List

- Earth-up potatoes as the plants develop – covering stem with soil encourages potato growth.
- Put protective barrier around your carrots to thwart the dastardly carrot-root fly.
- Regularly hoe weeds, and mulch.
- Water outdoors if required and also continue your watering and ventilation routine in the polytunnel or greenhouse.
- Support tomato plants as they grow and remove the side shoots as they appear (in the angle between the main stem and the leaf stem). As plants start to flower, tap the flowers to spread pollen and improve fruiting.
- Be vigilant for pests and diseases (eg carrot-root fly, aphids, caterpillars, rabbits, slugs and snails – complete gits, one and all).
- Support your pea and bean plants – twiggy sticks, pea netting, timber supports with chicken wire, or existing fence or hedge. Pinch out the growing tips of broad bean plants to help prevent blackfly.

Sowing Seeds

- May is the last chance for the tardy souls among us to catch up on our seed sowing. It's a good month for sowing, especially if you get the seeds in before the middle of the month, as many of the crops you sow in May will catch up with seeds sown in earlier months.

- *Sow indoors for planting-on later:* basil, dill, coriander, courgette, cucumber, sweet corn, melon, pumpkins, marrow, summer savory (great companion herb for growing and cooking with broad beans).
- *Sow outdoors:* winter cauliflower, cabbage, kale, spinach, sprouting broccoli, leeks, beans (French, runner, climbing French), beetroot, parsnips, turnips, swedes, radishes, lettuce, peas, broccoli, rocket, carrots.
- You could also try an extra harvest of early spuds by planting an additional row wherever you can accommodate them.

Planting Out

- Harden off and begin to plant out seedlings you have lovingly raised indoors – tomatoes, cucumbers, peppers, chilli-peppers, celery, celeriac, brussels sprouts, sprouting broccoli, cabbage, sweet corn, leeks.
- Sweet potatoes – not related to the humble spud (and therefore not susceptible to blight!), they prefer a sandy soil and do not like a rich soil. They must be harvested before the first frosts in winter and, like pumpkins, left to dry for about ten days in the sun before storage.

GRUB'S UP – WHAT'S IN SEASON

May is another tricky 'gap' month as stores continue to dwindle. You may, however, start getting some new spuds, particularly if you put down an early crop in the polytunnel back in February.

Continue picking asparagus, radishes, rhubarb, cabbage, cauliflower, spinach and chard.

May is likely to see the first real bumper crop of salad leaves, like lettuce and rocket, as well as the first garlic, beetroot and globe artichokes.

The end of this month sees the first of the real (ie outdoor reared, grass fed) spring lambs.

6

THE GUY WITH THE CHICKENS

MID-SUMMER: JUNE

salad leaves – cucumber – pigs again – our first ducks – home farm courses – home farm routine

Given that it's so easy to grow salad leaves, I cannot understand why so many of us are willing to pay for poor-quality, costly bags of leaves in the supermarket, which are sprayed with God-knows-what and invariably go limp (then wilted, then withered, then brown, then gooey …) at the back of the fridge. There is literally no excuse to explain an unwillingness to grow lettuce and other salad leaves, except, perhaps, just a genuine unwillingness – the seeds are incredibly cheap, they are easy to grow and you don't need much space (regular sowings of a compact lettuce like Little Gem in a couple of window boxes or in pots on a patio will give you salad leaves all summer long). The intense, peppery taste of your own rocket eaten just minutes after being picked is very, very hard to beat and a total revelation compared to the bagged stuff you buy in the shops.

It seems fitting to be discussing salad leaves as we move more deeply into summer on the Home Farm, but, of course, the cunning vegetable grower will have tasty salad leaves to munch all year round. Whether you want to tuck into corn salad, mizuna, land cress and the other leaves that grow well in the winter is another matter. Aside from the traditional ones like lettuce and rocket, there is a huge range of vegetable and herb leaves that can go into a salad bowl – mizuna, basil, coriander, sorrel, mustard leaf, chicory, endive – but, to be honest, we have, by and large, found enough to interest us so far in the various types of lettuce, basil and rocket. We also use baby spinach, chard and beetroot leaves to provide a splash of colour. The beauty of growing salad leaves is that they produce results so quickly – they are quick to germinate, so you see some action in the potting compost within days, and they are very quick to grow. You will be able to harvest some varieties of lettuce just six or eight weeks after sowing.

There are only two things that are a little tricky about growing salad leaves. The first is that you really do need to get into the habit of sowing 'little but often', which can be a challenge if you're perpetu-ally disorganised, like I am. I would much prefer it if I could sow my lettuce for the whole year in one afternoon, but, unfortunately, this just means that it would all be ready to eat at the one time and salad leaves do not store well (about three days in the fridge, if you're lucky). Lettuce doesn't keep well in the soil either and it's a fine line (basically about a week) between peak condition and bolting disas-ter. So, sowing fifty lettuce seeds in one go is not a good idea unless you've been asked to do the catering for a wedding. The best approach is to sow ten or fifteen seeds every fortnight or so. The other thing you have to watch out for with salad leaves is bolting – if your lettuces do not get enough water in hot weather they basically sense that they are about to die and go into crazy procreation mode, producing flowers and seeds in the hope of propagating before they shuffle off this mortal coil (which is kind of cool, you must admit). They are fit only for the compost heap at this point.

There are basically four different types of lettuce – butterheads are round and soft, cos are more upright and shaped like a rugby ball, crispheads have really dense and crunchy leaves, while loose-leaf lettuces don't have a heart at all, like the Tin Man from *The Wizard of Oz*. With the first three types you have to harvest the whole head, whereas loose-leaf lettuce is a cut-and-come-again type, so you can just snip off as much as you need each time – the more you pick the more it will grow. Within those four broad classifications there are hundreds of different varieties to try out, each with its own flavour, texture and colour. Interestingly, considering they are always associated with the summer, lettuces do not like very hot weather – we originally used to always plant all our lettuces in the polytunnel, but it's far too hot in there for them in high summer, so now we plant some outside too for summer growing and picking. Salad-leaf crops, like lettuce and rocket, stand outside the standard crop rotation plan, so you can basically shove them in anywhere you have a bit of space.

Lettuce and rocket germinate pretty well and even hackers like us can get a pretty good return by sowing directly into the ground. But still, you get pretty much a hundred percent results if you sow in modules. Drop two seeds into each module and once they have germinated, pull out the weakest seedling. If you are going to plant the seedlings outside you will need to get it used to the lower temperatures gradually by leaving the module trays outside for a few hours each day for about a week. Plant them out in a well-raked bed when the seedlings have four or five leaves, giving each plant about 20cm of space. In the height of the summer if the soil is too warm, lettuce seeds will often not germinate at all because the seed shuts down to protect itself from drying-out – you can get around this by watering the ground an hour before you sow and shade the ground afterwards. Your biggest threat at this point is the dastardly slug – slimy creatures from miles around will gather for a munch-brunch when they hear that you have put out a fresh row of lettuce – more on these buggers later.

Rocket is as easy to grow as lettuce (and can be grown the same way), but unlike lettuce it's nigh on indestructible. Although the leaves are at their best when young and tender, don't believe a book that tells you the older leaves are too tough to eat – I reckon they still taste pretty good, if a little bitter. We continued eating our rocket from the polytunnel last year even after it went to seed and it was fine – then it started to produce lovely white flowers and we ate them too (they look great in salads and taste like a hotter version of rocket). Because it went to seed last year, this year we had rocket springing up all over the place in one corner of the tunnel from around March onwards – I should have been mad over that, but instead I was just grateful to have them so early in the year (particularly since I didn't even have to plant them). The proper way to do things, of course, is to start picking the leaves when they are the length of your finger – the more you pick, the more leaves will grow.

Before I finish on salady stuff, I should mention cucumber, which provides a spectacular bounty for us every summer from just one or two plants. The poor old cucumber's reputation has taken a bit of a hammering over the past few years. It was the staple of the classic Irish and British salad for decades, but when we moved on and got all posh with our funny-named lettuces and spectacular dressings, the cucumber got left behind. No self-respecting restaurant will serve up a salad that has cucumber in it these days, which I think is a great pity because it has a wonderfully crisp, refreshing flavour. You will also get a great deal of satisfaction from growing whopping big cucumbers of your own – it's one of those plants that makes you feel you're a bloody good grower, even if you're not.

Our cucumbers won't be harvested until next month, but, believe it or not, we are still eating jars of pickled cucumber from last year and we absolutely love it (I think it's one of those things that you either love or hate). We have grown the standard, phallic green cucumbers and also strange-looking round yellow ones that look more like lemons than cucumbers. We start our cucumber plants in pots in March and then plant them in the polytunnel around May – they thrive in the warmth of the tunnel as long as you keep them well watered, as it is water that causes the fruits to swell to magnificent sizes. It also helps to give the poor cucumber plant a spray with whatever feed you are giving your tomato plants (an organic tomato feed, or, better again, a homemade feed such as nettle or comfrey tea). Incidentally, if you don't have a polytunnel or greenhouse, cucumbers will also do very well in large pots and containers indoors. When the plant is starting to harvest, you simply cut the cucumbers off when they have reached a reasonable size – the more you cut, the more fruit the plant will produce. Don't leave cucumbers to go beyond green to yellow – the whole plant will down tools and cease production if you do that. Older vegetable-growing books talk about cucumber being hard to grow and labour-intensive, but I can't say that I agree – ours works away in the corner of the tunnel, churning out fruit (up to thirty cucumbers from one plant) for about three months in the summer, with little heed paid to them, apart from daily watering. We haven't bothered with staking or putting up canes or anything like that – the plants just trail over the ground and seem quite happy that way. This year I already have my eye on one burgeoning cucumber I reckon is going to be ready shortly and will be our first of the season – as soon as it's ready it will be deployed as the core ingredient in a super-chilled *tsatsiki,* diced up and mixed with natural yogurt, olive oil, garlic, mint and seasoning, served with fresh white bread. The thoughts of it! Come on, cucumber, hurry up and grow!

PAULA MEE'S NUTRITION BITES: SALAD LEAVES AND CUCUMBER

Leafy green vegetables are great nutritional value for your painstaking gardening efforts. They are naturally low in fat and, because of their higher water content, they contain very few calories. Rocket and watercress, with their delicate textures and dark green colour, provide a myriad of nutrients yet a diminutive number of calories. In fact, the darker the leaves, the greater the nutrient content. So mix it up! Nutrition per Portion (80g):

Vegetable	Calories	Fat (g)	Salt (g)	Saturated Fat (g)
Lettuce	11	0.4	0	0.1
Cucumber	8	0.1	0	0

I had a funny kind of a day yesterday. It has been raining really hard for a few days (like that movie *Seven* where it rains in every scene) and when I went to feed the piggies I noticed that their run was a complete and utter mess, with the rainwater congealing with the soil and manure and urine and grass clippings and all manner of other mean and nasty stuff. The pigs were knee-deep in this soupy mess, looking at me forlornly, so I made the difficult decision to lock them up in their pigsty for a few days until the worst of the weather had passed. They never seem too unhappy in there, really, especially when it's wet. It's not huge, neither is it ideal (they can't root on concrete), but at least they are dry and they have a bit of space and fresh air. I know I shouldn't feel guilty about stuff like this, but I can't help myself. Anyway, it's only temporary until the weather improves (please God, let it improve).

My rather clever pigsty design has some flaws in it, not least of which is the fact that the gate into it opens out into their mucky run, rather than out onto the lawn. Big mistake. I don't need to go through the muck most of the time – I can feed and water them over the wall while standing on the grass – but, occasionally, I do need to go in, say, for example, if I'm mucking out and need to bring the wheelbarrow into the sty with me. I have a plank stretching from the fencing to the pigsty, which, in theory, keeps you out of the worst of the muck. There's a simple mathematical equation that every would-be Home Farm pig owner should familiarise themselves with:

wet weather+muck+pig excrement+pig urine x two heavy animals = extremely questionable soil consistency.

Yesterday morning I was walking delicately across the plank (like you would across a tightrope, I suppose) while carrying their food bucket in one hand and a watering can in the other and the two pigs were butting me from either side with their snouts and, of course, the inevitable happened. I could see it happening almost in slow motion in my mind's eye – one foot slipped on the wet plank and went out in front of me and because I had my hands full, I couldn't break the fall. So, basically, I just went down on my ass in the muck and dirt, and the pig bucket and watering can went up in the air and then splashed down in the dirt beside me. The pigs just stepped over me to get at the food, which was now in the mud. One of them was actually standing over me while feeding and I found myself contemplating her under-side, thinking to myself that maybe we should pack up and move to the city. It took hours of scrubbing to get the smell of pig off me. (Incidentally, last week I was at a meeting when I suddenly got a dis-tinct smell of pig in the air. I looked around at the other people, won-dering who was responsible for such a god-awful smell, when I suddenly realised that it was me. I looked down at my trainers and, sure enough, I could see some pig manure on them. I won't be invited back to meet that crowd in a hurry. *'Did you get a load of the pong off that journalist? Jeez, would he ever wash himself?'*)

Anyway, it's days like that when you wonder why the hell you bother with the whole malarkey – it can be such bloody hard, smelly, dirty work. Thankfully, I've found over the years that whenever I have a really bad day or a bad morning or just a bad incident, there's usually something pretty special just around the corner to help you get over it. Rummaging in the freezer for something interesting to eat yesterday, we came across packets of frozen ribs from last year's pigs. Most of the decent meat from last year's animals is well and truly gone at this stage. The sausages were gone in weeks, followed by the rashers, decent cuts of ham etc. Now, all we are left with are some dubious cuts – fatty-looking pork, the trotters – and a pig's head, which I take out of the freezer every now and then to scare visiting children. They say that you really should use up frozen pork within six months, but any we've used lately (which is nearly a year in the freezer) has been fine. Anyway, in that context the spare ribs were quite a find. We defrosted them and prepared a marinade and ate them with some home fries and a few beers – absolutely gorgeous. They were just what I needed to remind me what this whole project is about: self-sufficiency and great grub.

After dinner, I went off down to feed the pigs with renewed pep in my step, the animosity between us dissipated. They were standing up on their back legs with their front legs up on the wall of the pigsty, looking out for me, waiting impatiently for their supper (four legs bad, two legs good?). I'm not blind to the immense ironies in all this – eating ribs from last year's animals and then going off down the garden to fatten up this year's – and I do wonder about how mercenary I have become and how comfortable I am with killing animals for meat, especially when compared with the relentless introspection of previous years. It's not like I was thinking: Oh I've just had lovely ribs and look at the lovely ribs on you – I shall eat you shortly! I guess I wasn't thinking about it at all, which is just as it should be. Right now, our pigs are being looked after, given shelter and food. I'm falling into holes filled with muck and crap for them, for God's sake. But soon the whole project will move up a notch and turn from animal maintenance to food production and then, JOY TO THE

WORLD, food scoffing. As I headed back up the garden to the house, the sun shone momentarily and when I looked back at the pig run there was a rainbow off in the distance that seemed to be arching right over their house. Not sure what that meant, if anything, but it made me smile anyway.

We had an interesting time of it trying to introduce ducks to the Home Farm. For my birthday earlier this year, Mrs Kelly bought me two beautiful Khaki Campbell ducks. There was a time before all this madness started when she used to buy me normal presents, like a nice sweater or an interesting pair of socks. Not any more. The present *de rigueur* these days usually comes in a cardboard box that is quacking, grunting, chirping, squawking or dripping pooh.

Anyway, for some reason, which I will never fully understand, our first two ducks seemed to be very stressed out, like Woody Allens of the duck world. When we got them home, one of them escaped as I was putting her into the old hen run in which we planned to keep them for a few weeks while they were getting used to the place. I had an awful job rounding her up – she ran in behind the polytunnel (those little legs can move at quite a speed when they want to) and I only managed to catch her because she inadvertently got tangled up in a gorse bush. I am sure this little kerfuffle didn't help her nervous disposition. When I eventually reunited her with her buddy, the two of them disappeared into the house and stayed there for at least two days, which was a little alarming as they weren't eating or drinking anything. Eventually, they were bold enough (or hungry and thirsty enough?) to come out, but they would scurry back inside whenever we came within fifty paces. On the third day, I left them out for a few hours and they seemed quite happy – waddling over and back between their house and the pig-run and stopping occasionally to hoover up some of the food we had left or to take a splash in the water we'd left for them. They returned to their house as soon as it got dark and I locked them in, happy that they were starting to settle in. On the fourth day, I let them out for the entire afternoon and they made some slightly more adventurous sorties up the garden, returning at great haste to their house when the hens started to come towards them. On the fifth day, they were out for most of the day again, but this time when Mrs Kelly went to lock up their house, there was no sign of them. She thought she heard them in the ditch, but since it was dark she couldn't locate them. We decided to leave them be, hoping they would make their way back to the house at some point. Next morning, still no sign of them. A few times during the day, we went out into the fields with the dogs to look for them (if anyone could sniff them out, the dogs could), but came back duckless and generally forlorn.

We don't think that a fox got them – touch wood, we have not had a visit from a fox for a long time on the Home Farm, but perhaps they wandered off and *something* got them, like a large bear or the head chef in the local Szechuan restaurant. Unlike hens, who can't really do any flying worth mentioning, ducks can fly at considerable altitude and for long distances – so they may have decided to abandon the Home Farm and fly off in search of a warmer climate, a large lake or a better life. You can, by the way, clip a duck's primary flight feathers as you would with a hen (see Chapter 9).

Anxious and disappointed about our ducklessness, we were

chasing shadows and generally acting like crazy people for the next few days. For example, I was putting some vegetable scraps on the compost heap one day, and I was sure I heard a quack in the ditch beside me. I ran to the house to call Mrs Kelly. 'The ducks are back, the ducks are back!' I shouted through the kitchen window, and she came running down the garden, whooping and hollering like we had won the lottery. We searched the ditch around the compost heaps, but there was still no sign of them and I had to accept that maybe I was hearing things. The following day, she called me out from the house because she thought she heard a quack overhead – but it turned out to be two birds (or perhaps noises coming from inside her head?). Finally we decided to move on, before we went completely quackers, and accept that the ducks were gone for good. I was pretty disappointed about our first attempt at keeping ducks, mainly because I felt mad that they clearly hadn't enjoyed their time here on *our* Home Farm, when the rest of us residents like it just fine.

Anyway, just like when you fall off a horse, the best approach, when you've suffered a growing or rearing setback, is to get straight back up, dust yourself off and start again. About three weeks later, we got two more ducks and, for some reason, they seemed immediately more comfortable than the previous two had been (and because they looked pretty much identical, we could sort of pretend that the first incident had never happened). While the first two ducks didn't emerge from their house at all for two days, the new arrivals were out splashing around in a tub of water within hours. On the advice of the breeder, this time we left them in the run for a week and they seemed far more content when we finally started to leave them out for a few hours. Within three or four weeks, they were basically part of the hen flock (the two species integrate commendably well, though it's worth noting that a drake may try and 'get it on' with your hens if you don't have a rooster).

The Khaki Campbell is one of the most common Home Farm ducks, particularly amongst people who are keeping them for eggs. The breed was developed in England in the late 1800s and its rather strange name comes from (a) its colour – it has beautiful khaki-brown plumage and (b) the name of the woman who developed the breed, a certain Mrs Adele Campbell. This rather grand lady (I'm sure) crossed an Indian Runner duck with a Rouen duck to get the impressive egg-laying ability of the former and the size of the latter. Some Campbells will lay an egg a day all year, contributing food for the table even when your hens have given up laying in the depths of winter.

It took about two months for us to get our first duck egg and there were a few scary moments when we actually wondered whether they were, in fact, not ducks at all, but two drakes. We were told by the seller at the fair that they were 'point of lay' females, so you would have a reasonable expectation that they would lay pretty quickly, but months went by and there was still no sign of an egg. Drakes would be absolutely no use to us, of course, apart from becoming the main ingredient in Duck à l'Orange. Then, one day, I saw one of them trying to 'get up on' a hen, which I took to be a very bad sign in terms of their likely gender. I read everything I could find on the internet about 'sexing' ducks, but could not find anything satisfactory. Some articles I read suggested that male Campbells have a different-coloured head than the females and we thought we could detect a slight change in hue around the neck area in our two, but it was frustratingly subtle and so we weren't sure. Then, someone else told me that male ducks have a more 'raspy' quack, but I listened intently to our two and still wasn't sure – it sounded raspy enough, but maybe they'd been smoking Woodbines down at the end of the garden. They are kind of rebellious like that.

About a week later, I witnessed one of the ducks trying to get up on the other one – he was getting up on the wrong end and it looked like something you would see in a perverted duck version of the Kama Sutra; nonetheless, we took it as a positive sign that perhaps at least one of our ducks was female (either that or we had gay ducks). We decided that one of each sex wouldn't be too bad; we could hatch some ducklings ourselves and maybe sell them on. The following day I saw the same thing happening, but this time the 'drake' seemed to have worked out the 'right end'. And then, one glorious morning, I went to let them out of their house and there it was, on the bed of straw in their house – a big, perfect, marbly white egg. I swear I was so delighted, you'd think I had laid it myself. Duck egg heaven! This development confirmed that we had one female duck at least; the other turned out to be a drake, after all, and I decided to call them Mork and Mindy.

Duck eggs have a poor reputation, a legacy of the fact that they caused a salmonella outbreak shortly after World War II. Their shells (which are like marble to touch) are porous and will absorb impurities from the surrounding environment and it is important to keep this in mind if you have some ducks on your Home Farm. A duck egg laid on the bank of a dirty pond is not something that you want to eat; a duck egg laid in their house on a bed of straw, on the other hand, will be perfectly safe. Collect the eggs daily so that they don't get fouled by the ducks poohing on them in the house and clean them before you put them in the egg tray. Duck eggs will not last as long as your hen's eggs – roughly ten to twelve days is about the longest that you should keep them. As with hen eggs, duck eggs do not need to be kept in a fridge.

The eggs are much larger than a hen's egg and are therefore perfect for baking and cooking. They are certainly richer than a hen's egg, and for that reason many people don't like to eat them. I'm inclined to think that they are good to eat if you scramble them or use them in omelettes, but I am not a huge fan of a poached duck egg, which is how I generally prefer my eggs cooked, as the white tends to be a bit rubbery.

Duck eggs are higher in nutritional content than hen eggs by virtue of their larger size. They are high in zinc, calcium, potassium, sulphur and vitamins A, B, D and E. They contain about 20 percent of our recommended daily allowance of protein and just 7g of fat. The yolk contains cholesterol, but it's probably worth waiting about fifty years until scientists *really* understand what cholesterol is for, before worrying about this.

The Khaki Campbell egg is considered to be quite mild, as duck eggs go. You can, of course, eat duck meat too, so if you want to fatten birds for the table, you buy them as day-old ducklings, feed them up on barley and kill them at ten weeks old (they will give about 1.4kg of meat at that stage). I've never done this, incidentally, but I would like to try it at some point in the future. I reckon ten or twelve ducks would make a fine addition to the freezer and, given how rich the meat is (it's not an everyday meal like chicken would be), such a quantity of birds would surely suffice for a year or so. Khaki Campbells, incidentally, are a good dual-purpose bird (they are a good meat bird as well as being prodigious layers), which is a rare thing indeed with modern poultry. The ubiquitous Rhode Island hybrid hens, for example, which most people have for egg-laying, are a travesty when it comes to meat.

Ducks are sorely lacking in maternal instinct, as evidenced by the fact that nature has not been able to teach them that their little offspring cannot actually swim until they are two or three weeks old. Many a duckling has been encouraged by its mother to enter a pond only to drown moments later. So, if you are breeding them and have some fertilised eggs, you are better off putting them under a good broody hen to hatch, or, probably better still, in an incubator. It's a very bizarre and slightly worrying quirk of nature that hens make better duck-mothers than ducks do, and sometimes, while cleaning out their house, I find myself pondering how on earth ducks survived over the millennia if they are such rotten mothers.

There is a rather vexed question about whether to keep ducks if you do not have water (a pond or stream) in your garden. It is actually incredibly cruel to keep ducks in an environment where they have no access to water as it is the environment they were designed for. If in any doubt about this, there are three features of the duck to take a look at. First, you will notice that the nostrils are located to the back of the beak, near the head end – this allows them to 'root' for food in shallow water and breathe at the same time. Secondly, their feathers fit like a glove, overlapping each other in layers and appearing almost seamless. Courtesy of this incredible waterproofing, when a duck gets out of the water, they are completely and magically bone-dry. And finally, it's also pretty obvious when you look at their feet, that the duck is ultimately made for a life spent on or near water.

Aside from the fact that they love water, they also will not be able to keep themselves looking sleek and pristine without it. If you are lucky enough to have a stream running through or around your property, then you are on the pig's back. But if you don't, the obvious solution, on the face of it, would be to build a pond. There are two problems with this approach, however: firstly, a pond is a dangerous thing to have in the garden if you are going to have small people running around the place at any point in the future. Secondly, ducks will foul stagnant water and your pond will, within a very short time, become a stinking, green mess that is very difficult to clean out. So, in my humble opinion, giving them access to clean water in a large container is a better and ultimately a more humane way to do things, as long as you have only a small number of ducks. We have a big old Belfast sink filled with water for our ducks and we replace the water in it every couple of days to keep it fresh. It's got a stopper in it so that we can empty and wash it out and it's located close enough to an outdoor tap so it's handy to refill. Don't laugh at this, okay, but I even made some steps for them out of old red bricks so they can climb up to get into the sink.

I happened to be looking out the window the day Mork and Mindy 'discovered' the sink – it was about three weeks after we got them and I was perpetually worried that they didn't have enough water and wondering would they *ever* use the sink. They started craning their necks to look in and have a bit of a drink, and I was tense with excitement and shouting: 'Go on! Go on!!' from inside the house. Then one of them waddled around to the other side and figured out that she could climb up the bricks, and, all of a sudden, in she plopped. Then the other one figured the whole thing out as well, so she got in too and joined in the fun, and I was inside jumping up and down with joy like a madman. They spend some time in their swimming pool each day, splashing about a bit and ducking their heads under the water and then they get out and follow the hens around for the rest of the day. It's such a joy to watch them having their daily bath that I moved the sink to a point in the garden, just beside the vegetable plot, where I can see it from the study where I work (it's sort of like Duck TV).

Strangely enough, the hens seem to tolerate the ducks pretty well – their own pecking order doesn't seem to be threatened by the two ducks following them around all day long. If the ducks try to eat from their feed bowl, they might have a bit of a go at them, all right, but they seem to reserve their real viciousness for poor Luidín, and generally leave the ducks be.

We have an area down at the end of the garden where we have let the grass grow long, and the ducks like to snooze in the long grass in the afternoon. Incidentally, another nice thing about having ducks about is that when the weather is particularly awful and all animals on the Home Farm, including the human beings, are completely and utterly miserable, the ducks are delighted with themselves. Rain really is great weather for ducks.

Ducks, like pigs and unlike hens, are very talkative animals, which lends them a considerable charm – they always seem to be giving out or fed up about something. I don't exactly know why ducks quack, as opposed to, say, chirping or tweeting, but perhaps God makes them quack because he knows that it will always make human beings smile! Anyway, whatever the reason – I am mighty glad they do. Ducks also wag their tails or whatever the equivalent duck version of tail-wagging is (they sort of wag their entire back-side), though I haven't yet figured out whether they do that because they are pleased to see me or consider me a threat. They have taken quite a shine to our goofy Labrador, Sam – they waddle after him and give out to him a bit, and then he plays with them a little, chasing them all over the garden. Then he gets bored with that and heads off, and they follow him to give out a little more. I don't understand this inter-species relationship just yet – I can't make out whether they are giving out to him because he is playing with them or because he isn't playing with them enough. I love our ducks more than our hens – again, I think it's because they are so responsive (and, of course, because they quack). I love the fact that when they are on the move the two of them move in concert. One of them darts to the left and the other immediately does the same. They are like synchronised swimmers in the Olympics. Because their eyes are on the side of their heads rather than the front, ducks have almost 360 degree vision, so they are relatively easy to 'round up' if you have to – they spot even the slightest of movement from you and turn accordingly.

DUCK BREEDS AND EGGS

Most ducks that are bred for eggs or meat these days are descended from the wild Mallard and were first domesticated by the Egyptians for religious sacrifice about three thousand years ago. Southeast Asians and the ancient Romans also raised ducks in captivity for their meat – in fact, the focus remained on meat until the nineteenth century when people started to realise that the eggs didn't taste half-bad either.

The most common duck breeds are the Indian Runner (good layer, poor meat, doesn't really like swimming, stands upright like a penguin), the Aylesbury, (hardy, heavy, great meat, poor layer), the Khaki Campbell (a brown bird, excellent layer, good meat), and the tiny Call Duck (will lay only seventy eggs a year, but makes up for it by being adorable). For smaller duck breeds (like the Call Ducks, for example) a garden of 10m x 10m will suffice, but bear in mind that they enjoy eating grass, so the smaller the space you give them the more damage they will do. Ducks are generally more vocal than their hen friends, which is worth bearing in mind if you have neighbours who tend towards unnecessary litigiousness.

Despite our initial problems, we now find ducks easier to keep than hens. Whereas hens will get agitated and generally throw a hissy-fit if they don't have their perch to sleep on and a row of identical nesting boxes in which to lay (maybe!), ducks will be happy as long as they have a dry little house with some straw in it (they don't roost at night); they are incredibly reliable layers and typically lay right through the winter – plus, eggs are obediently laid in their house *before* you leave them out in the morning (none of that inconvenient hunting around in ditches as with hens). We give our ducks the same feed as our hens (a mixture of layer's pellets and a bit of wheat thrown in for good luck) which is very handy. They also fight for their share of the kitchen scraps, depending on what it is. Our ducks don't seem to like cooked potato, for example, whereas the hens will kill each other to get at it. It must be said that the ducks are generally harder on the ground then our hens – Khaki Campbells, in particular, are excellent foragers and love to snuffle around looking for grubs, slugs and insects. Hens will scratch in the grass and occasionally eat some of it, but they don't really do much damage if they are truly free range and have a good bit of space to run in. But ducks are far more efficient grazers and will nibble a lot more lawn. In my opinion, this is no bad thing – the more grass they eat, the less I have to mow. In the winter, however, when there is no new growth in the grass, they may cause an occasional bald patch, so, if you are very proud of your croquet surface, maybe it's best to steer clear of keeping ducks.

Most importantly for the Home Farmer, ducks (unlike hens) LOVE slugs, which means that we, in turn, LOVE ducks. We've tried letting Mork and Mindy into the vegetable patch for an hour or so at certain times of the year to initiate a cull on the slug population and that seems to work out okay – they generally seem more interested in the beasties in the soil rather than what's growing in it. How convenient is that? Ducks rock!

Last June things took an interesting turn here on the Home Farm when I started running courses for people keen to keep hens in their garden. For years, I've been trying to encourage anyone who will listen to me to keep hens, but the idea of doing this on a more formal footing came from a friend of mine who was doing something similar in Dublin. I'm no hen expert, but we've been keeping them for about four years now, and I reckon I know a fair to middling amount about them, enough to get the novice off the ground, at any rate. I'm hopeful that what I lack in knowledge, I make up for with my freakishly over-zealous enthusiasm for the subject. I sent a notice to the local papers, more in hope than expectation, thinking that I might get a handful of people interested – I couldn't believe it when my phone started ringing and then kept on ringing. Bookings came in thick and fast, so much so that we had to run several courses over six weeks to keep up. Just goes to show you the phenomenal level of interest there is out there in the 'good life'.

There's a fair amount of work in getting the content ready and the days of the courses themselves are just frantically busy. We are up at the crack of dawn, baking and cleaning, and head chef Mrs Kelly has to get the lunch ready while I am doing the morning session (another fine mess I got her into). We had a long debate about what to give people for lunch – I thought a lasagne or a big pot of chilli would be the easiest thing – but Mrs Kelly told me that was a silly idea, that people were coming on a hen course, so the logical thing to do was to make something out of eggs. She was right, of course, as she almost always is. She made wonderful quiches from our eggs and we served them with salad leaves and homemade bread. Given the amount of work involved, this year we scaled things back a bit, running just a handful of courses over the summer months. We like an easy life, you see.

We've had a huge mix of people from all walks of life on the courses – men and women, young and old. People with loads of land and people with none. Mostly they are people who just want to keep a couple of hens in their garden for eggs and just don't know where to start. There was a woman on the first course who used to keep hens when she was a young girl, but hasn't thought about them in forty years. At the other end of the scale, there was a young girl (eight years old) with her mother, and I found it wonderful to think that she might be inspired to keep hens as she grows up. The common strand is that everyone who has come along, so far, is interested in growing and rearing their own food. The highlight of the course, according to the feedback, is always (a) the lunch and (b) when they get to pick up the hens! There was a chef here one weekend who told me he had been working with chicken all his life, handling it almost every day, but had never held a live chicken in his hands before. How cool is that? We had an elderly gentleman here one Saturday who had kept hens all his life – I was worried he would be asking me questions that I couldn't answer and I wondered what he was doing here, but during the break he told me that he just came along to meet and talk to like-minded people. The same man was able to get a hen to go to sleep by tucking her head under her wing and rocking her from side to side! The strangest thing I ever did see.

The most interesting part of the day for us is always the lunch break. The people who come along are always food lovers and invariably some have tried growing their own vegetables. We love getting to talk to people about the projects they have tried in their gardens, what has worked and what hasn't. I love that idea of a network of people who are interested in the same things, exchanging ideas. Sally and her husband Eric came along to one of our first courses and I was intrigued to discover that Sally is a beekeeper – we had a fascinating discussion about the precarious state of beehives, and how the importing of foreign bees is having a massive impact on the hives, bringing in viruses etc. Her own queen bees had not been laying and she was concerned about how much honey she would have as a result. Sally invited me over to see her bees and a few weeks later I did that, getting suited up and all. She even gave me a pot of precious, delicious honey to take home. It's a fascinating area and I would love to get into keeping a few hives at some stage in the future.

Anyway, the Home Farm courses have been a wonderful process for us – incredibly hard work, but very exciting and it's been great to meet so many like-minded individuals and to feel that we are not ploughing a lonely furrow. Seeing them heading off afterwards, full of the joys of spring (well, okay, summer) and all fired up about keeping hens is fantastic. Occasionally, I will bump into someone who was on a course and they invariably start by saying, 'Oh you're the guy with the chickens!' and they give me an update on their hens and ask me a few questions, which I just love. If I fall over dead tomorrow, surely 'The Guy with the Chickens' will be writ on my tombstone.

A few months after our first course I got a frantic phone call from Sally. Her new hens – Faith, Hope and Charity – were scratching around in her garden that morning and one of them (think it was Hope, ironically enough) got mauled by two dogs. Sally was quite distressed, obviously, and wanted to know should she put her out of her misery. After mulling it over for a while, we agreed that she should leave her be and see how she got on. Thankfully, after a few days of R&R, Hope duly recovered – and, with a name like that, how could she not?

There was a lovely English couple on the first course who went off that very afternoon to make their own hen house, using a picture I have in the course handouts of a homemade hen house and run as a blueprint (a dog kennel with a run attached). She sent me an e-mail shortly afterwards saying that she got had got four hens, and she sent a picture of the newly constructed house. A few weeks later, I received an excited e-mail announcing the arrival of her first egg. It weighed in at just over 30g and she was pleased to report that mother and egg were doing well.

OF MICE AND MEN …

I read an article in a newspaper recently extolling the considerable virtues of keeping hens, but which finished with a sentence about how hens attracts rats and other rodents. I was so mad I nearly fell off my chair, because while the article had surely got its readers all fired up about keeping hens, that one sentence probably turned them right off the idea (who among us would deliberately bring something into the garden that will attract rats?). The reality is that keeping hens, in itself, does nothing whatsoever to attract rats or mice into your garden. Leaving hen or duck feed lying around the place, however, almost certainly will. Rats and mice are highly opportunistic feeders and they will thrive if there is a constant, reliable source of food around for them. Galvanised and plastic feeders (which you fill from the top, and then gravity pushes more feed to the bottom as the hens eat it) may make feeding your poultry a whole lot easier, but as well as feeding your hens you will also be feeding an array of other animals too – dogs, magpies, robins, and yes, rats and mice. Hanging the feeder from something so that it is suspended perhaps 20cm off the ground should make it accessible to your hens but inaccessible to most other animals. However, I'm still not convinced by this method – rats are cunning and would surely organise themselves into a vermin equivalent of a human pyramid to get access to the feed. The only sure-fire method of ensuring you don't encourage vermin is to put your hen feed out in a dog bowl or some other container, and then put it away when they are finished eating. We have a galvanised feeder suspended from the underside of the hen house, but we only use it when we have to – if we are going away for a few days, for example.

I love the routine that comes with having animals about the place. My mother's favourite phrase when we were kids was 'Sure, isn't it great to get back into the routine.' She used it any time we were feeling glum and in need of a pick-me-up – it could have been after Christmas when the decorations were being put away and we were all sad that the festive season had passed, or maybe after the school holidays when we were facing back into a new term at school. She would utter it with what I am now sure must have been an entirely manufactured false optimism, and we would all just groan. My sisters still cringe when they hear it, but deep down I always kind of agreed with my mother that getting back to routine was no bad thing. Anyway, having animals on the Home Farm imposes lots of routine on you because, of course, they have that annoying quirk of requiring twice-daily feeding and watering. You are very tied down by this fact.

Still, if there is a lot of work to do, at least we have plenty of daylight at this time of the year in which to do it. We don't have any blinds or curtains in our bedroom, preferring to go *au naturel* with regard to waking-up time. During the summer months the wisdom of this approach is called into question because the daylight wakes me at about 5.00am and if the light doesn't do it, then Roger the Chivalrous Cockerel surely does. He crows about twenty minutes before daybreak and, though the chicken's house is down the end of the garden, I can still hear him from somewhere deep down within my slumber. Summer solstice – the longest day (and shortest night) of the year – takes place on or around the twentieth or twenty-first of this month and at this time of the year we can enjoy up to seventeen hours of daylight, stretching from 5.00am right through to nearly 10.00pm. The biggest challenge is getting enough sleep because, of course, when it's daylight there really isn't any excuse to be indoors. Allowing yourself to be woken by natural daylight means you have incredible variation in the length of your days – in August I am awake by about 5.30am, but in November and December I usually don't wake until nearly 8.00am, a difference of two and a half hours. In my youthful naivety, there's a part of me that thinks this is how nature intended it – that she wants us to be up early at this time of the year because there's so much bloody work to be done and, besides, there's loads of vitamin D beaming down from the sky and we should be out there absorbing it rather than lying in bed. There's another part of me that thinks that's all a load of nonsense and we should invest in those really heavy drapes you get in hotel rooms so that we can sleep just as long as we want. Of course, I don't actually get up at 5.30am in the summer months, but I do lie there drifting in and out of sleep and feeling mighty guilty that I am still in bed. I usually get up around 6.30am if I can drag myself out and take the dogs for a walk around the fields before the day begins.

SUMMER SOLSTICE

Civilisations have celebrated the great power of the sun at the summer solstice for millennia, but this time of the year was also thought to be a time when evil spirits and potent magic were at their most prevalent, and pagans of old wore protective garlands of herbs and flowers to ward them off. They also celebrated midsummer with bonfires, forcing unsuspecting just-married couples to leap through the flames – the belief was that the crops in neighbouring fields would grow as high as the couples were able to jump. The hotter the bonfire the higher they jumped and the better the crops were ...

Back to the routine! If we are rearing chickens for the table, they are usually the first to get fed, purely because they are the most in need of it (we keep a batch of about twenty chickens at a time, and they are kept separate from the hens and ducks). It's a rather sad consequence of their breeding that they seem to get really hungry through the night and by morning they are riotous with starvation and practically killing each other, and me, to get at the food. While I am filling their feed tray with a broiler's pellet, they peck at my wellies in the vain hope that maybe the rubber is edible. There are two water containers to fill for them – one inside their house (which is almost always empty by morning) and one outside. I don't really enjoy feeding the chickens so much – they are way too insistent and I am consciously trying not to get too attached to them or to dwell too deeply on their plight.

After the chickens, I move on to feed the hens at the other side of the garden. The hen's penthouse is an old dog kennel up on stilts about a metre off the ground, which keeps them safe from the foxes (touch wood). I open up the door and the hens all descend down the ladder at speed, with one or two of them trying to overtake the others by leaping off the top rung. We feed the hens a layer's pellet in the morning, and they attack it with gusto. Again, their water container usually needs to be filled (a hen will drink a surprising half-litre of water on a hot day). At this stage, I will do a quick check in the nesting boxes for eggs – depending on the time and the mood they're in, you might have one or two warm eggs on the straw already.

Before I close up the hen's feed bin, I take a small jarful over to the ducks, which they snaffle up noisily. We usually feed the ducks some of the pig's barley at night time because the variation does them good; but they seem to digest that very quickly and they too are starving by morning. The ducks have access to two water containers – a small plastic container, which they drink out of but also splash about in. This is always dirty and has to be cleaned out. They also have their posh Belfast sink for swimming in and this needs to be cleaned out and refilled every other day. Mindy will usually have laid her egg by this time.

Last up, the pigs. Again, their water has to be changed or at least filled up and their chow dished out. At this time of the year, they are horsing through their barley/soya mix. I keep a big bin beside the pigsty in which I keep the grain and every few days I have to take it over to the garage, fill it with grain and then drag it back across the garden. I have a smaller bucket that I use to measure their feed and mix it with water before dishing it out to them.

In the summer months, early morning is a great time of day to get the polytunnel watered and, in really dry weather, I might have to water the outside beds too. It's relatively cool in the tunnel at this hour and it always *smells* fab with all the tomatoes plants in full flow, so it's a pleasant chore. I also love the moisture-laden smell of a freshly watered polytunnel. A full watering of the tunnel and the veggie plot takes about twenty to thirty minutes, depending on how much day-dreaming I do while watering.

That lot done, I feed the dogs and then ourselves. After breakfast I go out and put all the feed away if there's any left. With the pigs or the chickens there won't be, but there might be with the ducks and hens. There are several reasons why we do this – firstly, as I mentioned, leaving feed around is a sure-fire way to attract vermin into the garden and, secondly, our dogs (stupid animals that they are), love the hen's feed even though it makes them sick. The hens, incidentally, will sometimes stroll over to have a look at the dogs eating their own food and sometimes one of them is brave enough to try and reach in and grab some. We have four large black plastic bins around the place, filled with grains – one each for the chickens, pigs, hens and dogs. At this time of the year, trips to the local co-op for grain are frequent (and expensive).

During the day, there are various odd jobs to do around the place – and before you say it, I know, I am really lucky to be working from home and able to do them. I should point out that we don't mind any of these chores – I list them here not so that you will feel sorry for us, but just to highlight that producing your own food, particularly when there are animals involved, is time-consuming, so you do really need to love doing it. Anyway, during the day I usually check the nesting box once or twice and take any eggs that are laid – leave them lying around and they may well encourage a hen to go broody. Sometimes a hen may have started laying out in the hedge and if I am lucky enough to discover where, I will climb in and find the eggs there. With the considerable hours of daylight, the hens are usually in fine fettle when it comes to egg laying at this time of the year. They are also spending far longer each day out foraging in the grass and consequently the eggs are usually larger and the yolks yellower.

By lunchtime, the chickens usually need to be fed again (as do I) and I will usually let the pigs out into their little patch of ground to have a root around for the afternoon. They are usually pretty happy about this and run around a bit to show their appreciation (if you ever get to see a pig running you will know how cruel it is to keep them in stalls where they can barely move). Every two or three days the pigs' concrete sty has to be cleaned out – a most unpleasant, smelly task (particularly if it's raining), the details of which I will not get into here. It's a job for the afternoon when the constitution is at its strongest – I would retch and put myself off my breakfast if I did it first thing in the morning. Still, our time with the pigs is short, so you try not to hate them too much for being such prolific 'poohers' and, of course, it's all good stuff for the compost heap. The other animal houses are cleaned out maybe once a week or so. A full cleaning of all animal accommodation (ducks, chickens, pigs and hens), including changing the straw and putting it on the compost heap, takes about an hour and generally requires a shower afterwards.

The daily routine starts up again around dinnertime when all the animals get another bit of grub. The pigs get a bucket of scraps, if available, instead of the grain and they have great fun rooting through that to find the most interesting morsels and tossing the less interesting ones out onto the ground. I fill the chickens' water containers and then lock them in. The hens don't return to their house until much, much later in the summer months – they will be wandering around until dusk. Roger is first to scale up the ladder and his women-folk follow him, one by one. Luidín is either unable, or too lazy or scared, to climb up the ladder and she either goes into the small little house that's left on the ground specially for her or she goes in with Mork and Mindy (in fact, the three of them seem to have formed a kind of 'We Hate Hens' club and started hanging out together all the time). If she's not with the ducks when I go around just before dark to close things in, I have to lift her up and place her on the perch in the main house. If she is with the ducks, I leave her be. As far as I know, she has not laid a single egg since she got here, so she's very lucky that we allow her all this indulgence. I close the door of the duck's coop and the gate to the pigsty, and then turn off the electric fence that surrounds the pigs' yard. And some evenings, if we think of it, one or both of us will do a quick scout around the tunnel for slugs.

Phew. Reading that, you can imagine how difficult it is to get any time away from this place. Not that we want to. But you know what I mean: how many friends or relatives do you know who would take on that lot, even for a few days?

JUNE GROWER'S CALENDAR

Prep Work
- Prep work now gives way to real work, but you still need to keep preparing those outdoor beds that will take vegetables later in the summer.

To-do List
- Watering and weeding duties step up a notch – the tunnel/greenhouse, in particular, will require a good deal of water from now on. Watch the weather and water outside too as required. Water in the morning if possible. Add a good dressing of mulch around plants to reduce moisture loss and keep down weeds.
- Continue to earth-up potato plants to prevent the spuds becoming green.
- It's time to get really seriously vigilant with your tomato plants – mulch, water and continue to remove side shoots that appear in the leaf axils. Train the plants carefully on strings or strong canes.

- If gooseberry and red currant bushes are very leafy, start summer pruning by shortening back the new growth.
- Tie up beans and peas to stop them falling over – mature pea plants become like a canopy and could take off in the wind, bound for next door's garden. Stake everything that grows tall – raspberries, peas, beans, tomatoes etc.
- Net soft fruit against birds – it's worth the effort, I promise. They will eat your entire crop, practically overnight, if you let them.
- Thin beetroot in rows to single plants – for large roots space about 10cm apart – for mini-beets space at 3cm. Eat the leaves in salads – but sparingly. The beets need them too.
- Strawberries – runners are produced as fruiting peaks – to increase your stock of strong new plants for next year, direct the first big runners that are produced into the soil near the parent plant or into pots. Once the runner has established a root, you can snip it from the mother ship.

Sowing Seeds

- At this stage, any remaining sowing can most likely be done outside. Sow courgettes, pumpkins, summer and winter squash, fennel, chicory.
- Don't think your sowing duties are over – succession-sowing is vitally important to keep a regular supply of produce coming. So, continue sowing: beans (French and runner), kale, peas, spinach, spinach beet, summer broccoli, carrots, swedes, leeks, lettuce, brussels sprouts, beetroot, chicory, endive, turnips, kohlrabi, fennel.
- Sow parsley now to provide a late supply in autumn and some of the plants can then be lifted, potted and brought indoors for winter use.

Planting Out

- It's time to plant out pretty much anything else that has been raised indoors or under cover and needs transplanting – leeks, brussels sprouts, cabbage, autumn cauliflower, calabrese, sprouting broccoli, celery, celeriac, cucumbers, pumpkins, courgettes, marrows, runner beans, aubergines.

GRUB'S UP – WHAT'S IN SEASON?

June is a busy month for the Home Farmer, but it's also the month when we really start to see some payback – the first broad beans and peas, as well as new potatoes, new carrots, soft fruit like gooseberries, cherries and strawberries. You may even see the first tomato (but more likely in July). Herbs are in full flow.

Wild garlic – now is the perfect time to use the new leaves to make wild garlic pesto.

Also harvest broad beans, peas, kohlrabi, cabbage, cauliflower (month end), spinach, spring onions, shallots, salad leaves, elderflower, rhubarb, salad leaves, onions, carrots, beetroot, garlic, sea-kale.

7

SALAD DAYS

LATE SUMMER: JULY

tomatoes – conserving water – buying organic chickens – rearing chickens

July, really, is the first of what might be called the salad months. We've had salad crops, like radish and lettuce and so on, for months now, but it is the arrival of the first tomatoes of the year that really signals the presence of summer. This is a special time for the Home Farmer. There are some vegetables that you grow yourself and you really wonder whether it's worth the hassle, particularly if there are good commercial alternatives available (take a bow, potatoes). But given the fact that most of the tomatoes in our supermarkets are the super-bland, all-year-round Dutch variety and taste of ... well, nothing at all, having a good crop of your own tomatoes is really most rewarding. When the nerdy garden geek that I am sits down at the start of the year to write down the list of veggies to be grown for the year, tomatoes always go top of the list, like the boy that always gets picked first for any school soccer team. In fact, if there was a law brought in tomorrow morning that restricted people to growing one vegetable, after very little soul-searching I would pick tomatoes.

The reason is, quite simply, their taste. Tomatoes that you grow yourself taste a million times nicer than anything you will buy in the supermarket. Period. This is because the overwhelming majority of commercial tomatoes are grown for superficial uniformity, rather than flavour. With your own tomatoes, you are not likely to care if you get an occasional less-than-perfect knobbly one because you know they all taste as great as each other, whatever they look like. A supermarket wouldn't even allow such a tomato on the shelf, but they will take thousands of lifeless, insipid-tasting ones as long as they look good (and the same as each other). You are more likely to eat your own tomatoes as you would an apple rather than slice them up and put them in a sandwich. In fact, you will be lucky if they make it to the kitchen at all. They are a sweet, sumptuous treat, best eaten warm and freshly picked. Refrigeration, by the way, does nothing for the flavour of tomatoes – when cold, a tomato just tastes, well ... cold.

I like being in touch with the *seasonality* of tomatoes, though it is a bitter-sweet affair, given how short the season is. Tomatoes are basically in season for just a quarter of the year, four short months. Ours are starting to ripen now in July and the plants will go on producing, hopefully, into mid-October, and then they will be no more and we will shed a tear. We try to extend their season a little by getting the first seeds going on a warming mat in early spring at one end, and by preserving the produce at the other end (storing, bottling). If we have a glut of nice big ones (like the mighty beefsteak tomato, for example) they may go in a drawer, individually wrapped in newspaper where they will store for a little longer and take us into late autumn. There will be tomatoes on the vine come autumn that cannot develop fully because of the shortening days and will have to be picked green – these are, ironically, our most valued picks because they end up in a rather superb green tomato chutney (see recipe below). Other tomatoes will be made into sauces and purées for the freezer and will provide the base for many a fine and handy pasta dish in the winter. Finding ways to store tomatoes is a vital way of getting some much-needed nutrition in the winter months (arguably, we need them more then than in the summer months when there is so much fresh food around).

Tomatoes are relatively easy to grow, but there is quite a lot of work involved, so when you start to eat your tomatoes, it's worth recalling what has been a long and arduous growing season: seeds were sown expectantly in compost back in February or March and the pots placed on heating mats in the study trying to get them to germinate; the little plants were nurtured in the pots over months before eventually being put out in the soil in the polytunnel when they were about 30cm tall; they were trained to grow up lengths of string hanging from the top of the tunnel so that they wouldn't fall over when they got heavy, and the plants eventually thrived and practically took over the joint, growing up to 150cm tall. They were mulched and watered. Side shoots (that divert the plant's energy away from fruit-ing) were pinched off. We looked on with satisfaction and consider-able anticipation as the clumps of green tomatoes started to form, and then, eventually, one day earlier this month, we got the reward of a single ripe tomato. It was cut in half and shared and savoured. And then a day later, another few were ready and so on until, eventually, we were basically struggling to keep up and eating them every day in salads and sandwiches, and making *bruschetta* and so on.

Having gone through all that, it's hard not to feel a little odd about buying and eating supermarket tomatoes out of season because, as a tomato grower, you will know that to produce a tomato in February and ship it from Holland or Israel or South America to Ireland and have it appear ripe on the shelf in the frigid winter months, you have to bend the rules – a lot. In the commercial world, they use all manner of little tricks to prolong shelf life – the tomatoes are often picked green and then ripened in storage or in transit by gassing with a hydrocarbon gas called ethylene, which triggers the ripening process. These tomatoes will keep longer, but they will not taste as nice and will have a starchier texture than naturally ripened ones. Vine tomatoes (the ones you see in the supermarket that are attached to a vine) are an improvement on this – they too are picked when unripe, but ripen gradually in storage because they are still, essen-tially, attached to the plant.

Anyway, my point is that when you get scientists and food pro-ducers trying to devise ways to cheat seasonality and nature in order to grow out of season and prolong shelf-life, you have a situation where the food you are buying has been profoundly messed with. Scientists have developed a way to manipulate tomato genes to increase shelf life, but commercial producers are reluctant to go down this route because of the widespread resistance among the buying public to GMO foodstuffs. In the 1990s, a company called Calgene (now part of the biotech giant Monsanto, which is behind the market-leading herbicide glyphosate, otherwise known as Roundup) developed a tomato called the 'FlavrSavr', which was genetically modified to slow down the rotting process. It was the first genetically engineered food to be granted a licence for human consumption by the Food and Drug Administration (FDA) in the United States. The genetic tinkering that they did on the FlavrSavr meant that the tomato could be properly ripened on the vine and, even though it was soft and ripe when picked, it basically stayed that way; it had a shelf life that would make a tin of beans blush. Problem was, it tasted crap, and because it was so soft, much of the stock got damaged in transit. It didn't sell well and was pulled from the market in 1997, a rare example of consumers voting with their wallets to halt scientific meddling in the food chain.

Surely it is only a matter of time before GMO tomatoes (and God knows what else) are revisited – with what consequences, I wonder? When you produce a tomato that can be shipped further and left on the shelves for longer, what is the impact on flavour? On nutrition? So, in protest, we embrace the seasonality of tomatoes, though it is, of course, a double-edged sword, given how damned short the season of fruitfulness is. If you want to really embrace seasonal food consumption, you could do worse then starting with the tomato. Grow as many plants as your space will allow – nurture them, harvest, eat and store. Enjoy them fresh from July until October, and then in the winter enjoy your own 'processed' tomatoes in whatever form you have converted them to – then give yourself a break from them. They are not in season, so don't be tempted to buy them. When you have sampled the delectable taste of your own, I promise you that you won't find this hard.

Green Tomato Chutney

The beauty of this recipe is its exclusivity. Because you generally can't buy the primary ingredient (green tomatoes) in the shops, it can really only be made by the Home Farmer. Make it in autumn when your tomatoes can't get enough sun to ripen. It also uses up some of your un-ripened peppers and lots of onions. Don't tell Mrs Kelly I gave you this recipe.

- 3kg green tomatoes
- 6 large onions (about 1kg)
- 3 or 4 large green peppers
- 700g brown sugar
- 1.2 litres of vinegar
- Spices: 3 tbsp mustard seed, 1 tbsp coriander seed,
  ½ tsp celery seed, 1 tsp turmeric

Chop the onions and slice the tomatoes finely. Layer them in a very large bowl – start with onions, then tomatoes, then onions etc, seasoning each layer with plenty of salt and a little pepper as you go. Leave to stand for a day or so – then drain off the liquid (and discard) and transfer to a large stockpot. Add the rest of the ingredients (chopped green peppers, sugar, vinegar, spices), bring the whole thing to a boil and let it simmer on a low heat for two or three hours. Put it back in the bowl and let it sit for another day. Put it back in the stockpot and cook it for another half-hour so that the liquid reduces down further – you want just enough liquid to cover the vegetables when they are transferred into pots. Sterilise some jamjars and ladle the chutney into them. Don't be tempted to eat any for about a month – it's like a fine wine, it will get better with age. This chutney is particularly great served with meats – sausages in particular.

The first thing that you will have to decide with tomatoes is where you are going to grow them. There are varieties of tomato that will grow outside – but be careful; tomatoes are essentially a Mediterranean fruit, so it stands to reason that they will not do particularly well if you grow them outside in a cold, wet Northern European summer. If you want to try planting outside, you really need a site that is sun-drenched and sheltered and, let's be honest, there aren't too many of them around these parts. Far more successful is growing them under glass or plastic. As discussed elsewhere, tomatoes are an ideal plant to grow if you don't have a huge amount of space as they do very well indeed in pots and containers indoors or in hanging baskets on a sunny deck. A tomato plant in a pot (it will need to be a big pot, 25cm deep at least) will make an attractive feature in the porch or conservatory for the summer months and it will do very well there; in fact, many growers believe that tomatoes do better in pots than they do in open soil. The majority of Home Farm tomatoes, however, are grown in greenhouses or polytunnels. Every year we seem to plant more and more tomato plants – in our first few years of growing we started with, maybe, two or three plants, and gradually increased it each year. We just can't get enough of them. This year we sowed about fifteen plants and we can expect a yield of about 3.5kg of tomatoes per plant, which is considerable.

Though you could opt to buy tomato plants in your garden centre in late spring or early summer, I can't see the point in spending your hard-earned dosh on plants when they are so successfully and easily grown from seed (unless you forgot!). We get ours going in modules or pots (you can sow three seeds in one 8cm pot) on a heating mat indoors in February or March – tomatoes like a bit of heat coming up from underneath them. If you are growing more than one variety (and you should) it's a good idea to label the pots when you sow, so that you will know what's what later on. The seeds will germinate within about ten days, usually, and once they are well established (about 15cm high, usually around May) we plant them into the beds in the polytunnel. Lots of people will say the best way to grow them is in specially designed tomato grow-bags, but I like to think that the sweetness of flavour in ours comes from their unfettered access to soil (I'm probably delusional on that count). If you are planting them, as we do, in the soil in your tunnel or greenhouse, they will need a well enriched soil, so add plenty of well-rotted compost the previous winter. Be really careful when transplanting the plants – hold them by the root ball as opposed to the stem and try and bring as much of the compost that is clinging to the roots with the plant into its new home. We have, so far, successfully avoided disease build-up in the soil by planting in a different place in the tunnel each year in our incredibly unreliable imaginary quadrant system.

Essentially, there are two basic types of tomato plant – a vine type, which will grow to about 2m tall, if allowed to do so (and which con-sequently needs support), and the bush type, which is more compact. We have focused mainly on the vine varieties. When you are planting them into their final growing position in May, it's easy to be fooled by their size and end up planting them too close together. In our first year of growing tomatoes we put them in the soil in the polytunnel at the recommended 45cm apart, stood back to admire our handiwork – and we were thinking, bloody hell there's so much empty, wasted space between the plants. We were tempted to lift them up and plant them closer together – thankfully, common sense prevailed and we left them be. Of course, the plants grew huge by the summer and if they had all been planted on top of each other the lack of air circulating around them would probably have guaranteed a 'healthy' dose of diseases. You should also put your support canes or twine in place before you plant them so that you don't damage the roots of the plants by shoving them into the ground later on. Like a naughty dog, tomato plants need to be trained – our approach is to anchor some twine in to the ground beside the plant and then attach it to another piece of horizontal twine that's running along the roof of the tunnel – we then wind the main stem up the vertical string as it grows. The main stem produces leaf stems and also trusses on which the lovely tomatoes will grow. A tomato plant is just as interested in growing leaves as it is fruit, and so it also pushes out what are called side shoots, which grow in the angle between the main stem and the leaf stems. These side shoots will take much-needed energy from the plant and therefore need to be pinched out (with your thumb) as soon as they appear. Many growers recommend that you only allow the plant to form seven to ten trusses and then cut off the growing tip of the main stem to prevent the plant growing further upwards – this focuses the erratic tomato plant's mind, so to speak, and encourages good crops of intensely flavoured tomatoes rather than huge quantities of late-maturing, low quality fruits.

As I mentioned earlier in this chapter, tomatoes are hard work at the height of the summer. They are sort of like divas – they demand tender, loving care. The most important thing of all is water; they are incredibly thirsty and the ground that they are planted in needs to be consistently moist, so you need to water well every few days and sometimes more in the really hot mid-summer days when the inside of the polytunnel is basically Death Valley. If you water lazily or intermittingly, the soil will alternate between really wet and really dry, and the resulting tomatoes will tend to rupture and split, which is really, really annoying. Do not go on holidays for two weeks in August and expect your tomatoes to be fine when you get back – they won't be (believe me, we know this!). You will have to get someone to come in and water them for you. As with peas and beans, a good mulch around the base of a tomato plant will help to retain water.

Once the flowers have started to form fruits, it helps to give them occasional doses of a good fertiliser – a homemade one that involves immersing comfrey leaves or hen droppings in water (see below – it will be absolutely stink, but it works wonders), or there are lots of good quality, organic, commercial tomato feeds available. Pick off any yellowing leaves on the plants as the summer progresses, which will improve ventilation, and where clumps of tomatoes are forming near the ground, put some clean straw under them to prevent them from rotting on wet soil.

You can start picking the tomatoes as soon as they become ripe, and at the end of the season (late September or early October, probably) you can store green tomatoes in a cool, dark place where they will gradually ripen, particularly if you store them with a single red one. The ripe tomato gives off the aforementioned ethylene gas, which will help the others along.

Now, I know what you are thinking – this all sounds like a lot of hard work, but believe me, it's worth it. After five summers of growing, I think I can fairly safely say that tomatoes remain our most treasured produce here on the Home Farm – there is simply no greater taste of summer. Incidentally, it's nice to experiment with different varieties. Perhaps indicative of mankind's obsession with them, you will find tomatoes of literally all shapes, sizes and colours. So far we have stuck with the vine varieties such as Matina (early-cropping variety with medium sized, bright red fruits), Gardener's Delight (bite-sized tangy fruits, full of flavour), Brandywine (chunky beefsteak tomato, light pink in colour – last year we had one that was so big I considered entering it in a competition), Roma (oblong, plum, bright red – ideal for sauces) and Moneymaker (standard, smooth, medium-sized fruits – as the name suggests you get a huge crop, but perhaps a little blander taste-wise).

PAULA MEE'S NUTRITION BITES: TOMATOES

Tomatoes just blush with goodness! They are good sources of vitamin C and beta-carotene and the richest source of the antioxidant lycopene. Low lycopene levels are associated with prostate and breast cancers. Tomatoes contain other phytochemicals, which, together with their lycopene levels, make them an excellent addition to your salad. Interestingly, this is one case where processing can actually enhance the availability and absorption of nutrients. So, not only can you enjoy fresh tomatoes, you can also benefit from a little tomato purée, tomato soup or even tomato sauce! Lycopene appears to have the ability to help protect cells and other structures in the body from oxygen damage and has been linked in human research to the protection of DNA (our genetic material) inside white blood cells.

Nutrition per Portion (80g):

Calories	Fat (g)	Salt (g)	Saturated Fat (g)
17	0.3	0.02	0.1

COMFREY TEA

You can't drink it yourself, I'm afraid, but your fruiting plants (and anything else that needs perking up) will absolutely love comfrey tea, and it is a thrifty, environmentally friendly alternative to buying nasty chemical fertilisers. Comfrey is a deep-rooted, incredibly hardy little wonder-plant that's a cinch to grow, and was traditionally grown for its virtues in healing wounds. A very kind neighbour of ours gave us a little plant a few years back and it's thriving – you can harvest leaves from it about three or four times a year and use them to make dynamite liquid fertiliser, rich in potash and nitrogen. Stick 500g of leaves in 13 litres of water and let it stew for a month or two. It will stink to high heaven after a few weeks, so invest in a bin with a tight-fitting lid. Dilute it before putting it on your plants – holding your nose, draw off a small amount of this nasty brew into your watering can and then fill it up with water: 1 part tea to 10 parts water approximately. Something to mull over while your tea is brewing: tests have shown that comfrey tea has higher percentages of nitrogen and potash than a market-leading tomato feed. Talk about a no-brainer!

Having enough water for the vegetables and animals can become a real problem at this time of the year, even though for a few summers, there, we had the opposite problem – too much water. Dublin City Council was roundly ridiculed some years back for having advertisements on billboards and radio advising people to conserve water and not to hose their lawn. Their motives were good, no doubt, and they probably came up with the idea during a sunny spell back in the spring, but by the time the ads went on air, the nation was in the grip of a forty-day deluge of biblical proportions. The idea of conserving water by not hosing one's lawn when it looks like a paddy-field – my, how we laughed.

Our house is built on a bog, basically, and in really wet weather the lawn can be a rather unpleasant place to be because it gets all soggy. It feels strange to be donning wellies in the height of summer as we trek over and back to feed pigs, chickens, hens and ducks. Since we put in the raised beds and gravel paths in our vegetable patch, that area of the garden is relatively monsoon-proof, and you can get out and about if the rain breaks for a bit because the ground is dry underfoot. And, of course, there are *some* benefits to so much water falling from the sky: the duck's bath and the pig's water bucket do not need refilling, which is nice, and the outdoor vegetables don't need watering. In *really* wet weather, even our polytunnel manages to water itself – there's so much water in the ground around the garden that the soil in the tunnel gets wet from underneath. Handy. Still, it can be depressing not to have proper July weather in July. We tune in each night to the weather forecast, hoping for a glimmer of good news.

In regular summer weather, water conservation is an important consideration for the Home Farmer. A water butt is a great invest-ment – it sits quietly, attached to the downpipe of a gutter, a forgotten hero gathering up all the rainwater falling off the roof of your house, so that it can then be used for watering the tunnel. It's tempting, of course, to pull out the hose rather than ferrying buckets of water to and fro from the water butt, but your inner environmentalist will feel mighty pleased with itself when you do it the right way. You can even link up a number of water butts together to catch even more rainwater. Some people, who are far more ethically-minded than we are, go to the trouble of showering with the plug in so that they can collect up this 'grey' water for use on their plants. Frankly, life's too short. But we do occasionally divert water from the kitchen to the garden – the water in which you have boiled vegetables, for example, is great for watering your plants because it contains all sort of nutrients from the cooked vegetables (though that's probably an argument against boiling vegetables, if ever there was one).

The key with water conservation, I think, is to put a bit of thought into it. You shouldn't just stand there blithely spraying all and sundry with the hose for ten minutes every day. Different crops have different needs. In general terms, shallow-rooted crops, like lettuce, peas and beans, need frequent but light watering, whereas the deeper-rooted crops, like tomatoes, need more water but less frequently – this stands to reason, when you think about it. It's also worth sticking a spade in the soil to see whether it's still moist underneath the surface – if it is, you can head back inside for a cup of tea. When you do water, give those deep-rooted crops a good soaking – try and get the soil wet to about 15cm depth and if you do, you shouldn't need to come back to them for four or five days. You will, however, need to water your polytunnel or greenhouse almost daily, particularly if it's sunny. We generally water the tunnel in the morning – watering in the evening means that your plants have wet foliage overnight which encourages diseases, while watering at midday, when it is hottest, means you lose most of the water to evaporation.

Of course, in the first instance, the more organic matter you have in your soil, the more it will retain the water you pour over it. Once the soil is moist, mulch is also a really good way to prevent water loss caused by evaporation. Spread organic mulches, such as leaves, bark

HANDY WATERING

If you spray the leaves of a tomato plant with water they will burn in the sun – the key is to direct the water at the roots rather than the plant itself. Same goes for your spuds. A nice tip from my mate Feargal to assist with watering tomatoes is as follows: take a used, plastic milk carton (the big 2 litre ones) and cut it in half. Discard the bottom half, but keep the top half, the one with the spout. Bury this in the soil beside your tomato plant with the spout facing in towards the root of the plant. The carton acts like a funnel into which you direct the hose when watering, which ensures that the water gets straight to the root system of the plant. This is also a good way to measure how much water your plants are getting – if you fill the carton, you know they've got it all. Alternatively, sink a 10cm flowerpot in the soil near the base of the tomato plant and fill this when watering.

or compost, a few centimetres thick on the soil around plants to prevent sunlight from getting to the soil. You can even put a few layers of newspaper down and put the mulch on top of that. Mulching also acts a weed barrier, which also conserves water, because weeds drink water too.

There's an organic chicken producer in these parts and his chickens sell for around €18 in our local supermarket. We buy one of them when we don't have our own in the freezer, though I have to admit to finding them expensive, especially in these leaner times. As most people would be aware, you can often buy a bog-standard chicken for less than €5 or so and a free range chicken from €6 to €12, so from that perspective it's not an easy argument to win trying to convince people that it's a good idea to part with the €18. Still, there are several things that set these chickens apart from the rest. First of all, there is the size. The commercial chicken industry has done a very good job of creating the impression that all chickens are identical in size, when they patently are not. Every chicken, large or small, has two legs, two breasts and two wings, so we tend to feel we get the same amount of meat whether we have a little *poussin* or the biggest chicken in the world. The reality, of course, is that they can vary hugely in weight – from just over 1kg to nearly 3kg – and you get nearly three times as much meat on a bigger one. The organic chicken that we buy is basically the size of a small turkey – the average weight is about 2.5kg, and sometimes, if you are lucky and happen to pass the supermarket the day they're delivered, you could pick one up that tips the scales at nearly 3kg (they charge €18 regardless of weight). That's a lot of chicken. It's very unfair that we look at two chickens on the supermarket shelf and judge 'chicken A' as expensive and 'chicken B' as cheap, when we should be comparing them kilo for kilo, as we would with any other type of meat. So let's do that. A 2.5kg bird at €18, works out at €7.20 per kilo, whereas the 1kg bird at €5 is €5 a kilo. Now, you have grounds for a real comparison. The organic chicken is €2.20 more expensive per kilo than the bog-standard chicken – so what are you getting for the extra money?

Well, first of all, these organic chickens are reared for a 'normal' amount of time, and when I say normal I mean the amount of time that chickens have been reared for hundreds of years – about twelve weeks. This is about twice as long as a conventionally farmed chicken, and four weeks longer than most free-range birds. Those four to six additional weeks are expensive for the organic producer –

the chickens are out and about, scratching and foraging in a field, and they are mighty hungry as a result. The farmer can feed them only organic broiler's pellets, which cost almost twice as much as normal pellets (which I can verify, because I've bought them for our own chickens). I can't tell you how much profit the producer is making on each chicken, but, having reared chickens myself, I can tell you that in the last weeks of their lives, they are voracious eaters. We keep twenty chickens at a time for the table, and by the time they are ten or twelve weeks old, they are going through a bag of broiler's pellets a week between them – a bag of organic pellets currently costs around €20, which means that each chicken is increasing in value by a euro a week. Even for a Home Farmer like me, the difference in the cost of rearing for an additional six weeks is €6 per bird. The organic feed is so expensive, in fact, that this year we reluctantly decided to rear our chickens on regular, free-range pellets at half the price. So, basically, the organic producer is rearing his chickens for twice as long (resulting in a larger bird), and using a feed that is twice as expensive.

THE MISERABLE LIFE OF A COMMERCIAL CHICKEN

Figures from Compassion in World Farming on the state of the global chicken industry make for depressing reading. According to that organisation, around 70 percent of chickens raised for meat globally are raised in intensive farming systems. As I mentioned, these birds reach slaughter weight in just six weeks, but, given the conditions that they live in, that's probably six weeks too long. Literally tens of thousands of birds can be crammed into dimly lit sheds. An EU Directive from 2007 enforces a limit of 19 birds per square metre – that means that each bird has a space about the size of the surface area of this page in which to live their short lives. Fantastic! European chickens must feel very relieved that the powers that be in Brussels are looking out for them.

Lights are kept on in the shed most of the time because, of course, chickens don't eat in the dark and if they are not eating they are not getting fat. But the lights are kept sufficiently dim so that the chickens never get too active. And so, this is how they live out their lives – in a strange twilight world, trampled by their peers. Their innate need to forage is not accommodated in any way, nor is there any attempt to make their life even remotely interesting. There is nothing in these sheds apart from water, food and other chickens – lots and lots of other chickens. The chickens never get to develop any of the behaviours that come quite naturally to them (foraging, scratching, dust baths) and they never get access to fresh air or sunlight. Because there is nothing to do and no space in which to do it, they generally opt to stay sitting down. Bad news for the quality of the meat.

As is the case with pigs, intensively reared chickens require a cocktail of antibiotics and hormones administered in their feed to keep them disease free. The ammonia from their droppings is a pollutant (particularly when there are so many of them) and it damages their eyes and respiratory systems. It can also cause burns on their legs and feet, which you can often see on the chickens in the supermarket (sometimes they cut off the bottom part of the leg so you can't see it). Because they are bred as eating machines and have to put on sufficient weight to get them to the supermarket shelf in just six weeks, lots of them suffer from heart problems and leg deformities – it is estimated that up 120 million chickens die from heart failure in the EU each year. Another 20 million die as a result of injuries sustained in the battle that ensues from trying to round them up to get them to the slaughter.

The incredible flavour of an organic bird comes not just from the fact that it is fed top-quality nosh, it is also due to their longer lives (if twelve weeks can really be considered a long life) – during that additional six weeks spent out and about, doing what chickens do, they develop muscle tone and therefore flavour. A free-range chicken that's reared for just six or eight weeks equally doesn't have the chance to build up that same intensity of flavour. And with organic birds, you also know that they are not taking in any nasty chemical stuff – hormones, antibiotics and the like, which are routinely used in intensive rearing systems to fight disease and promote growth.

As you're probably already aware, many commercial processors inject chicken breasts with water to bulk them out (you can usually spot the offending items a mile off because they look sort of glassy and wobbly rather than firm). This is perfectly legal, by the way, and harmless enough on the face of it – but still it is a con job, designed to make us think we are getting a really big, fat, juicy breast when we are, in fact, getting a really small one. This fact will be revealed only when the water evaporates during cooking and we end up with a breast half the size of the one we bought. In my opinion, we shouldn't allow processors to take us for fools, like this. As is always the case with these food production sleights of hand, there are also health implications. The problem with injecting chicken with water is that eventually the water will go right ahead and leak out again, so they have to inject something else too to 'help' the meat retain the water – and it is with these so-called binding agents that potential health issues arise because they are typically based around animal proteins. An investigation by the BBC's *Panorama* programme in 2003 found that some chicken fillets contained as much as 50 percent added water, retained in the meat using injected beef or pork protein. That's just what we need – intensively reared chicken that's been injected with protein from other dead animals.

Now, I know what your thinking: Well, it may be delicious and it may be healthier, but I still can't afford €18 for an organic chicken when there's a free-range bird sitting on the shelf beside it for €6. Believe me, I share the pain, and ultimately it's everyone's own choice how much they want to pay for the meat they buy. Our approach, for what it's worth, has been to eat a smaller number of bigger birds instead of buying lots of smaller, cheaper ones. It's worth asking (politely) whether we are perhaps eating far too much chicken (and meat in general) anyway. Back in the 1950s, chicken was such a treat that most Irish and British people ate less than a kilo in a whole year. These days we eat almost 2kg per month each, on average. There seems to be an emerging consensus about the health benefits of meat – that it is a great source of iron and protein, but that we eat far too much of it (particularly the highly processed forms of it). Most nutritionists believe that eating a little less meat and a lot more fruit and vegetables is good for your health, as well as your wallet. And, finally, we might bear in mind that, at €7.20 per kilo, even organic chicken is exceptional value when compared with other meats – pork loin, for example, will cost over €10 a kilo; a leg of lamb could cost upwards of €13 a kilo; a striploin steak will typically cost a whopping €25 per kilo. It's no surprise, perhaps, that the two cheapest types of meat – chicken and pigmeat – come from animals that can be intensively reared, while the two most expensive – lamb and beef – come from those reared outdoors on grass.

I can't tell you how many arguments I have had with people over the years about the price of chicken and it's an argument I almost never win, particularly in the face of the economic woes that we currently suffer. Still, I'm a sucker for punishment, and I have fun trying. The fact that I can never seem to win these arguments, makes me very worried indeed for organic chicken suppliers – I think that in a world gone mad they are providing a top-class product that they are passionate about, and they should be fêted, not condemned. I prefer to give my money to someone who appreciates the importance of rearing a bird the way it used to be reared, rather than giving it to someone who is happy to sell chickens at a derisory profit – and that's what it must be. Derisory. I know my little chicken rearing project here is not representative of the commercial world in any way, but I just don't see how it's possible to sell chickens for €4 or €5 when they are costing me over €7 per bird to rear myself at home. Since the feed accounts for the vast majority of the cost of rearing a chicken, that is really the only area where commercial producers can make savings and that makes me very suspicious. What can they feed their chickens that costs so little? Or worse, what are they being given instead of food to promote growth? Rearing chickens is not an easy undertaking – if you go through that and come out at the end of it with a derisory profit, then you are going to be very unhappy indeed. Apart from anything else, a state of unhappiness is not what you want in the people who are producing the food that you eat. I know, however, that these are not particularly popular points of view.

I guess, all I am suggesting is that we all ask questions of our local butcher about the chicken we are buying. Most supermarkets do, in fact, employ a butcher, and in my experience they are generally very happy to answer questions about the meat that they sell. We might ask them where the chickens come from, what they have been fed and how long they have been reared for. Whether the breasts have been bulked up with water. If we are not happy with the answers, then maybe we just should not buy that chicken. And if the butcher doesn't know the answers, don't buy the chicken. We could try farmers markets, farm shops and country markets in our own area – there might well be someone in the locality producing chickens the way they should be produced. When we are lucky enough to find them, I think we really should pay them whatever the asking price is, even if it is more than we're used to. We're getting a far superior product.

Readers of my first book, *Trading Paces*, may recall my first forays into the world of rearing chickens for meat. It happened quite by accident, really. We have a cockerel to keep our hens in order, essentially (a cockerel is like a manly chaperone, escorting hens around the garden and keeping them safe-ish from predators), and, of course, if a cockerel is doing his duties, then all the eggs being produced by the hens are fertilised and, given the right conditions, will hatch chicks. One of our hens went broody, which means she sat on a batch of eggs, and lo and behold, some weeks later we had three little chicks. Faced with this *fait accompli*, I decided to rear them myself and about a hundred days later I went all hunter-gatherer and killed them for the table. It was not a happy event. I won't go into it again.

Of course, in times past, people kept chickens in the garden and killed them as they needed them. This is a nice idea, but unfortunately, the older a chicken gets, the tougher its meat becomes. As Mrs Beeton said in her household management guide, first published in 1859, 'in no animal, however, does age work such a change in regard to the quality of its flesh, as it does in domestic fowls.' These days, with the glorious technology that is the freezer, you can fatten a batch of chicks all at once and pop them in the freezer to preserve their youthful tenderness and use them as required. My brother-in-law was getting rid of an old garden shed last year and I took this as a sign that now was the right time to start rearing chickens properly; I requisitioned the shed for use as my *Palais Poulais* and erected it at the side of the garden, behind our garage. I then sourced twenty-two Hubbard chicks from a local supplier. These are a good meat bird and grow quite slowly, making them ideal for the Home Farmer. I only ordered twenty, in fact, but he threw in two for good luck, which made me feel (a) half pleased as I was getting a bargain and (b) half bad about how disposable this seemed to make the chicks.

They were freakishly cute the day I collected them – tiny, fluffy yellow, and cheep-cheeping to their hearts' content. At only a few days old, they were far too small to be given the run of a garden shed, so I put a wooden box in the corner for them into which went about 20cm of wood shavings. Nicky gave me the loan of an infra-red lamp, which you hang from the ceiling to keep them warm. At night time, the lamp sent an eerie red glow out the window of the shed into the surrounding gloom – from our bedroom window, it looked like someone was operating a brothel down at the end of the garden. During the first week or so, I was concerned that I wouldn't be able to kill them at all, they were so damned cute. I would go out there about three times a day to check up on them, to give them feed (a special starter food called a broiler's crumb) and make sure they had enough water. Sometimes I would go out just to look in the window at them.

Initially, they were very skittish, running and flapping around whenever I was anywhere near them; disappointingly, the fact that I was providing for their every need did not seem to create any level of bond between us. Perhaps deep down they knew my motives were not pure ...

One day I went out to find that two of them had managed to get out of the box and were huddled on the cold ground in the shed, shivering and generally helpless. One poor little fellow was in such bad shape I thought he would surely die – I placed him carefully back under the lamp and a few of his buddies came over and stood beside him – they seemed happy to see him, as if they had missed him. I could almost imagine they were saying: 'Where were you? What were you up to? What's it like out there?' Perhaps I was reading too much into it.

Two of the chicks went on an exciting excursion one day – they were taken in a cardboard box to visit the local school where Mrs Kelly works. There was much excitement – I gave out lots about how it was inconvenient and was eating into my day and that the chicks might never recover from the ordeal, but deep down I was delighted at the way the kids reacted – the sheer joy on their faces at these little bundles of yellow fluffiness was a sight to behold. Of course, I didn't tell them that we were keeping them for the table – perhaps they knew this anyway, or perhaps it doesn't matter.

One of the chicks died after about a week. I had been feeding them from a small tray and I reckon the competition at the trough was just too intense and maybe this little lad wasn't getting his fair share of grub. But, then again, maybe it was my friend that got stranded outside the box for the night. Either way, the poor little fellow didn't make it, which I felt bad about because it was a waste of one tasty chicken. After a few weeks, they had outgrown the box and I gave them the run of the shed, which they seemed to appreciate. There was a mixture of cocks and hens, and you could see the cocks starting to square up to each other, presumably an early sign that they were trying to establish a pecking order. The all-round cute fluffiness quickly disappeared and they started to get their first white or russet feathers. We had a pleasing mix of reddish chickens that basically looked like our Rhode Islands, slightly yellower ones that looked like a Buff Sussex, and pure white ones. After another week or so, the infra-red light was gradually phased out and then, eventually, switched off altogether, and we started to let them out of the shed for a few hours a day if the weather was fine. Myself and a buddy of mine spent a manly day constructing a chicken-wire run for them, which they could get out and about in, in relative safety. By their second month we were leaving the shed door open all day long and they were able to come and go as they pleased. Every morning when I opened the door they would all run out en masse, flapping their wings as if to embrace the new day.

It was interesting to see them starting to develop regular 'chicken behaviour' – when you are focused on rearing them for meat, you tend to forget that they are the same animal as your hens. I put a perch in their house and they started roosting on that at night, just like our hens do. Then, shortly before they were killed, some of the cocks started to crow in the morning, which upset Roger the Chivalrous Cockerel something awful. He would pace up and down outside their run and start crowing manically, and then they would all be crowing together, trying to drown each other out – it was like a dance-off scene from a bad R&B video. It was strange watching Roger interact with them at the chicken wire fence like that, and I couldn't help thinking about how 'sweet' or 'not-sweet' life is for chickens in our garden, depending on which side of the fence they happen to live. The poor meat birds live for just over eighty days, which is a terribly short existence, really (we have one hen who must be four or five *years* old). And though they have a lot of space in their run, we can't, unfortunately, give them the run of the garden like we do for the hens and ducks because there would be an unmerciful row – and Roger's head would surely explode at the idea of ten other cockerels on his turf. But, through it all, through eighty days of feeding and watering and mucking out their house, we try to keep a sense of perspective about it. Our chickens are well looked after, and, compared with the miserable existence of a commercial chicken, I reckon they do very well indeed. Any chicken that you eat has had its life ended prematurely – that's the plain black and white truth of the matter. We could let our chickens die of natural causes and, no doubt, they would have a marvellous time of it here on the Home Farm, but they certainly wouldn't taste very nice at the end of it. So, basically I suppose, we try to keep our eyes fixed on the prize: twenty-one chickens in the freezer, which represents over €350 worth of meat, and at our current rate of chicken consumption perhaps eight months' worth of eating.

You might wonder how on earth it cost us over €7 to rear each bird. Well, here are the maths. For the first four weeks of their lives the chicks are fed a broiler 'crumb' and they will get through around 1.5kg to 2kg of it each in that time. That's two 25kg bags. For the remaining eight weeks of their lives, they are fed on 'finisher' pellets and they will devour between 10kg to 12kg each. That's eight or nine

25kg bags (we actually had a little bit left in our eighth bag when they were killed). So the total cost is:

Quantity	Description	Unit Cost	Total Cost
20	Day Old Chicks	€2.00	€40.00
2	Broiler Feed – Starter (25kg bag)	€9.28	€18.56
8	Broiler Feed – Finisher (25kg bag)	€11.28	€90.24
	Total		€148.80
	Price per Bird		€7.44

I am being a little disingenuous with these figures in that I left out two other items of expenditure which should really be included – I bought two bags of woodchip shavings to line the floor of their house, which cost me over €20 and a bulb for the infra-red lamp to keep the chicks warm, which cost €10 – the former went on the compost heap, providing some value there, while the latter is re-usable. Including these items would bring the price per bird to over €9 – really makes you wonder about those €4 supermarket chickens, doesn't it? Even though the price of rearing them was pretty high, we still reckon that rearing chickens is a thrifty enterprise for the Home Farmer, particularly when you consider the amount of meat we got from the end product. Our chickens weighed in at between 2.5kg and 3kg each (that's plucked and gutted weight, incidentally). A 3kg bird at €7.44 is a breathtakingly cost effective €2.48 a kilo, which is actually cheaper per kilo than the piddly little €4 supermarket chickens.

During the time they were here, we wrestled with a decision about whether or not to kill them ourselves. There's a meat processing plant near here that will take in the chickens live, and return them to you in a plastic bag ready for the freezer, for the princely sum of €2 a bird. This sounds like a paltry amount in the scheme of things, but when you are watching your pennies to make sure that your chicken-rearing project is worthwhile, €2 per bird is actually a lot, and as a percentage of the total cost of keeping each bird, it's a huge amount. I also had the feeling that we would be doing it out of laziness – or worse, to salve our consciences. It also seemed a little spineless – like we weren't willing to go through this last, most difficult, step with them. And so, we opted to do the evil deed ourselves – well, when I say 'ourselves', I mean the two of us and anybody else we could drag in to help! We are lucky that we have family and neighbours who are extremely well up on these things and happy to lend their time and expertise – there were seven people in total, including Mrs Kelly and myself, which made the whole thing quicker, more efficient and far less daunting. We started at 9.00am and all birds were safely in the freezer (killed, plucked and gutted) by midday.

I could write a whole chapter on the process itself, but it would be a most disagreeable piece of prose that would put you off your supper, so don't worry, I am not going to (if you really want to read about the brutal process of killing chickens, try Chapter 7 in my first book, *Trading Paces*). There's a knack to it, you see, a way of going about it that makes things simpler for the person doing the killing and more humane for the bird being killed. But it is the details that make it *sound* absolutely awful – the implements and accoutrements used, the noise and flapping that ensues, the blood and gore; bad enough to describe it in relation to the two I dispatched in *Trading Paces*; multiplying it up to twenty-one – that's just not on. Suffice to say that the process of turning twenty-one live birds into edible meat is a most unpleasant one for all concerned (particularly the chickens). Killing them is not a bit nice. Plucking them is equally unpleasant – and gutting them, well that's just about the most unpleasant thing of all.

That evening, though exhausted, we felt very grateful that the whole endeavour had been successful and that we had the freezer stocked to the brim with a huge supply of top-quality meat. Meat that has darker flesh than any chicken we have ever tasted. Meat that has real chicken flavour. Meat that is plump, as opposed to being pumped with water to make it *appear* plump. Meat that is, ultimately, guilt-free. And in the context of what we'd been through in the process of killing them, that really is saying something.

JULY GROWER'S CALENDAR

Prep Work

- Any ground that has finished cropping must be quickly cleared away to take more vegetables – this is the essence of a productive Home Farm.
- Keep your Home Farm diary/notebook handy and honestly jot down your successes and failures ('It was *that* big, honestly') – these records will be invaluable for next year.

To-do List

- Use your produce – eat it, freeze it, process it, exchange it, give it away. Do not let it rot in the ground or end up on the compost heap.
- Continue to water and feed plants and practise good weed control. Continue to pinch out side shoots on your tomato plants and remove the lower leaves.
- Earth up brassicas such as brussels sprouts – these plants will grow tall and require a good deal of support.
- Prune raspberries and gooseberries when they have finished fruiting and apply a mulch.
- Cut down legume plants that have finished cropping and compost them. Leave the roots in the soil as they fix nitrogen in the soil.
- Keep an eye on the blight forecast and spray potatoes (if you have decided to do this) if required.
- Inspect all brassicas regularly for creepy things – it might be a good time to cover plants with fine plastic mesh or fleece.
- Summer-prune over-vigorous apple, pear, plum and cherry trees by shortening the vigorous shoots.

Sowing Seeds

- Continue successional sowings and use quick maturing varieties for autumn use – Swiss chard, lettuce, rocket, salad onions, radishes, turnips, peas, French beans (dwarf), carrots.
- Sow for winter use – spring cabbage, Hungry Gap kale, parsley, perpetual spinach (God, could it really be that time of the year again?), chicory and coriander.

Planting Out

- Anything else that's left indoors in a pot. As the song says, it's now or never.

GRUB'S UP – WHAT'S IN SEASON?

July is a peak month for produce – enjoy it! Pick early and often as some vegetables stop producing if not continually picked.

First crops of French and runner beans, tomatoes, peppers and chilli-peppers, cucumbers, courgettes and aubergines, marrows, beetroot, globe artichokes.

Continue to harvest new potatoes, calabrese, cauliflower, cabbage, spinach, carrots, turnips, shallots, garlic, radishes, spring onions, salad crops, strawberries, raspberries, tayberries, currants (black, red and white), gooseberries, loganberries, peas and broad beans.

Ask yourself – do you *really* need to go to the supermarket?!

8

EATS SHOOTS, AND LEAVES

EARLY AUTUMN: AUGUST

slugs – other scavengers – slaughtering the pigs – the department inspector – elderflower and elderberry – peppers and chilli-peppers

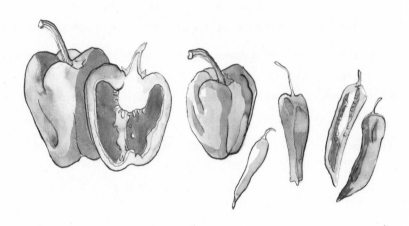

Hatred is never a wise emotion to harbour, particularly at this beautiful time of the year, but it's hard for the Home Farmer to do anything other than absolutely *hate* slugs. The common garden slug does more damage in our vegetable plot than the rabbits, and that's bloody well saying something. Slugs are the drive-by hit-men of the pest world and thwart our efforts to become self-sufficient at every turn – they eat shoots, and leave. In a single sitting, they will devour a row of young lettuces that you carefully nurtured from seed. They are determined, resilient, ubiquitous, slimy and generally awful. So are snails, for that matter, but then at least you can take your revenge on snails by eating them – well, in theory ...

It's an unhappy fact of life that your vegetable patch is a slug's heaven on earth – it provides them with all the shelter and all the food they need to survive and thrive. So how can you deal with them? Well, the answer is, unfortunately – you basically can't. Not really. I am very suspicious of anyone who tells me that I can get rid of slugs entirely or that their garden is entirely slug free – in my opinion that's just not possible. Obviously, some people choose to go the chemical route and slugs pellets are, indeed, extremely effective, but for us they are an absolute no-no because they contain chemicals that would be washed down into the soil, absorbed into the vegetable plants and finally into the body. Most pellets contain an ingredient called metaldehyde, which, even in small doses, is dangerous to humans. The pellets will most assuredly kill lots of slugs – and you will probably take great pleasure from this – but they could also finish off your dog, cat, hens and any birds unfortunate enough to mistake them for food. Poison has that annoying tendency towards being profoundly unselective.

SLUG PATROL

There are some precautions you can take to keep your slug population to an acceptable minimum (if, indeed, there is such thing as an acceptable level of slugs) and minimise the damage to the meals of

the future growing in your plot.

TIDY! Keep your raised beds, polytunnel, greenhouse and vegetable patch clean. Leaving lots of pots and seed trays, bags of potting compost, piles of dead leaves and so on lying about the place provides slugs with lots of base camps from which they will launch their nightly assaults on your vegetables. Raking over the soil in late spring will also disturb hibernating slugs and expose their eggs – this will provide a handy meal for the birds in your garden and a grisly end for the slugs. *Effectiveness level: not very. More in hope than expectation.*

DUCKS! A common myth that gets bandied about a lot is that chickens like to eat slugs. I have put a slug in the chickens' feed bowl to test this theory and found that they completely ignored it and moved off to something else. If you throw our hens a juicy worm, they will practically kill each other trying to get at it. Throw a slug at them and they will more than likely throw it back at you. Ducks, on the other hand, absolutely love slugs (Indian Runners are a duck practically made for slug hunting) and having an animal in your garden that accomplishes something that would otherwise require human intervention is one of the central tenets of good permaculture. Apparently it is worth trying to give young ducklings a taste for slugs by ensuring it is among the first things they get to eat. If you are really daring you can even go so far as to let your ducks into your vegetable patch, particularly at this time of the year when there aren't any really young, tender plants in there. Let them in for an hour or so some day when you are in the garden and can keep an eye on them. Incidentally, hedgehogs and frogs are also predators of the common slug, but we don't seem to be able to attract either of these to our garden. *Effectiveness level: good (providing the ducks don't eat the vegetables too).*

COPPER! Apparently slugs get a tiny static shock from copper, which they don't like. Copper tape, old copper pipes or even old pennies can be put around beds to protect them – the problem with using this approach is that the slugs are already in the soil, so you are effectively hemming in some slugs as well as keeping others out. That said, we have in the past seen some success from copper pipe around particularly vulnerable and delicate seedlings, such as radish and lettuce. *Effectiveness level: moderate.*

ABRASIVE STUFF! Slugs don't like to cross abrasive material, so ashes, grit and crushed egg shells will usually force them to change course. We put in gravel paths around the raised beds in our vegetable patch, which also seems to deter slugs – you will rarely see a slug passing across that much stone. It was so successful, in fact, that last year we used to put seed trays out there in warm weather because they were safer there than in the polytunnel. You still have the problem of the slugs that are already in the soil in your raised beds, but if you are vigilant you may be able to clear the beds of most of them. *Effectiveness level: moderate to good.*

BEER! If there is one thing that is even remotely likeable about slugs, it is that they seem to share with human beings a love of beer. A shallow container of beer is certainly an effective slug trap, as anyone who has ever put one down will know. Dig a shallow hole first and put the container into it so that the lip of it is at ground level. Then fill it with beer (they aren't fussy when it comes to brands) and come back in a few days – it will be full of drunk, drowning, dying and dead slugs. Empty the containers out and refill. If you leave them soak in the beer for too long they will start to smell. Divert half-consumed cans or bottles of beer to the vegetable plot for the purpose – or better again, make a whole batch of completely undrinkable home brew and then use it to kill slugs rather than risk drinking it, as I did. *Effectiveness level: excellent (and the plus side is that you can drink lots of beer ostensibly for the good of your vegetables).*

NEMATODES! The latest word in slug extermination is bio-control and specifically a little critter called *Phasmarhabditis hermaphrodita*, a naturally occurring microscopic little nematode (eelworm) that devours slugs from the inside (cunning!). About 12 million little worms are contained in each pack which are then watered into the soil using a watering can. After application, each handful of earth will contain literally thousands of them. The worm enters the body of the slug and releases bacteria that are fatal to them but harmless to other organisms. They remain active in the soil for about six weeks. The only downside is that they are relatively expensive – about €20 to €25 for a tub which will cover about 40 sq metres – but given the amount of produce we lose to slugs each year, it could well be worth it. *Effectiveness level: apparently, very effective, but we haven't used it yet so can't comment. Brands such as Nemaslug are starting to appear in garden centres.*

SLUG PATROL! Unfortunately, the most effective means of keeping down slugs is the one that takes the most effort. Go out to your garden at night-time with a torch and pick them off wherever you find them. I know you might find this a little bit too hippy (and creepy) for your liking, but it's actually surprisingly effective. If you have rows and rows of freshly transplanted lettuce seedlings, for example, it is really worthwhile getting out there every night over a few weeks to protect them until they get a little bit hardier. Don't be tempted to show the slugs any mercy by throwing them into a ditch or down at the end of the garden – it's like one of those classic horror movies, **THEY WILL COME BACK TO HAUNT YOU!** Slugs travel considerable distances in search of food. There are any number of ways to dispatch them to their sluggy afterlife: squish them with your fingers (don't forget to wear gloves), or stand on them (don't forget to wear shoes!), or cut them in half and throw them on the compost heap. I detest slugs, but even I find putting them in salt and then watching them bubble and fizz to death to be a little too gruesome. Depending on how many times slugs have visited their destructive misery on your veggies, you will either find slug culling unbearably gruesome or wonderfully cathartic. Let's put it this way – it's them or your vegetables. *Effectiveness level: excellent, and revenge is a dish best served cold.*

OTHER STUFF! It's a good idea to avoid watering your vegetable patch at night-time (Mrs Kelly always says that plants, like humans, should never go to bed with a wet head) because slugs just love to slither over wet soil. You could also try putting used halves of citrus fruits (oranges, grapefruit) upside down in your soil – the slugs love to hide under them and then you can come along and squish 'em all. Other methods, which I can't stand over as I haven't tried: smear some vaseline around the top of pots, which they apparently don't like; plant lots of marigolds as slugs love them and will collect around the stems; you can then cull them as per previous point. Plant loads of rhubarb – again, slugs apparently love the leaves but don't know (yet) that they are poisonous to them.

The slug is probably the biggest pest we have in the garden, but there are others. We've never had an issue (that we've noticed) with mice or rats, but perhaps we are just not looking close enough. Rabbits, on the other hand, are a complete nightmare and we have loads of them in our garden. In sheer frustration a few years back, we put a picket fence around our vegetable plot, only to discover that rabbits would go to the trouble of digging under it if they thought they might get a meal on the other side. Then we put a wire fence on the inside of the picket fence and dug this down about 30cm into the ground. That sounds easy – it wasn't. Our vegetable patch is pretty sizeable and I had to dig a 30cm-deep trench the whole way around, muttering and cursing rabbits as I did so. For about a week after that, I used to lie in

bed at night, smiling to myself while imagining the following scenario: rabbit spends several moonlit hours digging a tunnel under the
fence – only to discover? A wire mesh a foot under the ground!
Ha-ha! At the time of writing, rabbits have so far not been able to
breach Fortress Vegetable Patch, so I can heartily recommend this
approach. You can try to protect individual plants from rabbit
damage by making a makeshift *cloche*: cut the bottom off a soft
drinks bottle and push the base into the soil around the plant. I've
never tried this and I suspect that if a rabbit can dig under a fence,
they can probably dig under a soft drinks bottle. Perhaps the cleverest
way of keeping rabbits away from your vegetables, from a food-production perspective, would be to get up early in the morning, shoot
them from your bedroom window and then prepare a healthy rabbit
stew. Or is that a bridge too far?

Our hens are some of the worst offenders when it comes to damaging our vegetables – they just love scratching around in the soil of a
nicely cultivated vegetable bed and they also have been caught once
or twice picking at nice young shoots. Thankfully, the picket fence
seems to work a treat on the hens, though I am not sure why, given
that it is only about a metre high and they could easily power-leap
over it. Regular birds can also be a problem and we resort to putting
nets around our raised beds, depending on the crop that's in them. We
had a particular issue last year with our fruit patch – birds helped
themselves to our entire crop of blueberries and gooseberries, almost
overnight, and did the same with our cherries and plums. We had a
lovely batch of cherries that we were checking every day, and I swear
to God one day I checked them and said, 'Yep, I'd say they will be
ready tomorrow' – we came out the next day and they were all gone,

every last one. This year, we are considering making a fruit cage to keep them out – surrounding the entire fruit patch with chicken-wire fencing. (Our vegetable patch will eventually look like a heavily fortified prison camp and we will employ armed guards to shoot intruders.) A scarecrow is a traditional but very effective way to keep birds out – it cracks me up that it works, but work it does. You can also try hanging old, unwanted CDs from threads in the vegetable patch. Birds hate the flashes of light that bounce off the CDs – and, of course, no self-respecting bird would go within a hundred yards of a Garth Brooks album.

It's never pleasant taking animals to the slaughter, but over the few short years that we have reared pigs and chickens for the table here on the Home Farm, we've more or less got used to the idea. When you rear and kill an animal yourself for food, it puts a whole plethora of omnivore's dilemmas literally front and centre. Up until the day I first killed a chicken with my own hands, I had eaten meat practically every day of my life and never given a thought to the plight of the animals that gave up their lives to provide those meals. I had never thought about whether it was *right* to kill an animal for meat in the first place. Most meat eaters are the same, I think. We buy sausages and bacon in nice plastic packaging, but don't stop to think about the living, breathing intelligent pigs that had to die to provide those products; we buy a leg of lamb for Easter, but don't stop to think about the four-month-old lamb that just a few days previously was frolicking happily in a field with its mother; we buy a packet of twelve chicken breasts (great value at €15), but definitely don't think about the six chickens that were reared indoors in cramped conditions for just six weeks before being slaughtered; and, God knows, when we spend five minutes eating a burger or a steak, or a nice beef stew, we certainly don't want to think about the cow (or cows) that were reared by some farmer for nearly two years before being slaughtered.

Meat-eating has become almost completely sanitised, and perhaps necessarily so, because in reality it is an entirely bloody and brutal business. At its most basic, it is an act where one type of animal kills another to derive the energy it needs to survive, and there is nothing more brutal or cold-blooded than that. Home Farmers can comfort themselves somewhat with the notion that the animals they have reared have had good lives – they have been well treated, well looked after, well fed. They have been given a good deal of space to wander around or forage on and unlimited access to sunshine and fresh air. This is all important stuff, but at the end of the day, let's not kid ourselves – these poor animals have had their lives cut tragically short to become one of the ingredients in tonight's dinner.

When you rear animals for the table yourself, you really don't have the luxury of pushing these things to the back of your mind because the living, breathing animal that is about to become your meal is quite literally staring you in the face every day. So your choice at that point is to be so appalled that you resolve to never eat meat again (which would be quite valid, in my opinion), or to get comfortable with the whole thing and just get on with it. We have opted to do the latter, but it has been somewhat of a journey to get to this point and, in the process, we have come across lots of people who occupy a strange mid-point between these two positions – they continue to eat meat, but are upset or outraged when brought face-to-face with the realities of being an omnivore. I can't tell you how many times I have been showing the pigs or chickens to someone, only for them to say, 'Oh God, that's so cruel' or 'How could you?', or something along those lines when I mention that they are for the chop. At this point, I will always ask them whether they are vegetarian and they will (almost always) reply that they are not. I can understand a vegetarian being appalled – they have a set of principles and are sticking to them, and fair play to them. But I can't understand a meat eater reacting this way, making a brief foray into righteous indignation before rushing back to blissful oblivion. Perhaps it's a necessary defence mechanism.

Shamefully, our own attitude to eating the animals we have reared ourselves is different to the ones that we haven't. I find myself being a little more *thankful* when it comes to eating the meat from our own animals. I take a little more time eating it, for one thing – I mean, you don't wolf down a chicken breast from a chicken that you have carefully reared over a twelve-week period and it's unlikely to be used as a quick and handy supper that you throw together in twenty minutes. You want to savour and celebrate it, down to the last morsel. And, of course, given the amount of effort you have put into the process, you also do your best to try and use up every last bit of the animal. This is thrifty, but it's also a display of respect at some very small, insignificant level. You're doing the animal the terrible injustice of killing it for food – at least, pay it some respect by not wasting anything. It's terrible hypocrisy on our part that when we buy meat in the supermarket, we don't show the same respect and quickly revert to eating in a deeply unthinking way. We could, of course, try to be thankful, regardless of whether we reared the animal ourselves or not – but in some ways I think it's impossible to be *as thankful* when you haven't produced the meat yourself. And maybe that's why the commercial meat industry has been allowed to get so badly out of control – there just aren't enough of us around who have experienced rearing and killing an animal for meat. Go back a thousand or five hundred years to a time when pretty much the only way to access meat was to catch and kill it yourself. Go back fifty years to a time when lots of people kept a few chickens in their back garden, and consider how rare and special an event it was for a family to kill a bird for the table. In the modern world, eating meat has become far too commonplace and we've lost that sense of appreciation as a result.

The first year we took our pigs to the abattoir, I felt pretty bad about it. There wasn't any crying or anything like that, and I certainly never even came close to second thoughts, but it was a pretty abhorrent experience all the same, made more so by the fact that I watched the whole process from start to finish out of a sense of misplaced loyalty to the poor pigs. The following year, however, it was like I'd had an emotional lobotomy – I didn't feel a thing. We loaded up the pigs, transported them to the abattoir, filled in the paperwork and drove away without a backward glance.

We have some good moments with our pigs while they are alive and I certainly miss not having them around when they are gone, but there's part of me that's always sort of relieved too that the pig project is moving on from rearing to the best part – eating. Having fattened them up over five months or so, the pigs are by now very large animals and they require a lot of feeding, watering and mucking out – it is, quite frankly, bloody hard work. By August, they are ploughing through sacks of barley like they are going out of fashion, which means much lugging and hauling of grains about the place. As a natural consequence of their greediness, there is a huge amount of mucking-out to do in their pigsty too, which isn't very pleasant either. In addition, five months of hard-core rooting has exacted a heavy toll on the corner of the garden that they occupy. So, in some ways, delivering them to the slaughter will be a happy release (for us at least) from the daily drudgery of looking after them. That sounds terrible, I am sure.

Before we get to the point of re-stocking the freezer with beautiful pork and bacon, however, there's the small matter of transporting them to the abattoir, and we are always a little apprehensive about this because it's fraught with potential disaster. Essentially, the pigs have to be moved from the end of the garden to the back of a trailor, then they have to be driven to the abattoir (which in our case is nearly 100km away), and finally they have to be unloaded from the trailor at the other end. This might sound pretty straightforward, but pigs that are ready for eating are pigs that have put on enormous bulk and possess considerable strength. The cute little weanlings that joined us back in the spring could be carried in our arms from the trailor to their new home. Five months on, the same pigs can't be carried anywhere – they have to be *coaxed*, gently, and in the hope that nothing goes wrong, because if it does, and they decide they want to go to AWOL, there's very little you can do about it. The end of the garden has been their home for five months and they feel safe and comfortable there. Suddenly, we are pushing them into leaving it, which they are obviously not particularly happy about, and, of course, we are trying to encourage them to walk *over* the electric fence, which they have learned to steer well clear of (they don't know it's switched off this time). It helps to have someone with experience of these things on hand and, to his eternal credit, the old-man-in-law always steps up to the plate.

The first year we had pigs, we got a loan of his trailor and parked it over beside the pigsty for a few days before they were due to leave. We put some straw and food in it, and they eventually decided that the trailor was nicer than their own house and started sleeping there at night. Once they were inside, we would lock up the door of the trailor, which, of course, meant that on the morning of the slaughter we could just attach the trailor to the car and drive off with the pigs in the back. Unfortunately, this year the ground was too wet to bring the trailor or the car across the lawn, so we had to find a way of getting the pigs across the garden to the driveway, which complicated things considerably. The key to getting a pig to do something it doesn't want to do is to have it hungry – a hungry pig is generally a compliant pig. Having been starved since the previous morning, they would have walked off a cliff to get at some grub. We opened up the gate of their pen, Mrs Kelly rattled the bucket of grub, and they set off across the garden after her while I walked along behind with a stick (so that I could beat myself over the head if they escaped). It's a worrying thing, indeed, to be moving two enormous animals across your garden with only a bucket of feed to keep them from losing interest and starting to tear up the lawn. Every now and then they would stop, as if sensing a ruse, and they would have a little root, but a quick rattle of the bucket and they were off again. The whole thing was freakishly easy and within minutes they were in the pen, and we took a rest and had a cup of tea to calm our nerves.

After that, however, things took an interesting turn – maybe they smelt a rat at that stage, but they just point-blank refused to go up the ramp and into the trailer. You really cannot understand how strong and loud a pig is until you have one cornered and are trying to get it to do something it doesn't want to do (then multiply that by two). Anyway, after much huffing, puffing, heaving and a whole lot of shouting (at them and each other) we got them in the trailor, where they settled down in some straw, oblivious to their fate. I set off and about an hour and a half later, the doors of the trailer were opened and the two pigs wandered down the ramp into a waiting pen in the abattoir, where they would spend the evening getting good and relaxed before a dawn rendezvous with the slaughterman.

If I felt one pang of guilt in the entire day, it was right at that moment, just before getting back into the car to drive off. I was standing at the pen looking in at them, relatively satisfied that the job was finished without undue stress on us or them, and, wouldn't you know it, one of the pigs trotted over to me, looking for a scratch behind the ear. It was 'the outgoing one'(not surprisingly, none of those stupid names mentioned earlier stuck!), and she was doing something by now quite natural to her, since she and I had gone through the same little routine almost every day for five months. And, of course, I felt wretched. How could I not? These lovely animals had shared our garden and our lives for nearly half a year, and they did so with plenty of humour and good grace. It wouldn't have done at all to start bawling my eyes out or dropping to my knees to beg the abattoir owner not to go through with it. It was a moment to show a steely nerve and rock-solid composure. So I gave 'the outgoing one' a quick scratch behind the ear and then quickly got into the car.

A funny thing happened on the way to the abattoir. While I was in the car, I got a call from Mrs Kelly, back at base, telling me that a department inspector had just arrived at the house. I kid you not – a Department of Agriculture, Fisheries and Food inspector had taken a few hours out of his day to come and inspect our two pigs! See, in order to take pigs to an abattoir, you must have a herd number; the abattoir will literally send you packing if you don't have tags on your pigs' ears, with your herd number on them. To get the herd number, you have to contact the Department, who, in their infinite wisdom, then consider you a 'herd owner'. Now, I know that the Department has a job of work to do in controlling diseases like swine fever, blue tongue and all those other nasties, and it makes absolute sense to me that they keep track of where farm animals are being reared. But the problem that I have with the whole thing is that they apply the same parameters and rules to the Home Farmer keeping two pigs for their own table as they do to the commercial pig farmer who is rearing thousands.

Once you get your herd number you are on a computer some-where in the bowels of the Department's headquarters, which every now and then spits out some useless (in this context) mail to you, starting with the immortal words, 'Dear Herdowner ...'. Once a year or so, your name also pops out for 'inspection' where an intrepid Department man is dispatched from the cosy confines of his office to seek you out to nose around your premises. Now, I know the guy is just doing his job, okay, so I won't be hard on him because it's the system that's screwed up and not him. But let me tell you a few things which he did (as told by Mrs Kelly). First of all, he told her that he drove up and down our road for about half an hour looking for a commercial pig house and was bemused when he couldn't find it. Perhaps this is understandable, given that we have a herd number and all, so he is quite reasonably expecting to find an actual herd. When he eventually did find our house, he was, no doubt, quite disappointed to discover that not only was there no herd worth speaking of to inspect, but our TWO pigs were already on their way to meet their maker. So he had some choices: he could head back to the office and do some real work, or he could stay and poke around our house for a while. Of course, he chose the latter.

The inspector asked to see where the pigs were kept, so with admirable patience (I can't imagine what madness would have come over me, had I been there) Mrs Kelly took him over to see the now empty pig pen. 'It's very mucky,' he says, with considerable understatement. 'Well, you know, they're pigs,' says Mrs Kelly, '*they like mucky*.' And, of course, she's thinking about the fact that commercially reared pigs are kept in concrete stalls, where they can't root or get access to sunlight or fresh air, so *they're* never mucky. But in the interest of keeping things from becoming adversarial, she doesn't say anything about that. 'Yeah, we will probably have to deduct points from you for that,' he says. Deduct points from *what*? Mrs Kelly was wondering.

Next up, he asked her to show him where we kept our feed – she took him to our garage and showed him bags of rolled barley, which he surveyed grimly, and then informed her that you are not allowed to keep pig feed in the same area as other feeds (we keep all the feed for the animals in the garage) because of the risk of cross-contamination. I kid you not. Mrs Kelly politely informed him that since we go to the trouble of rearing pigs for ourselves, we are hardly likely to make the mistake of feeding the hen food to the pigs and the pig feed to the ducks. But he wasn't impressed by this. Which begs the question: does he want us to build a separate garage for the pig feed? Would the Department give us a grant to do so, I wonder (you know what – it's scary, but they might). Then he asked to see the dockets for our pig feed. 'The what, now?' asks Mrs Kelly, looking around her to see was there a camera filming this for some type of Candid Camera TV show. The dockets, he informed her, with an impressive straight face – you are buying pig feed, so, for trace-ability, you need purchase dockets. 'You mean receipts?' asks Mrs Kelly. No, we don't keep the receipts, she told him. Why would we? Would you keep receipts when buying food for your dog or cat or pet hamster?

'I'm afraid we will have to deduct points for these infringe-ments,' says our man from the Department. Mrs Kelly bristled. 'Deduct points from what?' she finally asks. 'From your pay-ments,' he replies. 'What payments? We don't get any payments,' she says. 'We keep these animals for our own consumption.' But he didn't seem too bothered by this fundamental flaw in his argument and continued to insist that he would be deducting money from our subsidy payment.

That night, with our pigs safely dispatched in the abattoir, we laughed a lot about the whole inspector incident. It could only happen in Ireland, was the general consensus. It is pretty funny, you must admit, but on another level it also makes me really angry. There are people like you and me and thousands of others out there who are trying to do the right thing – trying to live *slowly*, disengage from the commercial food production universe, trying to produce as much of our own food as we can and live healthier, more outdoorsy lives. So why is our government trying to make it hard for us? Why are they wasting resources and money, sending inspectors out to the homes of people who keep a few pigs for their own table? Why can't they use their computers to differentiate between commercial producers and Home Farmers who are keeping animals for food? 'I'll bring that up at the next management meeting,' the inspector promised me when I asked him that very question a few days later over the phone. We can but hope that he will.

One of the women who attended a hen course here on the Home Farm recently got me interested in the idea of elderberry wine. Like most people, I love the notion of a good homebrew, mainly because of the tremendous ancientness of the craft, especially when wild and free ingredients are being used. Last summer, I made my first foray into the weird and wacky world of homebrew by creating a batch of my very own lager, which was enormous fun until we cracked open the first bottle and discovered that it tasted like smelly socks. I've drunk some god-awful beer in my time with little complaint (it seems the later it is in the evening, the less discerning I am), but this was on another level of wretchedness altogether – and there are still thirty bottles of the stuff out in the garage that I am using up gradually as slug bait, and that I occasionally fed to the unsuspecting (and, frankly, very unfussy) pigs before they left. They had a good old slurp from their trough, then snoozed it off in the sun for the afternoon. Not a bad life – though I wonder what the inspector would have to say about that? It's worth bearing in mind, of course, that pigs will eat a plastic bucket if they're hungry, so the fact that they liked the beer is no great compliment to my skills as a brewer.

Still, passion undimmed by my beery blunder, my ears pricked up considerably when I heard talk of elderberry wine. I asked lots of questions and the woman was so impressed by my enthusiasm (bordering on mania) she sent me up a bottle of her wine that very evening, probably to shut me up. I wasted no time in opening it and drinking the lot. It wasn't merlot, that's for sure, but it tasted impressive nonetheless. Quite sweet, but very drinkable. You'd would be very pleased with yourself indeed if you had bottles of this maturing on a shelf somewhere (I would anyway). She also gave me the skinny (so to speak) on good locations for elder in the area. It's very treasured knowledge, so I am afraid I can't print it here in case you steal it on me.

There are loads of things you can make from the produce of the elder bush and it delivers its generous bounty from May to July. The flowers come first, followed by the berries later in the summer, which, incidentally, are very good for you; the eighteenth-century gardener and diarist, John Evelyn, charmingly called them 'a catholicon against all infirmities whatever'. Typically, the flowers are used to make cordials, ice creams, sorbets, jams and jellies, non-alcoholic champagne (what's the point of that, I hear you ask) and fritters (fried in some batter). Happily, the berries are best utilised in wine. You can pick the flowers right up to mid-July; after that they are on their last legs. You should pick when they are still creamy and before they fade to white; also try and get them on a country road (if you get them from the side of a busy road you will end up with a drink that smells of petrol).

I found it very exciting to bring home the beautiful cream-coloured sprays of flowers, thinking about the lovely drink I would make from them (and best of all, that it's totally free). Unfortunately, the smell of elderflowers is god-awful (a little like cat's pee, I reckon), but don't let this put you off – it is only the flowers that smell and once you start to process them, that will disappear. The wonderful flavour of the flowers can be infused into a huge array of drinks and foods. We bought a bottle of elderflower cordial last year and thought it tasted amazing – a little drop in a long, ice-filled glass, filled with water, and you have a gorgeous, lemony, fresh-tasting summer thirst quencher. So we decided to use our free bounty to make that. I suggest that you give it a try ... it's just brilliant having this concentrate in the fridge or freezer, and making up batches with water as you need it.

You will need about twenty elderflower heads, and a syrup made from 2 litres of boiling water and 600g white sugar. Strip the little elderflowers from the stalks with a fork into a large bowl. Add 4 sliced lemons and pour in the syrup. Cover the bowl and leave for 24 hours, stirring occasionally. Strain through muslin into small bottles and when you need to use it, dilute with about ten parts water or sparkling water.

Peppers and chilli-peppers are both members of the capsicum family, which I always think makes them sound like something from *Romeo and Juliet*. You could, perhaps, imagine the illicit union in your greenhouse between a fiery, young chilli-pepperette and a suave, but youthful aubergine. 'O Romeo, Romeo!' cries the pepper. 'Wherefore art thou, Romeo? Deny thy father and refuse thy name! Or if thou wilt not, be but sworn my love, and I'll no longer be a Capsicum.' OK, maybe not.

Peppers have one of the longest growing seasons of all the vegetables that we grow on the Home Farm. They were among the first batch of seeds sown back in the springtime, but it is only now that they are starting to bear fruit. They are tropical plants and need the deeply intense heat of the summer polytunnel or greenhouse to produce a decent crop. You would need a hell of a lot of pepper plants to become self-sufficient (each plant will produce eight to ten fruits if you're lucky), nonetheless, it's worth growing some just so that you get to see the sight of ripe peppers of all shapes, sizes and colours hanging in your tunnel or greenhouse. The contrast of a bright red, waxy pepper against the green foliage really is a beautiful sight. If you do happen to get a good batch of them, they can also be dried, pickled or frozen. We got a great crop of chilli-peppers last year and froze them individually – very handy.

Large, sweet peppers are known as bell peppers and can grow up to 20cm in length. Chilli-peppers are much smaller, but they pack a powerful punch in the taste department. Pretty much all peppers start off green and then ripen to different colours, like yellow, red, orange or even purple – from that perspective, a green pepper is essentially unripe and is, therefore, nowhere near as flavoursome as one that has been allowed to ripen fully. A fully-mature red pepper is an incredibly sweet affair – try baking them in a hot oven and then peeling off the skin, slicing them up and storing them in jars filled with olive oil.

Served on crackers – a little taste of summer heaven. The amateur pepper grower, however, faces something of a conundrum: if you pick the fruits when they are green, it encourages the plant to produce more fruit. If you let them ripen fully, the plant has begun to invest its energies in the ripening process and therefore produces a far smaller harvest. So what's it to be – flavour or volume? Ah yes, these are terrible choices we face.

Because they are nice and compact, peppers and chilli-peppers are perfect container plants, so if you really love them, you could fill a hot conservatory or south-facing room with pots and grow every variety imaginable. We plant ours out in the polytunnel around late May or early June, after growing them from seeds in module trays indoors in March or April. Like tomatoes, peppers benefit from being started off on a heating mat to encourage germination. Also like tomatoes, they will need regular watering in the summer months and will appreciate an occasional potassium-rich feed, particularly once they have started to bear fruit. We have never needed to put supports in place for our pepper plants, but some guides advise you to do so, particularly if you have heavy fruit growing on the upper part of the plant. They only need about 50cm of space when fully grown, so you can get quite a number of plants in a corner of the polytunnel. August and September are the two make-or-break months for pepper plants. If they get some decent sunshine, they will do very well. If they don't, they might not ripen at all before the cold weather sets in, and this will be a considerable disappointment. A fully formed green pepper takes about three weeks to turn fully red.

HOT STUFF

Courtesy of a combustible chemical called capsaicin, which lingers menacingly in the seeds and lining of the fruit, some varieties of chilli-pepper can be downright dangerous to eat if you're not used to them. Some of them are so lethal, in fact, you should wear gloves even to handle them. I have been launched into unstoppable fits of coughing, streaming eyes and an alarmingly runny nose just from slicing open a particularly fiery little red fella.

The heat in peppers is measured in units called Scovilles, named after a chemist called Dr Wilbur Scoville, who, in 1912, devised a simple test called the Scoville Organoleptic Test, which determines the heat in peppers by measuring how much capsaicin is inside. A bog-standard bell pepper has no Scovilles at all, and even poblano peppers only ratchet up a paltry 1,500 Scovilles. Most people would consider jalapeño peppers to be pretty hot, but they only manage between 2,500 and 3,000 Scovilles. Real chilli-heads scoff at these ridiculously meagre numbers and point out that the Jamaican Hot and the much revered Habanero pepper can reach up to 350,000 Scovilles. The Big Daddy of them all, however, is an Indian pepper called Bhut Jolokia, which weighs in at a hefty one million Scovilles – the advice, if you ever come across one, is to admire it from a safe distance and don't even think about eating it. Incidentally, drinking water will not have any impact if your throat is on fire from eating chilli pepper because capsaicin does not dissolve in water – far better to take some yoghurt or milk. The bigger question is why you would want to eat such fundamentally unpalatable food. Aficionados claim that eating a mega-hot chilli is basically like taking narcotics, such is the endorphin high that results. Capsaicin is also thought to have medicinal value, helping to burn fat, fight cancer and inflammation, relieve pain and promote heart health. Though, of course, you might also drop dead from the shock of eating a really hot pepper, which wouldn't be very healthy at all.

PAULA MEE'S NUTRITION BITES: PEPPERS AND CHILLI-PEPPERS

Red peppers are high in vitamins A and C, which are antioxidant vitamins. They are also a source of vitamin B6, which is essential for releasing energy from protein. To get the same amount of vitamin C as just half a red pepper, you would need to eat two oranges, three kiwis or forty cherry tomatoes! Like all vegetables, peppers are naturally low in fat, contain some fibre and small amounts of many nutrients such as potassium and some B vitamins. The capsaicin in peppers is a potent inhibitor of substance P, a neuropeptide associated with inflammatory processes. The hotter the chilli-pepper, the more capsaicin it contains.

Nutrition per Portion (80g):

Vegetable	Calories	Fat (g)	Salt (g)	Saturated Fat (g)
Pepper	26	0.3	0	0.1
Chilli-pepper	21	0.2	0.02	0

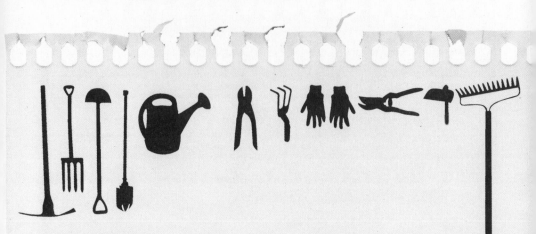

AUGUST GROWER'S CALENDAR

Prep Work

- Green manures are plants that are grown specifically to improve soil fertility. They are very useful when beds are empty, either awaiting a crop, or after they have been harvested (as is often the case in August). The green manure is grown directly in the bed (suppressing weeds at the same time), and then cut down and dug into the soil at a later stage, improving the soil structure and nutrient level, as well as preventing the leaching of nutrients. Green manures include mustard, buckwheat, radish, rye, alfalfa, clover and vetches.

To-do List

- Keep an eye on your pumpkins – give them plenty of water and regular applications of a homemade high-potash liquid feed, such as comfrey tea. Nip out the growing points to encourage the fruits to swell. Put something under the fruits if they are resting on soil to prevent the underside from rotting.

- Cut back any herbs that have finished flowering to encourage fresh growth – this will prolong their usage into autumn.

- Continued vigilance is required with your brassicas. Netting the plants is the most effective way of keeping butterflies and the cabbage moth away. Lift the netting regularly and inspect undersides of leaves, removing eggs and caterpillars. Hoe the ground around plants regularly.

- Protect the developing curds on your cauliflowers from the sun by bending a few of the larger outer leaves inwards (you can tie them in place around the curds if you want). This prevents them from going yellow in the sun.
- Keep weeding – in particular, don't allow weeds to go to seed as they will produce lots and lots of other weeds, which you really want to avoid. A good, sharp hoe is a great investment and makes the job a cinch.
- Keep watering – mulch around plants to retain moisture in really hot weather. A bucket of water placed beside aubergine plants will help create the right moist atmosphere.
- Keep an eye on your apple and other fruit trees – prune if they have made too much new growth.
- Pull up and remove crops that have bolted or finished producing – put them on the compost heap or feed it to your Home Farm animals. Warning: don't feed huge quantities of giant red mustard leaf to your pigs, it will make them cry and very thirsty!

Sowing Seeds

- Continue succession sowing.
- It's around now that you need to start thinking about sowing seeds to provide produce next year. Sow spring cabbage, red cabbage, winter spinach, salad onions (in polytunnel for spring crop), autumn salad mix, endive, parsley, and onion seed. The August polytunnel should be similar to the springtime one – resplendent with propagation trays.

Planting Out

- Strawberries – plant now for a good crop next June. You should aim to have strawberry plants at three different stages of maturity: three-year-old plants for heavy crops, two-year-old for medium crops and replacement plants from 'runners' off older plants. This would ensure a good supply of strawberries every year.
- Rosemary, sage and mint can be propagated from cuttings now.

GRUB'S UP – WHAT'S IN SEASON?

Depending on which system you follow, August is either late summer or the beginning of autumn – either way, it's truly a month of plenty in the garden, so enjoy every last minute. As vegetables and soft fruits continue, they are joined at the end of this month by tree fruits, like apples and plums.

Pick beetroot regularly as they reach the size you require – if left to grow too large they will lose their tenderness.

If you're lucky, each of your sweetcorn plants will produce two beautiful yellow cobs. Pick them as soon as the 'tassels' wither to brown and when a creamy liquid squirts out of the grains when you squeeze. Cook immediately – as the saying goes, 'Walk slowly to pick it, run back to the kitchen to cook it.' I cook it for just a few minutes in unsalted water.

Continue to harvest beetroot, tomatoes, carrots, cabbage, cauliflower, peas, broad beans, French and runner beans, salad leaves, radishes, turnips, potatoes, onions, peppers and chilli-peppers, aubergines, globe artichokes, courgettes, cucumber, gooseberries, raspberries and currants.

With the abundance of fresh produce, consider storing some for winter use – freeze, or make pickles and chutneys from onions, cauliflower, green beans, tomatoes, cucumbers, apples, plums. Make special vinegars from excess herbs, onions, chilli-peppers and garlic. Make jams, curds and jellies from strawberries, raspberries, blackberries, blueberries, gooseberries, currants (red/white/black), beetroot and mint.

9

PART OF SOMETHING

MID-AUTUMN: SEPTEMBER

GIY groups – harvest – wing clipping – squashes, courgettes, pumpkins

Trying to grow your own vegetables or to be in any way self-sufficient is a solitary pursuit most of the time – which is why it's called *self*-sufficiency, I suppose. In years to come, when I am an expert in these things, I guess that won't bother me so much, but as a relative novice I find it entirely disconcerting. Standing in my veggie patch, contemplating some sort of mysterious, freaky rust on my celery, I find myself pondering, with considerable envy, how sweet life must be for people in allotments and community gardens. Imagine how handy it must be when you have a query or problem to simply pop your head over the fence to get advice from the grower in the adjacent plot (I imagine him to be a crusty old fella, who has been growing for fifty years and won 'best-grower' awards for his prize cabbages).

The hen courses that we ran here on the Home Farm during the summer gave us a glimpse of how wonderful it is to be part of a group of like-minded individuals, sharing information, tips and war stories about producing your own food. We got tremendous satisfaction (and knowledge) from talking over lunch about all the different facets of food growing – what people had tried to grow, what had worked and what hadn't. People would also wander around our vegetable garden and comment on this and that – they would obviously learn some stuff and, in return, they would tell you how they did things at home, and you might pick up a little tip from them. I just loved that aspect of the courses and it got me all excited about the idea of setting up a food growers group in the area. Sometimes, I get a hare-brained idea and get all fired up and then, if I am lucky, after a few days I settle down and move on to something else, because my ardour is generally matched by an incredibly low attention span. But this idea just refused to go away.

Somebody mentioned to me that it would be a brilliant idea to be able to exchange produce with other growers at certain times of the year, and this struck me as particularly ingenious. Right now, for example, with the harvest in full swing, our thoughts are inevitably turning from growing to processing. It's obviously very satisfying to stash away the fruits of our labour, but it can be problematic and very hard work. Take a vegetable like courgette, for example: you use up the tender, slim ones, cooking them on barbecues and the like, but occasionally there's a courgette that slips under the radar – perhaps it's hidden behind the leaves of the plant and before you know it, it's about half a metre long. And now you have a problem – you have what's called a 'glut' of produce, in other words, more than you can eat. We use up our courgettes as best we can: we give some away, and they make a nice filler in a Bolognese sauce, but really there's only so much courgette a body can take and aside from making chutney, there's not a lot else you can do with it. (A Home Farming pal of mine says the best recipe for a big courgette is finely chopped and thrown on the compost heap!) When you run out of processing ideas, wouldn't it be great to be able to swap some courgettes for something that another grower has a glut of?

Ultimately, that was the idea behind the Grow It Yourself (GIY) network here in Waterford. My motives for setting it up were entirely selfish – and I continue to get more out of it than I put in – but I felt if it helped other people along the way, that would be great too. I wanted to learn from (more) expert growers and get tips and suggestions – you know those little nuggets of wisdom that growers have learned the hard way, but which would never occur to you or me in a million years? I wanted to try and recreate that allotment mood: you know, the '*My beets are bigger than your beets*' – competitiveness disguised as camaraderie sort of vibe with its friendly rivalry, banter and slagging. I wanted to meet people in my area who were up to the same things as we are. Most of all, though, I think I was hoping to be *part of something.*

I asked our local librarian here in Waterford would they give me a venue for a meeting, and they agreed – this was important because I didn't want to go down the road of having to pay for a venue and consequently having to charge people to come along. Ultimately, we've stuck with this cheapskate mentality ever since, and it has served us remarkably well. We are a business person's worst nightmare: we don't have an income and we don't have expenditure. We don't pay for the venue or facilities, nor do we pay speakers, and our meetings are completely free of charge. I think that ethos is vital in keeping the whole thing accessible to everyone. We rely a hundred percent on the enthusiasm and efforts of the people involved to keep the whole show on the road. Anyway, with a venue locked down, I picked a date for our first meeting and sent a notice to the local papers, expecting very few people to show up. I was thinking that if we got a core group of, say, twenty people we would have ourselves a ballgame. I didn't have any great plan in mind for the meeting except that I was going to get up and start talking about the joys of growing your own vegetables and why I felt a growers' group would be a good idea, and I was hoping things would catch fire from there. I was thinking: if you build it, they will come.

Just before the meeting started, I was talking to the first man to arrive about growing peas, and thinking to myself: My, this is going to be pleasant – a nice little group of veggie lovers, chatting about all things veggie. And then about ten people walked in, and a few minutes later, another five and then another seven. And before you could say 'hot-diggidy', we had three minutes to go to starting time and there were no seats left (we had fifty seats out) and the punters kept coming. Being incredibly nervous about getting up to talk in front of such a big crowd and altogether stunned by the turnout, I didn't do a headcount that first night, but I think a conservative estimate is that we had between eighty and one hundred people there. Imagine that number of people giving up two hours of their Wednesday evening when they could have been at home having a barbecue in the nice weather? It goes to show the level of resurgent interest that there currently is in this whole area.

I got people to indicate on their feedback forms that first night whether they would be interested in getting involved in running the group and, thankfully, about seven or eight said they would. They are the most remarkable, inventive, enthusiastic bunch of people imaginable. We met up the following week and agreed a rough format for future meetings; we agreed to meet once a month for about an hour and a half. We all felt that the network should focus on addressing the skills gap that exists when it comes to producing food. The skills that our parents and grandparents would have taken as a given have been more or less lost over the past twenty years while we were off doing other things, like buying holiday homes in Bulgaria and so on. So we wanted to provide practical instruction and information on how to grow or rear food, but, uniquely and where possible, to do this by drawing on the expertise from *within the group*, as opposed to getting people in from outside. As time went by, we discovered that we had about five or six really expert people in our network and gradually they started to get comfortable enough with the whole thing to share their expertise with the rest of us.

We now have a routine. We start the meetings with a talk from one of us on some area of food production – soil preparation, crop rotation, composting, making raised beds, home-brewing, keeping hens or pigs etc. Then we break the session into smaller groups of about seven to ten people for an informal discussion – one of our steering group came up with the name PODs for this part of the meeting, pure genius. Anyway, usually we talk about some seasonal fruit or vegetable in our PODs, so, for example, September would be the perfect month to discuss growing apples, so we get the PODs to talk about how they grow them, what varieties they use, what problems they encounter, and what they do with the harvest, and anything else that arises. The PODs are always the most popular item on the agenda, because the small-group format allows people to get to know one another, which is, after all, the main idea behind the network in the first place. And people are generally more comfortable talking and asking questions in smaller groups.

After the PODs, we have a session on the grower's calendar for the month ahead, which focuses on what we should be sowing, planting and harvesting in the month ahead – similar to what you have at the end of each chapter in this book. I put this together with Anne Cullen, whom I call our brain trust; she has been growing her own vegetables for years, so on top of the standard stuff that you always get in these calendars, we also get loads of really useful information and tips gleaned from a lifetime of growing. We try to get different people from within the network to stand up and 'present' the grower's calendar, which means that you get a flavour of their experiences as well. A lively conversation, or even debate, almost always ensues, for example: 'You mention that we should be sowing X this month, but in my experience it's way too early!' This is always a really useful segment, particularly for the novice growers, because they go away from the meeting with a handful of things in their heads that they have to do in the weeks ahead.

We have tried to make the meetings both inspiring and practical, because, in my view, that's the only way to keep things appealing for those who attend. I wanted to make sure we included some rearing projects as well vegetable and fruit growing, even though keeping hens, ducks or pigs may not be in any way practical for some people. I still think, though, the vast majority of Home Farmers are interested in hearing about these things. I have been consistently blown away by the attendance and enthusiasm at the meetings, and the mix of people involved. There are people who want to grow their own food, but are not sure where to start, as well as people like us who are already growing and rearing their own food, but want to learn more and get in touch with fellow foodies. And, thankfully, we have people involved who have immense knowledge – who have been growing for twenty, thirty or forty years and are happy to come along and share the knowledge they gained the hard way. We have young people and not so young people – people in their twenties and people in their eighties. People with acres of land and others with tiny gardens. People who are trying to become completely self-sufficient and people who couldn't care less if they never come within an ass's roar of self-sufficiency.

But amidst all that variation, there are things that unite us: we all love food; we all want to empower ourselves by growing our own; we are all concerned about food security, food quality, food miles, rising food costs and the impact of our food system on the planet, and we all have a sense that the solutions to these problems probably won't come from our politicians but from the ground up (so the speak). Above all, I think, everyone in the room is just happy to have the opportunity to focus on something that really matters – with the global economy going down the toilet, people are just mad keen to take a step back from the yawning ocean of negativity and get back to things that are real. The boom times made our lives increasingly frivolous and we were fixated on things that didn't matter a jot in the grander scheme of things. We became increasingly individualistic and selfish. The 'readjustment' in the global economy is forcing people to reassess their lifestyle and their priorities, and to admit that maybe we really do need each other, after all.

In addition to the monthly meeting, lots of informal extra-curricular activities have sprung up around the network. We do occasional visits to other members' gardens, which is always very educational and inspiring in the 'God, what the hell have we been doing with our time?' sort of way. On one visit, our host prepared dandelion and nettle smoothies, which has changed the way I look at dandelions forever (during the spring I see dandelions at the side of the road with their distinctive yellow flower and I now think 'health food' instead of 'weed'). We have done seed and seedling swaps, which are very thrifty and also a lot of fun. I think the result of all this is that we are all getting better results from our food producing. But there's so much more. We have made some great friends and become part of an incredible community of people. And there is, perhaps, nothing more important than that.

Shortly after we set up the network in Waterford, Dave, one of our members, established a second one in the village here – it's called GIY Dunmore. Dave worked in theatre for decades and is the closest our group has to a guerrilla gardener – he likes to go around the village planting raspberry canes at random because he just likes the idea of there being free fruit around the place. You gotta love that. At the time, I wasn't quite sure how I felt about the fact that we had another network. On one level I was delighted, but on another I was worried.

We were only getting started and we had a schism already! It was like the whole Judean People's Front/People's Front of Judea thing in *The Life of Brian*. But I needn't have worried. Soon after that, another network got up and running in New Ross, County Wexford, this one established by Will Sutherland, who runs the John Seymour School of Self-Sufficiency in Killowen. They had over sixty people at their first meeting. Then a fourth network got set up in Tramore, established by Sally, who was on the hen courses and was involved in our steering group in Waterford – they had so many people at the first meeting they had to move to a bigger venue for their second one. We have had contact through our website (www.GIYireland.com) from people all over Ireland interested in the idea and very gradually we are starting to see glimpses of a much bigger picture – GIY is an idea whose time has come.

There is phenomenal interest in food producing at the current time and these groups work on two levels – they give people the practical help they need to get started, and, perhaps more importantly, they create a sense of community so lacking in modern society. We recently set up a sort of national umbrella organisation called GIY Ireland to promote the idea of GIY networks, to help local chapters to stay connected and to share ideas. The organisation is still in its infancy – teeny, tiny shoots of potential, but who knows where it could go next? GIY Manhattan? GIY Rio de Janeiro? Yeah, you can tell I'm getting carried away. But there is genuinely a feeling in the air, a straw in the wind – and other cliches too.

If you allow it to be, the harvest can be a time of incredible celebration, and it is quite right that it should be so. We *should* be celebrating at this time of the year, even though it might be kind of quaint to be doing so. The joy of the harvest is another thing that the modern food chain's aggressive assault on seasonality has deprived us of, for if every vegetable and every type of fruit is available all the year round, then there is no reason to celebrate in the traditional harvest months. But, as Home Farmers who have been trying to eat seasonally all year, the joy of the harvest is truly ours to savour and we should really try to enjoy it. We should cherish the sights, sounds and smells of autumn – our apple trees laden down with ripe fruit and the polytunnel heaving with produce; the display of technicolour leaves that the trees are putting on in our honour; we should enjoy lifting crops and getting them into storage; we should delight in the *process of processing* – spending time shelling and dicing and chopping and pickling, secure and happy in the knowledge that we are putting produce away for the rainy, cold days that will assuredly come; we should take time to cook and then delight in heroic meals in the company and conviviality of good friends.

There's a strange irony to the harvest celebration, however. It is a time of joy and decadence, but it is ever so slightly tainted by a hint of sadness. There are still two good months of growing left in the garden, so it's far too early to go all melancholy, but there are dark clouds of barrenness gathering on the horizon, nonetheless. All the gathering and harvesting that we are doing at the moment is done in the knowledge that we are doing so because the pickings will soon be very slim indeed. The sight of the yellow leaves on our tomato plants, or the odd exhausted pod hanging from a bean plant, are enough to remind us of this fact and draw our attention slowly to the leanness of winter. Two things happened in the past few days that gave me pause for thought even at the height of abundance: first of all, I was sowing some spring cabbage and spinach seedlings. Given that there is so much wonderful produce yet to be enjoyed in the vegetable plot, it's strange to think of a time when we will really, really appreciate spring cabbage and spinach as the first greens of the next year's growing season. But I *could* imagine it, and it made me sort of sad. We also started to harvest the very first of our pumpkins and winter squashes, two vegetables, which, while traditionally associated with autumn, are really better utilised in winter. While they will taste great right now, they really come into their own as stored vegetables, put away until after Christmas when they will really be appreciated. And, carrying a basket of them up the garden, I found my mind wandering to last winter when we were enjoying squashes in stews – and that made me feel sort of sad again. The other day we lit the stove for the first time in about four months, and while we enjoyed sitting by it late on a cool autumn evening, it felt like a sombre occasion at the same time. All over the garden, scaly and furry things are stocking and bulking up in preparation for a long hibernation, and there is a feeling that perhaps we are too.

Ah nonsense! There is still so much to enjoy. All the great 'summer' produce like peas and tomatoes, courgettes and cucumbers, aubergines and peppers are still thriving in the September garden and we are also starting to harvest carrots, celery and parsnips. We're still busy. Since the chickens and piggies are now gone, we have less to do on the feeding front every day, but we are still busy watering and there is a huge amount of processing to do. As the evenings get slightly chillier, we don't mind spending evenings in the kitchen (rather than being in the garden) getting things into the freezer, making chutneys, preserves and the like.

HARVESTING APPLES

We put in six or seven apple trees when we moved here first, and though they are well established at this stage, they are really only getting started in terms of producing food. They are also, sorry to say, greatly neglected on the pruning and maintenance front. Unfortunately, apples are prone to quite a few diseases and greatly loved by pests. Still, despite this shoddy treatment, last year we had a reasonable harvest and I have high hopes that at some point in the future I will have enough apples to consider converting some into cider to keep me lubricated over the winter. Eating your own apples through the winter and into the following spring is a great treat, particularly when you consider that your supermarket will only be able to offer you highly travelled or heavily sprayed specimens at those times of the year (almost all commercially grown apples will be sprayed dozens of times before they reach the supermarket). Be particularly wary of apples for sale in the late spring and early summer – these are, most likely, eight to ten months old and you have to ask yourself how they have survived that long. Far better to steer clear of apples at those times of the year and get your vitamins and minerals instead from your own seasonal produce like rhubarb, and the great triumvirate of soft fruits – strawberries, raspberries and blueberries.

Back to the present, however, and the puzzle of what to do with whatever apples your trees have produced. You need to keep an eye on them for signs of ripeness – they reach maturity at different times, depending on the variety and the climate, so the best test is to take a bite. A mature fruit will be crisp and tasty and the flesh will be yellow or white – certainly not green. Only the perfect apples should be considered as candidates for storage – the less-than-perfect ones will let you down by rotting and will most likely take a whole tray of apples with them in the process. Wrap the good ones in newspaper and place them carefully in crates or boxes in a cool place. We stored wrapped apples quite successfully one year, carefully layered in a sealed black plastic bin, which we left outside where it was nice and cool. Then last year we did the same and most of them rotted – I suspect that some of the fruit that I put in was slightly bad. If you are careful about it, and get the conditions right, stored apples should last until the spring.

There are other ways to process your apple harvest. You can stew them and then freeze them, or, indeed, freeze them in segments (though they won't be great to eat this way). You can divert apples to jams and chutneys – a particular autumn favourite of ours is blackberry and apple jam, which is just exquisite. Apple juice can also be very successfully frozen in small portions. If you don't have your own apple trees or if you don't have enough produce to store, there's still a good argument, I think, in favour of buying good quality (organic, if you can get them) local apples in bulk in the autumn, and storing or processing them yourself.

Our harvest bounty is improved considerably when we collect the meat from the pigs. It's three weeks since the rueful day in the abattoir and we've been counting down the days to the moment we get to try the first cuts of meat from our own pigs. Will it be lean or fatty? Full of flavour or lacking? Collecting the pig meat is another slightly stressful occasion because the meat is frozen in portions and consequently there's no time to lose in getting it back to base, sorting through it all, and getting it into our freezer before it starts to thaw. Next year, I am hoping to do the processing of the meat myself, with the help of Nicky and some of my buddies from the GIY network. I would like to try my hand at making some sausages, and my own cures for rashers, hams and the like. But, for the moment, we are really lucky to have found a fantastic abattoir and butcher in County Wexford, who deals patiently with our requests about how we want the meat processed, and whom we trust to do a good job when it comes to curing the bacon and making sausages. There's very little point in going to the trouble of rearing your own animals only for the butcher to mess things up for you by loading your bacon with additives or making the sausages overly spicy. Our sausages and rashers, for example, are really, really basic, which is just the way we want them. We want to be able to taste the flavour of the meat to work out whether we have done a good job in rearing the animals and picking a breed.

The meat comes to us in two or three large, black sacks filled with individual cuts: hams, pork roasts, cuts of bacon, ribs, sausages, rashers of bacon, pork chops, diced pork, pork fillets. Freezer space is at a premium since we started keeping chickens for the table as well, and the large freezer out in the garage will be completely full of our own meat by evening. The freezer in our kitchen will be the same and some overflow often has to go to the black hole that is the mother-in-law's chest freezer, from which it will never, ever return (Tee-hee!).

The day we get our meat back, we always have a feed of pork chops with some apple sauce, because they are quick and easy to cook and they give a good indication of how the whole thing has fared. Commercially produced pork chops, in my opinion, are simply not worth eating anymore – they are just too lean, too dull and too tasteless. Our own pork chops have a wonderful, intensely porky, almost gamey flavour. The following morning we will usually have a good old-fashioned fry-up with sausages and rashers – any older person who has tasted a fry-up from our pigs tells us that it is like a taste of the old days. And so it continues, one artery-clogging week after another. And dear God, do we love it. As well as feeding our-selves, our own meat is also 'currency', and we use a small amount of it for barter. I already mentioned the pork-for-lamb swap. Our friendly local farmer also gives us a huge quantity of cow manure in exchange for a few cuts of meat, and, of course, we have to repay the friends, family and neighbours who contributed scraps to the pig bucket during the year.

Hens don't fly, but they can manage an impressive power-leap when the mood takes them. That means that most fences/barriers/ditches that you put in their way won't really keep them in if they really want to get out. A few years back, having had enough of our hens laying out in ditches (which meant we weren't able to find the eggs), I spent a macho weekend building a mini-fortress of 1.5m-high chicken wire, which closed them into an area of about 30 square metres. Were they happy with this sizeable plot of land to roam on? Were they heck. They were used to being completely free range and didn't like this poultry equivalent of Shawshank prison, so each morning a few of them would fly out over the top of the chicken wire and lay their egg in their favourite little spot in the ditch. Watching them foil my elaborate fencing job, and driven half-mad from the need to hunt for those precious eggs, I resorted to clipping their wings.

Wing clipping is a harmless way to prevent your chickens (and ducks if you want) from flying. It involves using a sharp scissors to cut off the first ten flight feathers on one wing. This causes a bird to lack the balance needed for flight and, in theory, discourages them from trying – it is also temporary, because it lasts only until new feathers grow after the next moult (maybe a few months in young birds, or up to a year for older ones). It is completely painless for the hen – rather like getting a haircut for you or me. It also won't be noticeable when they are walking around, since the primary flying feathers are hidden underneath when the wings are folded. We found that clipping the flight feathers on only one wing didn't work with some of the more determined Andy Dufresne-type characters among our flock, and so we had to revisit them and clip the other side too. If you feel bad about clipping wings (and you will), give yourself a stern talking to: the reason you keep hens, if you are a Home Farmer, is so that they will provide eggs. If you can't find the eggs because they are laying in a ditch or in the neighbour's garden, then you are wasting your time. Also, it's your responsibility to keep your flock safe. If they are able to leave the garden at will, you are putting them in harm's way.

Here's how to do it. Once you have spent three hours running around after your hen to catch it, spread one of the wings out to display all the feathers. You will need an attractive assistant to help you to hold the hen and keep it calm. The feathers you want to cut are the primary flight feathers which are the longest ones towards the front of the wing. You can leave the first one alone if you want, as it is visible when they tuck their wing into the body, and your hen might look a little odd without it. Cut about 6cm off the other nine, to bring them almost in line with the second row of feathers. Keep apologising to the hen in the process for the inconvenience you are causing – and *voila!* your work is done. You will need to carry this out again each time a hen moults as she will grow back new primary feathers to replace the ones that you have cut.

(PS: some smart guy will, no doubt, tell you that wing clipping means a hen is less likely to be able to escape a fox. Believe me, a hen wouldn't escape a fox if it had ten sets of wings and a jetpack.)

I mentioned elsewhere that growing cucumbers makes you feel like a really expert grower even if you're not – well, if you can get even one really enormous orange pumpkin growing, you will feel about ten times better about it than you did even about your finest specimen of cucumber. One of the women in our GIY group gave me a pumpkin that she grew herself, which was about twice as big as anything I had ever grown. The secret to growing such a giant, she told me, is that pumpkins love manure, so she actually grows hers in her compost heap. Very clever. This particular giant was so heavy it was actually quite a job to get it back to the car (and I had to put it on the front seat with its seatbelt on, for fear I'd have to brake suddenly and it would take off through the windscreen like a cannonball). It took us about two hours to process it – we had container-loads of delicious pumpkin soup in the freezer for months afterwards. There is something magical about the notion that a small seed, sown expectantly back in the spring, can produce something that enormous and provide so much food.

Pumpkins are only one member of a very delicious family of fleshy vegetables that are related to the aforementioned cucumber, and also include gherkins, marrows, courgettes and squashes. We have been harvesting courgettes (called zucchini by our friends across the pond) since July, and they are plentiful indeed – two or three plants will produce more than enough courgettes to see you though July, August and September. I like courgettes just fine, and appreciate that they are so easy to grow, but they can be bland enough, especially if they are left to grow too big (though if you peel thin slivers off, give a good dose of olive oil, loads of rock-salt and pepper and then cook on a griddle pan, they will be transformed). I have no time at all for marrows, which are simply overgrown cour-gettes. Pumpkins and winter squashes, on the other hand, are well worth growing and they will be starting to come into their own right around now. They are gaining popularity as vegetables to eat and it's quite right that it should be so, because they taste very good indeed and store incredibly well. They are, therefore, a really useful addition to the Home Farmer's culinary arsenal. Pumpkins will look great in your window at Halloween, but they are probably better directed to the larder or the kitchen, where they make a delicious addition to a soup or a tray of roasted winter vegetables. The nutty flavour of winter squashes (like butternut) is, to my mind, the quintessential taste of autumn.

PAULA MEE'S NUTRITION BITES: SQUASHES, COURGETTES AND PUMPKINS

Pumpkins and squashes are a source of vitamin A, in particular beta-carotene, a powerful antioxidant vitamin. Since they are largely composed of water, they are lower in calories than many other vegetables.

Nutrition per Portion (80g):

Veg	Calories	Fat (g)	Salt (g)	Saturated Fat (g)
Pumpkin	10	0.2	0	0.1
Squash	29	0.1	0	0
Courgette	14	0.3	0	0.1

Both plants look great at this time of the year, with their extensive leaf canopy tumbling across the beds and often out onto paths. You can grow some varieties vertically if you want, training them up support canes, but you will need to provide additional support for the fruits when they come, particularly the larger ones. We just let them sprawl along the ground. They are relatively low maintenance – the formidable leaf growth means that weeds simply don't stand a chance, which is very welcome, but, on the other hand, to plump up that lovely fruit requires lots and lots of water – they are exceptionally thirsty. A very large pumpkin needs as much as ten litres of water a week.

Pumpkin and winter squash seeds are sown way back in early spring – the earlier the better, in fact. The seeds are best sown vertically rather than lying them flat, to prevent them from rotting. We usually sow two or three seeds in each 8cm pot at a depth of 3cm in February, using a heating mat to get them started and then moving them on to individual, larger pots as required. After hardening off the plants, we put them out into the soil in late May in a bed that has plenty of manure in it – it doesn't even need to be particularly well-rotted as these babies love their muck. In fact, if you fail to give pumpkin and winter squash plants the nutrients that they need in the soil, they will produce terribly puny fruits that won't be worth storing. If you want to grow a really large pumpkin, cut off all but one of the fruits (the fastest growing one) on each plant as they develop – this will allow the plant to focus its energies on creating one big momma rather than lots of smaller little babies. Once the fruits have started to develop, you need to keep a close eye on them. They need sunlight, so cut away any leaves that are blocking them and make sure that slugs don't start to nibble on them. Don't let the fruits rest on wet soil or ground as they may start to rot, so put a roof slate or equivalent underneath them.

I don't think there's any point in eating squashes and pumpkins now in the autumn, when there is so much other stuff still fresh in the garden which doesn't store so well. They will store for up to six months and you will really appreciate them in January and February (or even later) when the only thing you have fresh in the garden is some boring old spinach (sorry, spinach, I really should stop putting you down like that). Taking a big, heavy fruit from storage in the grim winter will make you feel like

Simple Pumpkin Soup

Melt 20g of butter in a big saucepan, add a chopped large onion and two or three chopped cloves of garlic, and sweat over a gentle heat for five minutes. Dice 500g of pumpkin (discard the tough skin, but you can keep the seeds if you want – dried out they make a lovely crunchy addition to the top of a loaf of brown bread, or you can keep them to grow next year's crop) and add it to the pan, sweating for about five minutes. Then add 750ml chicken stock and plenty of seasoning. A bit of grated nutmeg or some fresh thyme leaves will also improve the flavour. Cover, and cook until the pumpkin is tender, which could take anything from 15 minutes to half an hour, depending on the size of the dices. Blend the soup in a liquidiser. You can make larger batches of this soup for the freezer if you have a particularly large pumpkin.

it's your birthday; slice it open in hushed reverence to (hopefully) reveal the moist, orangey flesh inside. If you want your pumpkins and squashes to store well, you need to leave them on the plants for as long as possible so that they are fully ripe and have developed the tough outer skin that will help them to retain water inside the fruit. It is that water retention that will make the flesh nice and moist to eat. Once the skin has started to crack slightly, cut the fruit from the plant, leaving about 10cm of stalk on it. You need to cure it by leaving it sit in the sun in the polytunnel or greenhouse, or any sunny spot, for about two weeks. After that, store it on a straw-lined shelf in a cool, dry place. Try to avoid the stored pumpkins being in contact with each other, don't stack them.

SEPTEMBER GROWER'S CALENDAR

Prep Work
- With the inevitable focus on harvesting, it's easy to forget about those important 'prep' tasks for the remainder of the season, or indeed for next year. Lift crops that have finished growing and remove weeds from empty ground before they set seed. Dress 'bare' soil with manure, compost or plant green manures.

- Don't neglect the compost heap – if it's ready, empty it out to make way for new material. If it is not ready, turn it over every few weeks to improve the decomposition rate.
- Late autumn and early winter is the best time to plant fruit trees and bushes, so if you don't have any or want to get more, now is the time to research them and prepare the ground.

To-do List

- Wasps can be a real problem as fruit ripens. Wasp traps made from jars of sugary water or the dregs of marmalade or jam in jars are effective. Pick up any windfalls or damaged fruit (feed it to the pigs) as they will attract wasps if left on the ground. Once the wasps finish munching those, they will probably move on to all the rest of your fruit.
- Pumpkins and winter squash continue to grow when other things are starting to fade, so you need to continue to water until the end of this month.
- French bean pods are most likely to be too tough to eat now, so you can leave the pods on the plants to seed – save the seeds for sowing next year.
- Remove old canes of summer raspberries once they have finished fruiting.
- Watering requirements often change slightly as we move into autumn. Continue to water regularly, but be careful not to over-water the foliage of tomato, aubergine, pepper and chilli-pepper plants, as that could encourage grey mould. Give a good soak once a week to celery, celeriac, marrows, courgettes, pumpkins, runner beans and leeks.
- It's a busy time in the kitchen, converting that hard-won harvest into fuel for the winter. Those tired vegetables that we threw on the compost heap really should have been put in the freezer – in a box, in a pot or in a jar. Shame on us.
- Start removing surplus leaves from your tomato plants, which allows air to circulate around the plants and sunshine to fall on the fruit (which helps them to ripen).
- Continue to check for pests and diseases in the greenhouse/polytunnel and in the garden.
- As the nights cool down, close up your greenhouse or polytunnel earlier to preserve heat.
- As the stems of asparagus begin to yellow, cut them back to 10cm high.

Sowing Seeds

- Last month for sowing perpetual spinach and oriental salads – these really will be worth it in the New Year when there's almost nothing else to eat, so get sowing! In the polytunnel/greenhouse, sow lettuce, mustard, cress, basil, coriander, parsley, radish, dwarf early pea (eg Feltham First), broad bean, cauliflower (seed, for planting next spring) rocket, chicory, onion seed and garlic.
- Outside, sow white turnip seeds to crop around Christmas, and autumn onion sets, eg Centurion and Sturon.

Planting Out

- Plant out strawberry runners as early as possible this month.
- Pot-up some strong parsley plants in a large pot for winter use.
- Spring cabbage plants can be put in this month, in a sunny spot.
- Woody herbs such as sage, rosemary and thyme often root where their stems touch the soil – separate these out and plant to give them time to establish before growth stops for the winter.

GRUB'S UP – WHAT'S IN SEASON?

September is a great month for harvesting because the summer vegetables and fruits are joined by those more traditionally associated with autumn/winter, eg parsnips, swedes and celeriac.

Lift your onions once the foliage withers and dies – leave them to dry out in the sun or in the polytunnel/greenhouse (but eat a few immediately to savour the taste of a really fresh onion).

The great autumn tree fruits – apples, plums, pears – are now ripening. Pears should be picked when ripe and then stored for several weeks before eating.

Continue to harvest salad leaves, tomatoes, shallots, radish, potatoes, carrots, turnips, beetroots, cauliflower, cucumbers, peppers and chilli-peppers, french and runner beans, courgettes, spinach, leeks, red cabbage, summer cabbage, aubergine, sweet corn.

Go berry picking! Blackberries, sloes etc are now in season.

10

EVERY SUCH THING
AS A FREE LUNCH

LATE AUTUMN: OCTOBER

rabbits – foraging – growing herbs – raised beds – slow food – onions

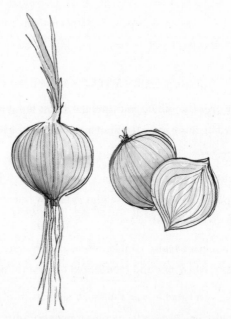

There are two types of people in this world – the type who think rabbits are cute, adorable and fluffy, and the type who think that all rabbits are the devil's spawn. It's no surprise that the people who think they are evil creatures are generally the people who grow their own vegetables. This year alone, rabbits have caused me more grief than just about any other pest in the garden, except perhaps slugs. But, as we all know, you can't *eat* slugs. Rabbits, however ...

Pretty much every morning when I wake up and look out the window there are a few rabbits out on the lawn, munching happily on the grass. This should be an idyllic picture (I will admit, if forced to do so, that they are a little bit cute), but instead of standing there marvelling at the diversity of God's earth, I can feel my blood pressure rising because I know the little gits have most likely been raising havoc during the night (or perhaps are planning it for the following night). Every morning, I think to myself that if only I had a shotgun I could take it out and take aim. Ah, who am I kidding? I'm a terrible shot, so even if the rabbit was the size of an elephant, I would still miss it.

I will give you an idea of just how destructive rabbits are. Last year, I spent weeks growing kohlrabi from seed in modules in the polytunnel. In early summer, I spent an entire day preparing a bed outside in the plot and then lovingly planted about twenty of them in two neat rows. I was immensely tired, but satisfied, at the end of the day, leaning on my shovel admiring my work. Next morning, I came out to admire my work again and, yes, you've guessed it, rabbits had eaten every single last one of them. Months of work, gone in one night of greedy bunny-gorging. Last winter I put in two new raised beds up at the top of the garden near the house. They are separate from the main vegetable plot and were designed specifically with rabbits in mind. They are made of railway sleepers and are a little under a metre high (apparently high enough so that rabbits can't get up on to them) and about 10m long. We put about 5 tonnes of soil into them, which, as you can imagine, is quite a bit of muck-hauling. And all because of rabbits. And wouldn't you know it – when we were finished and had started growing things in these new rabbit-proof beds, what did the rabbits do? They thumbed their noses at us, climbed right up on top of them and helped themselves to whatever was available.

As I mentioned in Chapter 8, rabbits were also the reason that we constructed a picket fence around our vegetable plot. Again, there was considerable expense and work involved (for me and the brother-in-law – well, okay, mainly the brother-in-law who's much handier at that sort of thing) – but unfortunately, it's the only really effective way of keeping them out. With the added wire I mentioned earlier, it mainly works a treat, but every now and then I will find one of the pickets in the fence scratched (or chewed?) away and know that they have been working at it overnight trying to get in, and reminding us that they are still there, lest we forget. Anyway, all that's by way of introduction as to why I am not at all squeamish about the notion of killing a rabbit for its meat. It's amazing, really, that I feel the need to justify myself when it comes to rabbits. I mean, each time I eat a chicken I don't feel the need to defend myself by outlining all the wrongs that chickens have committed against me. Just goes to show you, we have a very strange attitude to the meat we eat, one that is inconsistent and often illogical. Is there a taboo about eating rabbit meat because they are sometimes kept as pets? Or because they are so cute and cuddly looking?

It's strange that rabbit has fallen off society's meat radar (particularly in Ireland) because it is a meat that tastes very good indeed. Traditionally, they were much hunted for their meat and some smallholders even bred them. Rabbits are prolific breeders –

we all know the phrase about bonking like rabbits – well, that translates into about forty offspring a year. Just three breeding rabbits would provide a meal for a family once a week all year round. That's pretty impressive, given that they don't need a lot of space (you need approximately 8000 sq metres (about 2 acres) to rear a cow but just 1 square metre to rear a breeding female rabbit, who will produce 80kg of meat per year); they also require little time or investment, and the meat is reputedly better for you than chicken, pork and beef (according to a report by the Food and Agriculture Organisation at the United Nations, rabbit meat is easier to digest than most meats, is highly nutritious, low-fat, low-cholesterol and rich in proteins). It's pretty unlikely that Mrs Kelly will ever agree to have breeding rabbits around the place and, as I mentioned, I am an absolutely woeful shot, so I must look to other methods of capture. I tried laying a trap down at the end of the garden one time, but I am a complete wuss about trapping animals and I lay in bed that night racked with guilt: what if a rabbit got trapped and lay there in agony overnight? Eventually, I felt so reprehensible, I had to get up at about midnight and go down in my boxers with the torch to dismantle the device. I know – pathetic.

As it happened, fate was shining down on me. Last year, when our Springer spaniel Ozzie died, we got a new dog, a rescued Red Setter called Amber (personally, I think the name makes her sound like a lady of the night, but that's her name and we're stuck with it). She's a beauty, but completely out of control and possessed with a dangerous combination of boundless energy and incredible stupidity. But, as it turns out, she has quite a talent for catching rabbits. It helps that she's the fastest dog in the universe, of course, but she's also got a killer instinct, which Sam, our Lab, doesn't. I've seen him run down the garden after a rabbit and catch up with it, but then he stalls as if he's thinking: Bloody hell, I've caught up with it, what exactly do I do now? Amber, on the other hand, knows exactly what to do.

Last week I was out walking the two dogs in the fields and, next minute, I turn around and see her taking off like a bullet after a rabbit. She runs into a ditch after it and all I can see is her bum in the air, tail wagging furiously. To be honest, I'm not expecting much and I just walk past her. Next thing I know, she's trotting along beside me with the rabbit in her mouth. She dumps it at my feet and looks at me expectantly, waiting for praise, a treat, payment, I don't know what. The rabbit is clearly dead, whether from a heart attack or Amber breaking its neck, I am not sure. The fur is not damaged and there's no blood or anything like that. I give the dog a pat on the head and she picks it up again and trots along beside me, carrying it all the way home. (By the way, all this time, Sam, the supposedly intelligent one, is just standing there looking at me, the big useless article.)

It didn't occur to me to do anything other than prepare it for the pot. It just seemed the right thing. I mean, I don't want to get all new age or spiritual about this, but when an animal has given its life in a chase, I think it's only right that you celebrate that by putting it to good use. What's the alternative? Throw it over the ditch and let the birds/rats get it? There was also something about the time of year that made it feel right too – coming into autumn, evenings closing in, lots of root vegetables available in the vegetable plot to go in the pot with it.

Rabbits are 'paunched' or de-gutted to prepare them for the table and it's best to do this immediately, otherwise the meat can become tainted. It's not the most pleasant job in the universe, but it's a damn sight less smelly than gutting a chicken or fish, I can tell you. I guess this is because wild rabbits have a totally natural diet that consists only of grass and a healthy proportion of produce from your vegetable garden – ie, no processed grain.

All you do is make a cut down through the belly and pull out the innards, being careful not to pierce any of the organs. It is an entirely freaky experience to look at the bright red heart and lungs of an animal that, minutes earlier, were pumping air and blood around its body. Never mind these thoughts – back to work! Lots of people retain the heart, liver and kidneys to eat, but I'm only learning when it comes to being barbaric, so maybe another day. This time around, they went to Amber as a prize for being my favourite dog in the world (Sorry, Sam, but when have you ever provided me with a meal?). She didn't seem at all perturbed that all she was getting as payment for her ingenuity and speed were these tiny organs. Once you've gutted the rabbit, you can hang it for twenty-four hours – strictly speaking, a rabbit doesn't need to be hung because it's not game, but some people say it tastes better if left alone for a while. To be honest, after the gutting, I was quite happy to leave it be for a day before I needed to think about skinning and jointing. The rabbit hung from a beam in the garage for a day and Mrs Kelly gave out quite a bit about that, particularly when she went into the garage to get something from the freezer and came quite literally face to face with it – for a farmer's daughter, she can sometimes be pretty squeamish.

Skinning a rabbit is a lot easier than you would imagine. You make a nick in (or remove) the paws and then pull the skin down over the body. People say it's like removing a glove, and this description does fit the bill quite well. You stop pulling when you get to the head

and then just cut the head off, and *voilà*, your work is done. The jointing is a little trickier than for a chicken, and I was sort of feeling my
way along, to be honest. You need a very sharp knife. I removed the
front legs first, then cut the muscle that covers the gut; then I severed
the backbone and finally removed the back legs. Once you have that
done, you are ready to cook.

Rabbit can be cooked in a number of ways. It will make a good
substitute in any recipe that demands chicken, but bear in mind
there is far less meat and it is generally thought to be dry if roasted
(there is so little fat on rabbit meat that there is actually an illness
called 'rabbit starvation', a form of acute malnutrition that arises
from excessive consumption of very lean meats). Boiled is therefore
the norm. I fried up some lardons (the fat from the bacon is important
to counteract dryness in the rabbit meat), then browned the meat. A
trip to the garden produced some fine herbs and vegetables to accom-
pany it – garlic, onions, carrots, celery, thyme and parsley – the
hunter-gatherer excitement in me bubbling to a crescendo. I added
some stock and wine, and cooked it for about an hour. A nice way to
finish it off is to remove the meat and vegetables, reduce the cooking
liquid and add some cream and Dijon mustard.

A fine, comforting meal was had. Rabbit is a far more complex
piece of meat than chicken and this dish had a strong, gamey taste. I
thought it was wonderful, but Mrs Kelly could not be convinced to
try it, which was a pity. Perhaps it was her meeting with its head in
the garage that put her off. A certain person, who will remain name-
less, tried to get me all freaked out about eating the rabbit (warning
me that if I started to weep from the eyes after the meal, I should
immediately head for A&E because that would be the myxomatosis

setting in) but I didn't let their scaremongering get to me. My advice to anybody who wants it is: don't be tempted to feel any twangs of guilt as you tuck in – this is fresh, one hundred percent free-range organic meat at its absolute finest, and completely free too. So relish every single bite and remember – by eating this rabbit, you are doing your vegetable patch an enormous favour, so consider it your sacred Home Farming duty. If only the dog could catch the other five hundred rabbits in our garden, we would be laughing.

Rabbit Stew

250g streaky bacon or pancetta

1 tbsp olive oil

1 wild rabbit, skinned and jointed (1.5-1.8kg) – if you don't have a speedy Red Setter, ask your local butcher if they can source

Chopped vegetables – whatever your veggie plot has to offer you; a clove of garlic, a large onion, three good sized carrots and a stalk of celery would be good

Plenty of chopped herbs (thyme, parsley, bay leaf etc) and seasoning

600ml stock and glass of white wine (and maybe drink one as well after what you've been through)

Optional – cream and mustard

Cut the bacon into cubes and fry it in some oil in a large pan. Remove to a casserole dish. Put the rabbit pieces in the hot pan and fry on each side until golden brown. Add to the casserole. Then throw the veggies into the pan and get the juices from the cooked meat all over them before putting them in with the meat. Deglaze the pan with the stock and pour that into the casserole with the wine. Add the herbs and season well. Bring the whole lot to the boil, cover it with a lid and then transfer it to a hot oven. It will probably need about an hour and a half, but judge this carefully – an older animal will need longer. The meat will be meltingly tender when it's ready. If you want, at the end you can pour off the juice into a clean pot, de-grease it, and then add some double cream and Dijon mustard, or perhaps a serving of Mushroom à la Crème. This will make for an altogether richer dish. Serve with mashed spuds.

Of course, the stew described above, or any stew for that matter, would be a sorry affair without the addition of plenty of fresh herbs. Before we started growing our own food here on the Home Farm, we used to buy those packets of herbs that you get in the supermarket. Occasionally we have been known to do our shopping in an organised manner, ie buying only the ingredients we need to make four or five recipes to see us through the week. And let's say that those recipes required the Scarborough Fair foursome of parsley, sage, rosemary and thyme, and maybe basil and mint too – those five or six packets of herbs must have cost the guts of €20. Pure madness.

The cost of them is one thing – but you also have to consider the inferior quality and waste involved. They may look okay when you buy them, but within a day of getting them home, they start to deteriorate and in no time at all they are festering at the back of the fridge and you are trying to ignore them as you reach in to get milk for your breakfast each morning. You might use a portion of the herbs as required by the recipe, then the rest get left there and, of course, the next time you go to use them they are gone off. And while we are on the subject of waste, what about the five or six plastic cartons that you had to discard or recycle as a result? (Incidentally, despite years of government campaigns to get us to 'reduce, re-use, re-cycle', it appears that the packaging waste being produced by our food system is getting more problematic rather than less. Even vegetables like tomatoes and mushrooms, which we used to pop into paper bags, now seem to come in plastic cartons. As always, the best solution to these issues is to avoid the supermarket as much as possible and grown the vegetables oneself.)

Herbs make an unbelievable difference in the kitchen, especially when they're fresh and when you can pick large quantities of them. Sit a measly sprig of rosemary on top of your roast lamb and it will make very little difference, but pick an enormous bunch of rosemary from your garden and put the lamb sitting on top of it in the oven, and the lamb (and your house) will be infused with a wonderful aroma. Grow huge quantities of basil in the summer and you can enjoy basil pesto or Caprese salads of basil, mozzarella and tomato for months on end. Your own fresh mint will make a delicious tea, or a great accompaniment to boiled spuds or your first garden peas.

I wince when I think about the amount of herbs that we used to buy because, of all the things that you grow in the garden, herbs are by far the easiest and, of course, there is simply nothing more useful than growing them in your garden. Whether you have five acres or just a balcony, you should be able to get prodigious quantities of all the herbs you need, with little bother. They will do equally well in pots or containers as they will in the open ground of a vegetable patch. When it comes to working out which herbs to plant, have a think about what herbs you like the taste of and what uses you have for them. The herbs discussed below are mainly for culinary purposes, but you might, of course, grow herbs for fragrance or for medicinal properties.

A lot of the herbs we are familiar with – marjoram/oregano, lavender, thyme, rosemary and dill – are native to the Mediterranean region and will therefore need moderate warmth and sunlight to thrive. We grow most of our herbs in the polytunnel and we have never gone short. Some herbs, like parsley and mint, will do well in partial shade. Some herb plants (like rosemary, chive and thyme) will last for years, but others (like basil, dill and borage) have to be grown each year (though propagation using cuttings or runners from existing plants is an easy and thrifty way forward). You can prolong the season of herbs in many ways. You can dry and freeze them, for example – a nice trick is to chop herbs and put them in ice cube trays, then fill with water and freeze. Simply pop a cube or two into a stew for a quick herb boost. You can also lift some of your perennial herb plants out of the ground in the autumn, re-pot them and bring them inside for use over the winter.

GROWING HERBS

Annuals and Biennials

Basil: Nothing brings out your inner Italian quite like basil. Sow it in pots of compost in March and plant out in the polytunnel or greenhouse in June. Pinch growing tips regularly to produce bushy rather than leggy plants. Pot up plants in the autumn and bring indoors. The biggest barrier to a large harvest is that pest of pests – the slug!

Parsley: Parsley is a rather workaday herb, to my mind, but it is very useful, nonetheless, and I particularly love it in omelettes and scrambled eggs. And, of course, you couldn't make stuffing or garlic bread without it. Sow seed in spring for summer crop, and again in autumn to have over winter – but beware, germination is painfully slow, so you might want to buy a little parsley plant instead. It will grow well indoors or out.

Dill: The feathery leaves of dill are attractive in their own right, but it's also a stunning culinary herb, much used with fish. We also use it when pickling cucumbers, and in dill and mustard dressing (yum). As you might gather from its delicate physique, dill hates to be disturbed, so it's best to sow it where you plan to grow it. Sow in April, about 20cm apart. Harvest the leaves as soon as they start to appear.

Perennials

Rosemary: Rosemary is one of those herbs that pretty much goes with everything. It likes a sunny spot in the garden and once it takes off you will have a serious crop – so much so that many people use it as a border or hedge. Prune in spring to keep it in check. Probably easiest to buy a small plant of rosemary to plant out in spring. Renew it every three or four years as it tends to get a bit woody. It's a perfect accompaniment to all kinds of fish and meats, such as chicken, pork and lamb.

Thyme: Nothing says 'warming winter stew' like a sprig of thyme, and it is also the partner of parsley for stuffing. It's a compact, attractive little shrub with a beautiful little flower, and can be picked all-year round. Once you get a crop going, you will never need to buy it again, so it's a good investment to buy a sturdy little plant to put out in spring. We grow ours in the polytunnel and it does nicely there, but it will also be fine outside. Every three years or so, divide the plants and re-plant.

Sage: A beautiful shrub with grey-green leaves and blue flowers, sage is one of the strongest herbs and should therefore be used sparingly. It makes a fine addition to a stew. A single plant will be enough for most people. Plant it in the spring in a well-drained spot and harvest regularly. Though it's perennial, we found that our sage plants didn't fare particularly well after two years or so.

Mint: Have you ever made your own mint sauce? I made it recently for the first time, and I swear I simply couldn't believe that I had made something that tasted that good. To my mind, spuds and peas (especially the new-season ones) are simply not worth having without a very generous sprig of mint in the cooking water. We made a bittersweet mistake of planting mint in our polytunnel one year – we got a great crop of mint, but it absolutely took over and it has really strong, invasive roots. So be careful where you put it – or better still, grow it in containers. It will thrive in all but the worst of soils.

Marjoram/oregano: we have various little shrubs of pot marjoram around the garden in soil and in containers and it basically looks after itself. It is there all year round for us to pick as required. It's a really lovely herb, and perfect for sprinkling over soups before serving, or in tomato sauces, omelettes, salads or stuffings. Buy yourself a little plant and put it out in the garden in spring.

Chives: the chive is a member of the onion family, but it's like a distant cousin that only gets to see the other members at funerals and weddings. It's quite mild, and makes a great addition to salads, soups, omelettes and sauces. Lots of people, including us, use chives as a border in beds – it is an attractive plant with lovely pink/purple flowers. You can grow from seed in early spring and plant out in early summer; divide the plants every four years or so to reinvigorate.

Traditional kitchen-garden vegetables were almost always planted in beautiful, neat little rows, which, you must admit, looked incredibly impressive. But they were also incredibly time consuming. It's worth remembering that the beautiful walled kitchen gardens that you see in many stately homes had a permanent staff to keep them ticking over. Few of us have that sort of luxury these days. As you have probably gathered by now, we are not really a fan of the traditional rows and furrows system, and almost all of our planting is done in raised beds. Yes, indeed, the modern, lazy grower has arrived on the scene like a punk-rocker, throwing the old conventions out the window and replacing them with easier methods. The good news is that we have science on our side to validate our methods. Out go long rows of vegetables in open ground which have to be weeded daily. Out goes single-digging, double-digging – and, come to think of it, any digging at all. Out goes thinning out, pricking out and potting on. In comes raising seeds in modules and then planting them out into a bed system (particularly raised beds), with permanent paths that allow easy access. And scientists and horticulturalists nod their heads sagely and tell us that not only is this the most efficient way to do things, but because we stay off the soil and don't dig it, it does not become compacted and is therefore easier to grow in. Hurrah for science!

Putting in a raised bed system is a lot of hard work and, depending on the materials used, it can be costly, but it will pay enormous dividends in terms of time saved for decades to come. In my opinion, it also the best way for a novice to get going because it is more manageable and keeps things looking neat and tidy, even if you are not. Raised beds are accessible in every way – if you get a dry twenty minutes on a really wet day, for example, you can head into the garden and do a bit of work at your raised beds, whereas open ground is likely to be far too wet and mucky to even think about it. Before you start, have a think about how many beds you want to put in and what you are going to grow.

It makes sense to try and tie in the number of beds you have with some form of a simple crop rotation plan (see Chapter 5) so that it's easy to move things around. A very straightforward, easy-to-manage system would be to have four raised beds – three of them for rotating the three main vegetable groups (legumes, brassicas and roots) and the fourth for perennial vegetables like asparagus or rhubarb, which don't need to be moved at all. Again, the key is to start small – while it might be a pain to have to come back in a few years' time and build more beds, it will be even worse if you put in too many of them now and end up not using them at all. We started with four beds and have added to them each year since. We now have six large beds and four little ones, and I wouldn't rule out a few more popping up in the future.

You can let your creative juices go riot when it comes to the design of your beds. As I mentioned elsewhere, we have square, rectangular and triangular beds; my friend Dave has a nice C-shape bed, which looks really cool and is really handy access-wise. The important thing to remember is that you are not supposed to walk on the soil at any point, so you must be able to reach into the centre of the bed from the sides. We have one square bed that flouts this convention somewhat, and you have to try and tiptoe into the centre if you need to get at something – avoid this mistake at all costs. A 1.2m square bed is therefore considered ideal because the centre of the bed can be reached from both sides. The whole point of these beds, of course, is that you are raising the level of your soil above the ground level – this is particularly important if your soil isn't in great condition (very few people have the perfect loam that vegetables love) as you can bring in soil from outside and start to improve it every year by adding compost and manure. Most vegetables love a good depth of decent soil to grow in and it's a sad fact of life that very few gardens have such a luxury these days. In most housing estates, for example, builders come along at the end of building and toss a layer of poor-quality topsoil across whatever mucky, stony builder's rubble happens to be lying on the ground at the time. In our first house there was about a centimetre of topsoil and then nothing but stones. The only way to improve soil that bad is to add lots and lots of soil on top of it and that's effectively what a raised bed does.

In our situation on the Home Farm, our problem wasn't really soil depth, it was that our soil had terrible drainage. In our second summer here, we had dreadful weather and we would go down to the vegetable plot to find our veggies sitting in pools of water. Clearly, this is not conducive to happy, healthy vegetables. When you increase soil depth, you also increase drainage – in fact, a disadvantage of raised beds is that they drain *too well* and therefore need more watering than regular beds. But, overall, raised beds are basically an ingenious cheat and in no time at all you will have deep, fertile soil that's high in organic matter – perfect for planting.

They can be as expensive or as cheap as you want them to be. When we moved in here we discovered loads of old railway sleepers in a ditch down at the end of the garden and we used them to make our first batch of beds. Sleepers have the advantage of looking very pretty, but are incredibly difficult to work with (they are exceptionally heavy and you need a chainsaw to cut through them – or you could use a regular saw if you have a couple of weeks to spare). Real railways sleepers were sitting on railway tracks for decades and absorbing oil and other nasty toxins from passing trains, and many people are reluctant to use them for that reason. We lined the inside of ours with a black polythene material that you can buy in the garden centre and then we forget about it. Anyway, when it came to build our second batch of beds we didn't have any sleepers left and because I am a neatness freak, I decided to buy more – this is a really expensive way to do things, of course, because each sleeper will cost you about €20 or €30. Visiting other gardens since, I have seen the error of my ways – you can build wonderful-looking raised beds made from scaffold planks, wooden boards, bricks and even concrete blocks. It doesn't need to be expensive. On the other hand, I am pretty sure that the railway sleepers will still be around long after I'm gone, so it is worth thinking about the durability of the timber you use. Softwoods like pine will be cheap as chips, but you may need to replace them in a few years' time.

You do need to put a bit of thought into the construction. When filled with soil, there will be quite a bit of pressure exerted on the sides of the bed, so you should put wooden pegs firmly into the soil on the inside of the bed (they will be covered with soil so you won't see them) and then nail the planks to the pegs for support. How deep you go is largely a matter of preference. We have beds that are just a single sleeper high (about 25cm) and others two sleepers high. I'm inclined to think the latter are somewhat of an indulgence and perhaps even a total waste of soil. But, on the other hand, vegetables that appreciate deep soil, like carrots, absolutely thrive there. I'm not convinced that the deeper beds are all that much easier to work – the big argument in their favour is usually that they are so easy to weed, but to be honest, I think you have to stoop one way or another. You stoop standing up at a tall bed, and you stoop kneeling down at a not-so tall one, so it's probably all the one in the end. The deciding factor may well be how much good quality soil you can get your hands on – a large, deep bed will need lots and lots of soil.

Putting in paths around your beds is another important consideration. You can, of course, just leave grass growing around them. Two of our beds are out on the lawn and they are easy enough to keep tidy. But in the main vegetable patch, we have put in gravel paths, which have the advantage of being weed-free (black landscaping fabric goes down beneath the gravel, which allows water to drain away but prevents weeds from coming up). If we work around the beds on the lawn on a wet day, the grass around them quickly turns muddy, but there is no such problem on the gravel paths. There are lots of other approaches – brick, paving slabs, bark mulch etc. Whatever one you use, make sure that the paths are wide enough so that you can easily move a wheelbarrow around them. If you are considering putting in some raised beds, now is a really good time to think about it. If you get them built in the autumn and early winter and filled with soil, you can add in some compost and manure and cover them down for the rest of the winter so that they will be bursting with nutrients and ready to rock next spring.

ACQUIRING TOPSOIL

In theory, it should be pretty easy to work out how much topsoil you need, and, in any case, you don't need to be hugely accurate – you will, in my experience, always find a use for leftover topsoil. Many suppliers work in cubic yards, so let's work it out that way. A raised bed that is 8ft (2.5m) long, 4ft (1.2m) wide and 2ft (.6m) high has a capacity of 64 cubic feet (8x4x2). To get the cubic yard measurement, you divide by 27. Now, 64 divided by 27 equals 2.3 cubic yards. My advice would be to order less than you think you need. First of all, bear in mind that you don't need to fill your beds to the top with soil – in fact, it's a bad idea to do so because (a) you won't have any space left to add compost/manure and (b) the wind will tend to whip along the surface and dry it out. Far better to fill the beds to within about 10cm of the top so that the sides of the bed act as a windbreak of sorts. You should also aim to incorporate a good deal of compost or manure – a mix of about 60 percent soil and 40 percent compost would be ideal.

Where to get it from? Ask at your local garden centre, gardening club, grower's group or allotment organisation. Failing that, keep an eye on local papers. Be careful who you buy from and ask to see the soil before it's delivered. You do not want delivery of a big lorryload of subsoil full of stones and weeds. In terms of acquiring compost, some local authority compost facilities will give you compost free if you collect it.

The International Slow Food festival *Terra Madre* was hosted in Waterford last autumn, which was very exciting for all concerned – one of the highlights of the weekend for me was the opportunity to interview the founder and chairman of Slow Food International, the great Carlo Petrini, for a piece for *The Irish Times*. Petrini was a food journalist when he established Slow Food in 1989 in opposition to the emerging fast-food culture and, more specifically, in reaction to the prospect of a McDonald's opening up near the beautiful Spanish Steps in Rome. He was horrified at the idea of young Italians standing in line to eat fast food, not just because they would be turning their backs on their wonderful native food culture (what's not to love about Italian food?), but also because he abhorred *the very idea of fast food*. In Petrini's mind, fast food made a mockery of one of life's great pleasures: taking time to produce great food, taking time to cook it, and, most importantly of all, taking time to enjoy that food in the convivial company of others. In other words, instead of fast food, which turns the food we eat into a standardised, globalised, homogenised package (McDonald's makes a virtue out of the fact that a Big Mac tastes the same in Bangkok as it does in Boston), Petrini was advocating the very opposite: *slow food*.

What started as one man's protest has grown into an organisation that promotes local food economies, helps small farmers and food producers, and strives to preserve endangered foods and processes around the world. The organisation now has more than 86,000 members in 144 countries, organised into local groups, called *condotte* in Italy and *convivia* elsewhere. The convivia organise courses and tastings, promote Slow Food ideals, and link consumers with local producers. Over the twenty years since he established Slow Food, Petrini has refined his message to a mantra: Good, Clean and Fair. That is, food that tastes good, is produced in ways that doesn't harm the planet, and pays the producer a good wage. While the Slow Food movement is undoubtedly tackling serious issues: the pervasiveness of fast, cheap, unhealthy and processed food; the lack of sustainability in the food chain; the destruction of small farming and local economies; and the giant multinationals who control every aspect of our food chain, Petrini does not allow the organisation he founded to take itself too seriously. Why should it, he argues, when its core message is about pleasure and the enjoyment of good food in jovial company? Little wonder that chef Alain Ducasse dubbed him the 'Don Juan of the food world'.

This is one of a string of ironies that makes him such a compelling figure. Slow Food is not a political organisation and yet it has growing political power. He promotes a return to tradition and yet is thoroughly modern in his outlook. He wants to change our agricultural system and replace it with local economies, but he is not against globalisation, commerce or industry, as long as they are 'virtuous'. But what really blew me away about the fifty-nine-year-old Italian was just how uncompromising he is. Too often public figures aren't willing to rock the boat too much and are afraid to say things that might be controversial. During the course of our interview, Petrini rammed home a number of basic truths, and they were all the more forceful because of his generally laid-back style. For example, when I put it to him that many people consider organic food to be over-priced and generally elitist, he shot back with a statistic that should make us all stop and think about where our priorities are. 'I have to make an observation on the cost of food,' he said calmly. 'In 1970, in Europe, an average family spent 32 percent of their disposable income on food. Now, an average family spends about 15 percent of their disposable income on food and 12 percent on mobile phones. Perhaps we should make a couple less phone calls and concentrate more on food quality?' He didn't mention that the average income in the 1970s was a fraction of what it is now – so, basically, we are earning far more but spending less on one of the most fundamental things of all: the food that keeps us alive.

In his latest book, *Slow Food Nation*, Petrini places great emphasis on the importance of spending time breaking bread with friends and family. Though many people would question whether this is a realistic goal for a modern family in today's hectic world, he is, again, unapologetic about the need for us to take responsibility for how we live our lives. If we don't have time to dedicate to a family meal, then we have to *make time*, and if we have to cut other things out of our lives, then so be it. The family meal, he maintains, is sacrosanct, and we should be willing to jettison whatever it takes to keep it that way. 'Sharing food with family and friends in conviviality is a great ethical heritage that we have,' he said. 'If this heritage is not shared, this is a complete disaster. This is a fundamental part of our civilisation and also very important for our health and psychological wellbeing.'

Throughout the interview, Petrini talked about the need for each of us to take responsibility – responsibility for our own time, responsibility for the food we choose to eat and, ultimately, responsibility for how much we are willing to pay for it. These can be unpalatable truths for us because we are so used to being able to blame other people for the state of our food chain – blame the producers, blame the supermarket, blame the government. In the Slow Food world, consumers are called 'co-producers', which implies that they share responsibility with the people who produced the food. And as co-producers we should not always look to pay the lowest price for food, but rather the *right* price. If we come back to our discussion in an earlier chapter about chicken, what's the right price to pay? Is it €4? 'Co-producers,' he said, 'are consumers who are fully aware and sensitive to what's involved with regard to food production.'

Across Europe, Slow Food has launched campaigns to encourage hospitals, canteens, universities and schools to buy from local producers. This would be a revolutionary thing, of course, because large organisations have over the years clubbed together to use their buying power to drive hard bargains with the biggest producers on a national level, which sees small, local producers squeezed out. The

Slow Food approach is holistic – I hate that word, incidentally, but it's the only one I can think of at the moment to describe it. Rather than adopt an 'us versus them' mentality – a conflict between producers and consumers – they have tried to bring together all the stakeholders – the food industry, producers, consumers, chefs and even academia – to address the problems in the food chain. Petrini established a University of Gastronomic Sciences in Pollenzo, Italy, to encourage academic study in the whole area of gastronomy. In Turin, he set up the first *Terra Madre* (which means Mother Earth), a meeting of up to five thousand food producers from all over the world and these conferences are now spreading around the world (hence the Waterford event).

Remarkably, after all these years, and in keeping with his infectious *joie de vivre*, Petrini refuses to be pessimistic about the state of the global food chain. He points to the US, where Slow Food has 40,000 members. 'Even in that country, which invented fast food, malls and the supermarket, there is a sea-change happening.'

We grew a decent crop of onions in our very first year here on the Home Farm, which was pretty remarkable given that we were entirely and utterly clueless at the time. It's a stroke of wonderful good fortune that one of the easiest vegetables to grow is also by far and away the most useful in the kitchen – there are, of course, very few meals that don't involve the peeling and chopping of an onion, and, as we proved, there are very few people who can't grow a crop. What a happy coincidence. Onions are cheap and plentiful in the supermarket, and I would probably be exaggerating if I told you that our own ones tasted significantly better. So what's the point, you might ask. Well, to my mind becoming self-sufficient with any vegetable is an incredibly worthwhile affair, so when you come across one that's really easy to grow and stores well, it's silly not to try – just two well-timed sowings of onions (in April for harvesting in September, and then a sowing of winter-hardy varieties in late autumn for harvesting in early summer) will pretty much guarantee you a year-round supply.

Though they can be grown from seed, most people (including us) grow their onions from 'sets', which are immature bulbs that have been specially grown for the purpose of planting. Because they are much further developed, they mature much more quickly and take far less skill to grow. The only downside is the relative cost – it is much, much cheaper to grow onions from seed, but then again, it's still much cheaper to grow from sets than to buy onions in the shop. Next year, we are going to sow some onion seeds in module trays, just for the hell of it, and see how we get on – because, as you know by now, we are just mad rebels. We grew shallots very successfully for a few years, and while they are undoubtedly very sweet and tasty, I find them to be extremely fiddly in the kitchen, so I don't think I will bother with them next year.

An onion bed needs a bit of work before you sow anything in it. It will do your onions a power of good if you spread lots of manure or compost the previous winter (if you use fresh manure at the time of planting it will probably cause the sets to rot) and then give the bed a good digging over with a fork, then a raking just before you sow. If you rake over and back repeatedly across the top of the bed, eventually the soil succumbs to your charms, and breaks up into little tiny, crumbly bits. If it won't rake for you (if the soil just keeps sticking to the rake), it usually means that the soil is too wet to plant in. To plant sets, we make a shallow drill about 3cm deep, the length of the bed, and space the onions about 10cm apart, before pulling the soil back in around them and then firming them in; rather like garlic, with onion sets you just push the bulb into the soil, leaving the tip just peeking out. The only difficulty that we have had with sown sets is that you sometimes get what is called a 'frost heave', where the freezing and thawing in frosty weather causes the soil to expand and contract, pushing the poor little bulb right out of the soil, as if unwanted. Consequently, it's a good idea to check the bulbs for a few weeks until they get established and push back any that have been evicted. As already mentioned, most of our raised beds are behind a picket fence in a corner of the garden, which, amazingly, seems to keep the hens out of the plot altogether, but two are out in the garden away from the others (a planning error is what we like to call it) and the hens like to get up on these beds for a good scratch around. Depending on what's sown in the bed, this can be a major problem. If the onions are there, it's a complete disaster, so we net them, as half a dozen hens could easily ruin a day's work with five minutes of intense scratching.

Onions don't like competition from weeds and the bulbs won't swell if the soil around them is compacted, so the main work of looking after them is to keep the bed weed-free and the soil around them loose – a sharp hoe does the job on both fronts. They don't need a huge amount of watering, but you will need to give them a soaking if it's very dry (precious little chance of that). One of the most remarkable sights you will ever see in your vegetable plot is a bed of onions getting itself ready for harvest. In the last weeks of summer, a nutrient tug-o'-war of sorts happens between the bulb and its foliage, which, of course, you are hoping the bulb will win. The bulb starts to suck all the vitamins and minerals from the foliage until, finally, thoroughly beaten, the foliage turns yellow, withers and then topples over dramatically in a final act of surrender. Two weeks from the date this happens, your onions are ready to be picked.

It's worth eating a few of them at this stage, because they are literally bursting with nutrition and they taste fantastic. Supermarket onions are always dried, and a mature, luscious, fresh onion is therefore a surprisingly different taste sensation. The onions you are planning to store yourself will also have to be dried first. You put them on a rack in a sunny spot (we put ours inside the polytunnel if the weather is wet) for about two or three weeks, turning them occasionally, as if they were a big plump sausage on a barbecue. Alternatively, you can hang them from a clothes horse so you can move them in and out, depending on the weather. The onions are then tied to a length of string and stored somewhere cool and dry from where you can help yourself as you need them. In my opinion, a string of onions looks very cool indeed. Incidentally, we have been known to cheat and use the tops of the onions before the bulb is ready as salad greens – and very nice they are too!

PAULA MEE'S NUTRITION BITES: ONIONS

Onions have been revered through time, not only for their culinary use, but also for their therapeutic properties. The liberal use of the allium species, including garlic, leeks and different varieties of onion has been associated with beneficial effects on cholesterol levels and heart disease. Onions are one of the few vegetables that are a source of biotin, a B vitamin, which is important for healthy hair and nails. Biotin also helps your body to digest fatty foods.

Nutrition per Portion (80g):

Calories	Fat (g)	Salt (g)	Saturated Fat (g)
29	0.2	0	0.1

OCTOBER GROWER'S CALENDAR

Prep Work

- Pot up herbs so that they can be grown inside for use during winter.
- Continue to lift crops that have finished harvesting and clean up the beds.
- By now, green manures sown in late summer will be ready to be dug into the soil. You can also sow over-wintering green manures now.
- Try to find a good source of farmyard manure if you don't have your own – cow, horse, pig, sheep and chicken manure are all great sources of nitrogen, phosphorus and potassium. If you are going to cover empty beds down with manure for the winter, the earlier you do it the better. October or early November is ideal.

To-do List

- Pull up crops that have finished harvesting and compost.
- Plant fruit trees and bushes.
- Tidy away canes and supports that you used for your peas, beans etc, and you should be able to use them next year. Leave them in the ground or throw them in a corner, and you probably won't.
- If you have a pond, stretch a piece of netting over it to keep leaves out.
- Start collecting leaves for leaf mould.
- Start storing vegetables like carrots and beets – only store the perfect specimens. Try to process the rest.
- Your tomatoes are most likely on the way out now (sob) – this is a good time of the year to make the green tomato chutney discussed in Chapter 7.
- Check apples regularly to see if they are ripe (see Chapter 9) – early ripening

apples generally don't store that well, so you have a good excuse to scoff the lot.

- Cut autumn-fruiting raspberry canes down to the ground.

Sowing Seeds

- You can sow hardy varieties of peas and broad beans later this month for an early spring crop, but only do so in well-drained soil (we don't really like sowing peas outdoors in the winter, to be honest, but we think broad beans do okay).

- In the polytunnel we usually try and get a crop of cauliflower and carrots going over the winter.

Planting Out

- Later this month, plant selected varieties of garlic and winter onion sets. The former will benefit from a good frost, so it's good to get them in the ground before Christmas. (God, did I really just mention that word?)

GRUB'S UP – WHAT'S IN SEASON

Depending on the weather, the harvest may well continue into October – it's also a month when you are still harvesting many of the great autumn fruits and vegetables – pumpkins, squashes, courgettes, apples, pears etc. It's the last hurrah, however, for peas, French and runner beans, tomatoes, cucumbers, aubergines, lettuce, peppers and chilli-peppers. Parting is such sweet sorrow.

A good month to harvest wild mushrooms, elderberry, blackberries, sloes, celery, leeks, cabbage.

Crops, like carrots, parsnips, swedes, celeriac, turnips and beetroot, as well as your main-crop potatoes, should still be thriving. You can leave these in the ground for another while yet, and use them as you need them, or lift and store if you prefer.

Start to fall back in love again with old winter reliables such as chard and spinach. They will shortly become your very best friends.

11

EAT THE VIEW

EARLY WINTER: NOVEMBER

carrots – urban farmers – winter approaches – the manure pile

The Celts were right. November really feels like the beginning of winter. Things are becoming distinctly dreary around here and Christmas is bearing down on us – people have started to say, 'Oh, it's only X shopping days to Christmas', or worse, 'Have you done all your shopping yet?' in that incessantly annoying way that makes you want to beat them over the head with their shopping bags. The first Christmas ads appeared on the TV weeks ago and the other day I heard the first Christmas song on the radio. I'm no Scrooge – in fact, I love Christmas – but it's just far too early to be thinking about it. And besides, as far as the Home Farm is concerned, it's still the season of harvest.

As we transition into winter, the focus, in terms of vegetables, moves from dainty fruits and greens to the hardy root vegetables that supply us with much-needed energy at this time of the year, and which are doughty enough to survive in the cold soil. Vegetables such as carrots, parsnips, beetroot and celeriac are high in energy-supplying carbohydrates, and are rich in the vitamin B and C we need to fight off colds (even that most serious variant of a cold that affects only one gender – the 'man cold'). It is also worth bearing in mind, in terms of the importance of seasonal produce, that vegetables eaten fresh are at the peak of their nutritional content, so the root crops we are plucking from the vegetable patch at this time of the year are the healthiest thing we could eat right now.

Over the years, our attempts at growing carrots here on the Home Farm have been a little bit hit-and-miss. This is unfortunate because, to me, carrots are one of the most useful and tastiest of all vegetables and it would be just incredible to have a really bumper crop of them. They are also, of course, one of the healthiest to eat. Food scientists have recently zoned in on the anit-oxidant capabilities of a chemical contained in carrots called 'falcarinol' that is believed to have potent anti-cancer properties. Pulled straight from the ground in the winter months and put into a casserole or stew, their all-round earthiness is instantly comforting. They are also, of course, a vital component of stocks and soups. To my mind, the great winter root vegetables are the last glimpse of real *colour* from the growing season and are there-fore to be savoured as we count down to year's end. They say that if you are going to buy one organic vegetable, then it should be a carrot, because carrots suffer more than most vegetables from the rigours of mass-production. There is simply no comparison between the intense, concentrated sweetness, crunchiness and vibrant colouring of a home-grown carrot and the bland sogginess of the commercial alternative. So, there are compelling reasons to grow them. The problem, in my experience, is that they are just not that easy to grow. If you read a book that tells you that it's easy to grow carrots, jump up and down on it and then throw it out the window, for it can't be trusted.

The problem, I think, with carrots is that they are so annoyingly temperamental – they are the divas of the vegetable world. Carrots like a sandy soil and simply will not do well in regular, crappy soil – and heaven forfend that the root should happen to encounter a stone while it's growing because it will, of course, fork and turn into a zany-shaped mutant carrot that all your friends will laugh at. Carrots need fertilised soil, but you can't sow them in soil that has been manured in the past year. They also hate weeds, so you have to keep their bed weed-free, but you're not allowed to use a hoe as that might upset them. And – oh yeah – the seeds don't like dry conditions, but they also don't like being too wet either. Plus, the *only* water you can use is Evian natural spring water and it must be poured gently on to the surface of the soil by forty buxom virgins!!

And then, of course, there is the cunning carrot-root fly, which will come along and destroy all your hard work if you do manage to overcome the considerable growing difficulties and actually produce a crop. Along with potato blight, carrot-root fly damage is one of the most miserable growing experiences possible, and you can be pretty much guaranteed it will visit you at some point. The carrot-root fly can smell a carrot from a thousand miles away, even if someone is

holding its nose. So, while you are spending a nice afternoon thinning out your carrots, thousands of miles away a group of carrot-root
fly stop what they are doing, sniff the air inquisitively and then
immediately take off in formation, bound for your garden. The larvae
from this rotten little insect will burrow into your carrots and you
won't know anything about it until you go to eat them and find there
are horrible holes right through the centres.

The first time I tried to grow carrots, I spent a whole day getting a
bed to a 'fine tilth' – in other words, I abandoned my 'no-dig' philosophy and dug and raked the bed, and when I finished digging and
raking, I dug and raked it some more. By the time I had finished with
it, it was a thing of such utter beauty I didn't want to plant anything at
all in it. I marked out a drill with some string so that I would know
where to look for signs of growth and then I sprinkled the seed into
the drill as thinly as I could (but then, carrot seed is so small it tends to
come out of the packet in bulk and you end up with a clump of ten
seeds in the soil where there should only be one – aagggghhhh!). And
then? Then I waited. And waited. And nothing. Absolutely nothing
came up, except weeds. Well, as far as I know, nothing came but
weeds, but since I had never grown carrots, I didn't even know what
the foliage was supposed to look like, so as I weeded I may have been
plucking infant carrots, for all I know. Second time around, I basically dumped an entire packet of seed in three or four rows and had a
small measure of success – a few of the seeds germinated – but it was
hardly a harvest to write home about. Then I was in the local garden
centre and I noticed that they were selling module trays of well-
developed carrots – now, I have always read that you can't transplant
carrots because it damages the root, so I asked the guy there and he

said, 'Nonsense, my good man. As long as you transplant carefully from module trays the roots should be undisturbed, and everything should be fine.' I suppose you could argue that he *would* say that given that he was selling them. At €3 for fifteen or so roots, it's ridiculously expensive when you consider that you get two hundred seeds in a packet for about €2.50, but hey, I was desperate. And besides, it's still cheaper than buying carrots in the shops and, of course, I had the instant gratification of them looking magnificent in the garden while growing. Visitors would comment on them – 'God, you have lovely carrots growing there' – and I would just stare at my feet and say nothing.

Since then, things have improved somewhat. I have discovered that the main reason the seeds don't germinate is generally that the seed is sown too deeply; the recommended depth is just 1cm, which is far shallower than what you would expect, so it's easy to get it wrong. We also sow seed in old lengths of guttering in the polytunnel and then we transplant them when they're big enough to handle. This is more time-consuming, but we have found it quite effective. Finally, we also sow some dwarf varieties in containers (for example Parmex, known as the Windowsill Carrot, a little stubby root) and they do very well indeed. As with other vegetables, the key with carrots is successional sowing. If you sow a small number of seeds in containers every three weeks or so from March right through to this month, you should have a constant supply – each batch will be ready to eat about 10-12 weeks after you sow (and in as little as 8 weeks for early varieties). My friend Anne does a couple of sowings of carrots direct into the soil in her polytunnel over the winter, which basically means she has carrots all year round – a fine idea. Carrots do well in the polytunnel at any time of the year, in fact. You can even sow heat-resistant varieties such as Amsterdam Forcing in high summer and they will absolutely thrive.

THE PERFECT CARROT?

I picked up another tip for growing carrots in the open ground, which I tried this year with great success. You make a very deep, v-shaped hole with a crowbar or dibber, or some such implement of destruction, and then fill it with compost or sand, or a mix of both. Sow the seed about 1cm deep and you get award-winning, perfectly long cylindrical carrots about 25cm long. This makes sense because the root can grow down into the depth of compost unhindered and unobstructed. The downside to this approach is that it is terribly time-consuming compared to sprinkling seeds into a drill, but then again, given the results, perhaps it's worth the time.

If you sow direct into the soil, you are supposed to 'thin out' seedlings so that the carrots are 8cm or so apart. This is complicated by the fact (I think) that each carrot has a mop-top of foliage and it's hard to tell where one ends and the next one begins. Plus, thinning carrots sends an aroma into the air that is irresistible to the carrot-root fly, so it's basically like standing on top of a mountain and broadcasting to the world's carrot-root fly populace that you have a perfect spot for them to come and lay their eggs. The best time to do this job is on a wet, cool evening (which keeps the smells down) and you should take the thinnings away with you and lock them in the safe with the deeds of your house. Some people swear that intercropping is the key to thwarting the efforts of the carrot-root fly – the idea is to sow alternate rows of carrots and onions so that the dreaded fly is thrown off by the onions and the onion fly is put off by the carrots.

I've never tried this, so I can't comment on whether it works. In any case, the rules of our incredibly simple crop rotation don't allow for carrots and onions to lie in the same bed!

Again, it would seem that raised beds have an advantage when it comes to growing carrots. First of all, you have a good depth of soil for the carrot to grow in. The general rule of thumb when planting carrots is that the soil should be well cultivated up to the depth of a spade – this is far easier to achieve in a raised bed. (The no-dig policy falls down somewhat when it comes to growing carrots – you really do need to do some work on the soil if you want decent carrots.) We have two raised beds that are almost waist high and the best carrots we ever had were grown in one of those beds. A high raised bed may also foil the carrot-root fly because, for all their cunning, they can't, apparently, fly any higher than 50cm off the ground. Hurray! If the sides of your raised beds are higher than this, the fly shouldn't be able to get up to the carrots. *It's almost too simple.* This will work until they introduce a 'How to Fly at 60cm' course at carrot-root fly university. If your beds are lower than 50cm, you will need to put a fine-woven mesh around the outside of the bed to keep them out. In fact, it's probably a good idea to do that anyway. Alternatively, you can cover the crop with fleece; this keeps the root fly away and warms the soil at the same time.

Carrots store really well over the winter, which again makes them a really useful vegetable to have around – if you grow enough of them you could be eating them right up to March of next year (though our most successful crop of carrots ever lasted us only until mid-January). You can leave carrots in the ground over winter and simply use them as you need them (cut off the foliage and cover them with straw to protect them from frost if the weather turns really cool), but at this time of the year we normally take out whatever carrots are left and store them. This basically frees up the bed they were growing in to be manured or covered down, or whatever you have planned for it for the winter months. Carrots will keep really fresh in a box filled with sand, and there's great fun to be had rooting (ahem) about trying to find them. Cut the foliage off the top of them before you store them, only store the good ones and don't let them touch off each other in the sand. Carrots will keep like this until next March.

PAULA MEE'S NUTRITION BITES: CARROTS

Carrots are well known and loved by even the youngest children in many countries and the benefits of this root crop are legendary. Your mother probably told you that eating carrots would keep your eyes bright; that's because, of the commonly consumed vegetables, the carrot provides the highest source of betacarotene, a form of vitamin A, and vitamin A is essential for healthy vision.

Nutrition per Portion (80g):

Calories	Fat (g)	Salt (g)	Saturated Fat (g)
24	0.4	0.08	0.1

The most common excuse that you come across from people to explain why they can't or won't grow their own food is that they don't have the space. This is, I'm afraid to say – and you really will have to pardon my bluntness here – nothing more than an excuse. Don't get me wrong, if you have absolutely no interest in growing your own vegetables, that is completely and absolutely your own business and you won't hear any arguments from me whatsoever.

But, the space argument just won't wash – a small urban or suburban garden can be a highly productive food-growing enterprise if you want it to be, so long as you are in the right frame of mind. If you're interested in such things, there's a nice discussion about what exactly our gardens are *for* in my first book, *Trading Paces* – are they an outdoor entertainment venue or an asset that you can put to work for the benefit of yourself and your family?

Back in the spring, I was asking the owner of a garden centre how his business was faring this year; sales of decking, barbecues and other garden frivolities have plummeted, he informed me sullenly, scratching his head with the top of a hand fork. But on the other hand, sales of vegetable seeds and fruit bushes have gone through the roof. He completely underestimated the demand for seed potatoes, onions and garlic this year, he told me, so much so that all three were sold out in about two weeks. This, I am sure you will agree, is good news because it means that we are all starting to focus in on what's really important in life and realise that our gardens, regardless of their size, can become a productive Home Farm *as well as* a place for us to enjoy and hang out in.

An organisation called Kitchen Gardeners International, which promotes home-grown vegetables, got a hundred thousand people to sign a petition asking the newly elected President Obama and his wife to grow vegetables on the lawn of the White House; they had a great slogan encouraging the First Couple to 'Eat the View'. I think that sums up the Home Farm approach nicely. It's about having a garden where everything you grow is edible instead of being just nice to look at (but it's also nice to look at). Incidentally, Michelle Obama did set up a vegetable garden on the south lawn to provide home-grown food for her children and visitors to the White House – they grow over fifty varieties of fruit and vegetables, including spinach, peas, fennel, squashes, mint and berries. Apparently, America's powerful agribusiness lobby was furious at the First Lady's decision to grow organically and in a carefully worded letter urged her to use appropriate 'crop protection products'. The organic approach, you see, is bad for business.

The Eat the View mentality should apply to all of us, regardless of whether we're growing on the south lawn of the White House or the smallest space imaginable. Let's start with residents who are likely to have the least space – apartment dwellers. You might think that someone living in an apartment is not very likely to be able to grow much at all – and you would be right to mention that there's no soil to be found in an apartment. But if your apartment has a decent balcony that gets some sunlight occasionally, there are actually lots of things that you can grow. You could set a few potato and strawberry plants in planters, for example, which would be fun, and you could even grow some carrots and onions in a deep container. In the summer months, you could go mad altogether, growing salad crops like lettuce, cucumber, rocket, basil, spring onions and radishes. In addition, if you don't mind having things growing in your living room, you could grow lots of things in pots inside too, like peas and tomatoes. And, of course, you could almost certainly become self-sufficient in herbs and never again have to buy those expensive, wasteful plastic packets of herbs of generally questionable quality. In fact, with a little ingenuity, you should be able to produce some sort of crop of a great many vegetables. Does it matter that you will never be self-sufficient from a balcony or that you will still have to go to the shops to supplement what you grow yourself? Absolutely not. Any contribution that you can make to the dinner plate is incredibly worthwhile and you will get tremendous joy from it into the bargain.

MAKING THE MOST OF YOUR SPACE

A well planned balcony garden will allow you to make the most of a small space and will probably be a lot easier to keep and maintain than a regular garden. For a start, there's probably not going to be much weeding to be done and, of course, all the soil will be nutrient-rich (since you will be using potting compost to grow in). Most importantly, those great banes of the Home Farmer's life – the slug and the rabbit – are unlikely to be much of a problem when you live ten floors above street level. Slugs and rabbits are dogged, determined and generally ingenious, but they are not – as far as I am aware – much of a problem in apartment blocks (yet).

The key to maximising growing space on a balcony is to go vertical! A four- or five-shelf plastic 'greenhouse', for example, would be a great investment – each shelf supports five or six pots and it has a zippable plastic cover to keep your vegetables toasty warm on cold nights. Stash some gardening tools, compost etc on the ground beneath the shelves. You could also hang rectangular planters for rows of lettuce and other plants that have shallow root systems from the rails on your balcony. Take a bit of time to work out which plants should go where, based on which part of your balcony gets the most sunlight. Some plants need direct sunlight while others prefer partial shade, so check seed packets. Make sure that the pots you choose are large enough to accommodate the full grown plant – tomatoes, for example, will need a 45cm-deep container. Patio growers will also be able to use existing balcony features, such as a railing, to trail climbing plants up.

Many cities, of course, have tremendous traditions of urban farming, and readers of a certain age will, no doubt, recall a time when allotments, cow yards, dairies and even pig farms were an occasional feature in city neighbourhoods. Cities around the world have vast potential for Home Farm food production, given that an estimated 25 percent of their land is garden – but most of that resource remains untapped. Just how self-sufficient can you be in a city garden? Well, I've met some people over the past year who grow vegetables (and more) in small and sometimes tiny urban and suburban gardens and I've discovered it's possible to be very self-sufficient indeed. In fact, some of them are producing more food in small city gardens than we are on almost an acre in the country. Either they are just super-efficient or we are just really, really lazy! Whichever, it makes a non-sense of the excuse that a small garden means vegetable growing cannot be for you.

There's an eighty-year-old man, Joe, in our GIY group who is probably more productive in his urban garden than I am in my garden and I remain envious of his diligence. (So there's another excuse knocked on the head – I often come across people of a certain age who say they are far too old for all that vegetable growing malarkey!) His is a classic semi-detached housing estate garden, and from his vegetable patch and a small greenhouse he producers bumper crops of vegetables (potatoes, peas, onions, shallots, garlic, cabbages, kale, tomatoes and more), fruit (strawberries and rhubarb) and herbs (rosemary, thyme etc). The day I visited his garden he showed me an old crate in his garage that was still half-full of last year's spuds (it was early March and he still had hundreds of spuds left – hungry gap, my eye!). Anyway, this proves you can have a highly productive Home

Farm even in the smallest of gardens.

The bigger issue, I guess, is whether you're happy to do so – 80 percent or more of Joe's garden is given over to his vegetable growing and that's probably not for everyone. I went to visit it and I thought it looked great. I came away with bags of spuds, spring onions and a giant bunch of kale, all of which we were enjoying for about a week afterwards. I also came away with a few really good tips (see one below on wood ash) and feeling very much inspired.

WOOD ASH

An interesting nugget of advice gleaned from my visit to Joe's garden concerned wood ash. He advised me to save the ash from wood fires to sprinkle over the bed in which I am going to grow my tomatoes, which, he says, acts as a fine potash fertiliser. It makes perfect sense to me to put ashes to work in the vegetable garden rather than throwing them away. Wood ash works on two levels – first it contains nutrients, which wash into the soil when watered, and, second, it is slightly alkaline and therefore will reduce acidity levels in a similar manner to lime (though it is not as potent). Though it varies depending on the species of wood, the ashes from wood contain an array of beneficial nutrients including potassium, phosphorus and magnesium. Before you use it, it's probably worth trying to work out the existing pH level of your soil – you will find pH testers in most garden centres; if it's already alkaline, it wouldn't do to make it more so. The rule of thumb is that wood ash will be beneficial for fruiting crops (particularly tomatoes where potassium deficiency is a common problem, which results in the fruits ripening unevenly) and other plants that prefer slightly alkaline, rather than slightly acid, soil. Do not use ashes where you plan to grow spuds.

Horticulturist Bernard Wesenberg of Washington State University recommends using one gallon of ashes per square yard on loam to clay-loam soil, and half as much on sandier soils – I couldn't really tell you whether our soil is loam, clay-loam or sandy, and I have to admit to being a little confused about the idea of a gallon of ashes. But never mind, Joe and I reckon a good sprinkling of ashes on your soil will do the trick and if your plants do well this year, then you know you've used just enough. (If they die, you've probably used too much.) Keep your ashes dry while you are waiting to use them, otherwise the nutrients will simply wash away. Be careful of using ash from timber that has been chemically treated and never use ash from a coal fire. I would steer clear of firelighters to start a fire too – use kindling instead. And finally, it goes without saying that the ashes should be cool before use!

In 2008, when my first book was published, the Minister for Food and Horticulture, Trevor Sargent, very kindly came and did the honours at the book launch. He was telling me that evening about his own garden and the different things that he grows and rears – I was excited about that because (a) I had drunk way too much red wine and I was excited about pretty much everything, and (b) because it's rare that you find a government minister who is not only on top of his brief, but can walk the walk too. Anyway, I was telling him that I was interested in the whole area of productive urban gardens and he invited me to come and see his garden in north county Dublin. Each autumn, armed with an old apple press and the output of just one James Grieve apple tree, he churns out enough apple juice to last him a year. 'It freezes perfectly,' he said, offering us a glass during our visit. Very nice it was too. I'm an awful man for picking one little thing in a conversation and zeroing in on it relentlessly, but there was something so exciting about the idea of being able to become self-sufficient in apple juice from just one apple tree – I mean, he clearly knows what he's doing and is looking after the tree very well, but isn't that just the most amazing thing? He bottles up some of the apple juice for 'fresh' and he freezes the rest in little plastic containers with just enough for a portion. Three or four times a week, he takes one out of the freezer, defrosts it and drinks it the next morning. Fantastic.

Trevor turns the 'problem' of lack of space in his suburban garden on its head and views it instead as an opportunity. He has owned larger plots of land in the past, including at one point an entire acre, but felt overwhelmed by the amount of work required to maintain them. His garden is a model of efficiency and smart planning, which, given its size, it has to be. There isn't an inch of wasted space. Four small raised beds are used for an organic crop rotation of roots, brassicas and legumes, and surrounded by neat paths. Tomatoes are grown in a planter and there's a separate bed for herbs. Apple and plum trees provide shelter and interest, and he grows comfrey in the front garden, which is used to make an organic liquid feed. There's also an aesthetically pleasing pond, but it too has its practical uses, encouraging slug-nibbling frogs into the garden. His only concession to regular gardening is a minuscule patch of lawn in front of the kitchen window ('The cat likes to lie on it,' he explains), though that may shortly make way for an underground rainwater harvester and presumably the cat will just have to buzz off and find somewhere else to sleep.

'Investing the time creating the beds at the start was key,' he said. 'They are small enough to be easily planted and because of the paths I can go out there in hail, rain or snow, or even in a shirt and tie, and do a bit of weeding. When I have a Sunday afternoon free, I love to be out in the garden, chilling out. There is nothing as restorative to mental and physical health.' Growing his own, he says, gives him an appreciation for the farmers and growers he meets in the day job. 'By and large, supermarkets treat farmers with absolute disdain. It's horrific for a farmer to nurture a product and then see it selling in a supermarket at a loss. When I buy food I appreciate it because I know the effort that has gone into producing it.' Meanwhile, back in the garden, he's identified a corner where he wants to grow grapes and he is wrestling with the idea of keeping hens.

About forty minutes away by car from Trevor's house, near Dublin's outer ring road, Breffni and Kathleen Galligan take the concept of urban farming to another extreme, keeping chickens, hens, ducks and pigs in a tiny garden and a small, rented paddock. Spurred on by the desire to bring a little bit of country to their corner of suburbia (and a love of bacon), Breffni started renting a corner of a field about ten minutes away from their home about a year ago, and he sourced three Gloucestershire Old Spot weanlings from a rare-breed breeder in Galway. The Old Spot thrives on the outdoor life and produces top-quality meat. 'The meat from old breeds tastes far better,' said Breffni. 'The new breeds are mostly hybrids and they are bred for quick growth. Little attention is paid to flavour. When you buy supermarket meat you don't know where the meat has come from or how the animals have lived.' Breffni spends about an hour with the pigs each day, feeding them a mixture of pig nuts and scraps from the kitchen – vegetable peels, apples, stale bread and left-over biscuits. We laughed a little about the whole idea of naming pigs. I told him that real farmers would always shake their head in disgust if I mentioned that we called our first two Charlotte and Wilbur. Breffni called his boar Jasper. 'I knew all along that his fate was to end up in the abattoir, so I had no real qualms about it and I tried to make sure that I didn't get too attached to him. My wife was quite upset, though.' The two gilts were kept for breeding and Breffni recently 'rented' a boyfriend – another Old Spot boar – from a pig farmer down the country. If their tryst is successful, he plans to sell the piglets, keeping one or two animals for the table each year. He likes the fact that producing his own food gives him control over his food security. 'We've become so helpless as a society when it comes to feeding ourselves. Keeping a few animals is a great way to counteract that. It's a fantastic de-stresser, great fun and gets you back to basics.'

Back in their garden, his wife Kathleen keeps ducks and hens for eggs and is rearing chickens for the table. The ducks were reared in an incubator and spent their first weeks in the house under a heat lamp. She loves having them in her back garden (where they splash about in a paddling pool) but she admits they've turned her lawn into a series of bumps and hollows, completely devoid of grass. 'It's worth it,' she says, 'for the eggs. I'm sure our neighbours think we're nuts, but every road should have its eccentric couple!' And so say all of us.

Bruce Darrell, a Canadian architect who lives just two kilometres from Dublin City Centre, told me a very interesting and little-known fact about urban growing – because they are surrounded by buildings and walls, urban gardens generally enjoy a more benign climate than their rural equivalent, enjoy lighter winds and higher temperatures, and are less susceptible to frost. His own garden is a shining example of the benefits of such genteel weather and of just how much can be achieved in a small space – every available centimetre is given over to some useful food production enterprise. In raised beds, he is growing tomatoes (grown very effectively under some old recycled windows – there's no space for a greenhouse), potatoes, peas, runner beans, broad beans, lettuce, onions, radishes and artichokes. Containers are used to grow herbs and carrots, and there are also fruit trees and a productive-looking compost heap. Hearty greens, such as kale and cabbage, see the family through the lean winter months and he's completely self-sufficient in garlic, with two impressive braided bundles hanging in the kitchen. He is convinced that the primary limitation for most people is not space at all, it's lack of knowledge. His young daughter, he tells me, grew swedes last year and though she didn't like them much, she ate them anyway because she had grown them herself. As a result of their growing adventures, his children are less fussy about what foods they like and dislike. 'It's great for kids – to have a child who has picked peas and knows what a carrot plant looks like, that's just fantastic.' In his native Canada, a new fad is the idea of guerrilla gardening, where armies of urban farmers have taken over unused green spaces (such as grass verges) and planted vegetables in them. 'Now, that's exciting,' he says with relish. I tell him about my mate Dave in Dunmore and his guerrilla raspberry-cane planting.

The final urban farmer I discovered was Ella McSweeney, whose garden is hidden away at the bottom of a laneway in a leafy housing estate on the south side of the city. A walled vegetable garden with neat lazy beds at the back of the property is the venue for most of the serious growing, but there is evidence of a desire for self-sufficiency pretty much everywhere. A converted dog kennel, with a small run attached, is home to three laying hens, while a sun-drenched porch is chock-full of vegetable plants at different stages of development – tomatoes, peppers, courgettes and cucumbers. 'You get hooked into growing things,' says Ella. 'You put a seed in the soil, feed it, give it some sun and it grows. It works. I just love that. Making a dinner entirely from the contents of the garden is an amazing feeling because our day-to-day lives are so far removed from that. I find it connects you with your friends more. I know it probably sounds hideously middle-class, but we give eggs to our friends or swap produce with them. I know you can romanticise the whole thing and that a lot of people are glad to turn their back on it and be able to buy in the supermarket. That's fine. It doesn't fulfil everything in life, but if you can do a bit of it, it's a really nice thing to do. And, of course, food, especially organic food, is ridiculously expensive, so it's a really good investment.' Star performers in the McSweeney garden are tomatoes – last year, while expecting her first child, she grew sixty tomato plants in her porch. Sixty, I thought? Bloody hell. The tomatoes, she said were 'juicy, sweet, gorgeous', but as the pregnancy developed she discovered that the very notion of tomatoes repulsed her. Talk about sod's law. 'In the end we gave a lot away and made sauces for the freezer.'

Keeping a few laying hens, she says, is possible for most urban gardens, even the tiniest ones, though you shouldn't get them if you like a pristine lawn. 'They definitely make a mess. On the other hand, the eggs are amazing and it's very satisfying to eat an egg when you know what the chicken that laid it has been eating. They are a cinch to look after. I let them out in the morning and I close the hatch at night – both those things take about 30 seconds. You need to make sure they have food and water and every few days I clean out their house. But that's about it.' Her advice to anyone interested in growing or rearing their own food is quite simply to get stuck in. 'Make a decision to try it this year. Get a grow bag, put two or three tomato plants in it and keep it watered. See how it goes. What's the worst that can happen?'

One thing that we have been really poor at on our Home Farm is bringing nutrients back into our soil each year by adding organic matter. It's always been a chore that I have felt sceptical about – I am a great believer in the idea that nature will sort things out if left to her own devices and so the idea that soil is not self-supporting and requires help each year to allow things to grow has always jarred with me. But I can, indeed, report from the trenches that when you grow things in soil year after year, the things you grow suck the goodness from that soil and eventually it starts to get jaded. You might wonder (well, I do) – why did Mother Nature design it this way? Surely she could have found some way for the plants to put nutrients back into the soil so that it would replenish itself each year and put compost manufacturers out of business? Well, in some ways it does just that. Using crop-rotation schemes leverages off the inbuilt synergy that exists between vegetable types – peas take nitrogen from the air and leave it in the soil for cabbages to avail of the following year. That's the wisdom of nature. Another clue to the solution she must have had in mind can be found in the traditions of smallholding – namely that most smallholders would have some farmyard animals around (like a cow or a pig) to provide lots and lots of lovely manure that would keep the soil fertilised. Unfortunately, we don't have space for a cow, but we have our pigs, ducks and chickens to provide quite a bit of manure in their own right.

Adding manure and/or compost to improve the fertility of your soil is something that needs to be done every year, ideally in autumn or early winter. It doesn't really matter whether you use compost or manure or both, as they essentially achieve the same thing. When we started growing here first, our compost heaps were generally a pretty sorry affair – slimy heaps of sludge down at the end of the garden where food scraps (happily) disappeared, but which were about as much use in terms of composting the veggies as a slap in the face with a wet fish. Eventually, we got a decent attempt at a system going, using two heaps made from timber pallets, and we tried our best to add things to them in alternate layers of green and brown. The idea is that you fill one of the heaps and then leave it alone for six months or so while you fill the second one. This is working well, but there is a relatively finite amount of compost being produced. Our vegetable beds and the tunnel require a sizeable amount of manure to do them any justice, particularly since we are still working hard at trying to improve the fertility of our soil overall. Most Home Farmers are in a similar boat and have to beg, borrow or steal farmyard manure if they are to secure a decent quantity without paying a fortune for it.

The problem we tend to have is that we attack the job of manuring too late. After a busy growing season, we tend to power down for the winter and turn our minds to soil preparation the following spring, when, of course, it's far too late for the manure to work its magic for that year. If it is not sufficiently rotted down, the high levels of nitrogen in the manure will kill off your plants instead of helping them to grow. We put horse manure down in February one year, covering it with plastic in the hope of keeping weeds down and preventing the nutrients from the manure from leaching away, and when we started to use the beds later in the year, some vegetables did indeed thrive, but many just died because the manure was too fresh. This year, we are far more organised. I happened to be out walking the dogs in the fields around our house one day recently and I noticed a large pile of steaming, rotting cow-manure in one of the fields. I gave my farmer friend a call, asked him if I could have a consignment and promised him some bacon/sausages in return. Within a few hours he (very kindly) showed up at our house in the tractor, pulling a very large trailor full to the brim with manure. 'Where do you want it?' he asked. 'I think we'll dump it there,' I replied, pointing to an area in front of the polytunnel, wondering would Mrs Kelly object to a big pile of manure being deposited right beside the washing line? My farmer friend was amused at how grateful I was for this special delivery. I kept saying, 'Are you sure you don't mind?' and he kept looking at me with a look that said: Why would I mind; do you think I keep it to bathe in or something? But seriously, take a trip to your local garden centre and check out how much they are charging for tiny bags of 'farmyard manure' – as far as I am concerned, swapping some of our meat for tonnes of the stuff was a canny investment. And you know how much I love canny investments (see the story about the purchase of my beloved milk separator if you are in any doubt).

LEAF MOULD

Many a grower's calendar will tell you that late autumn and early winter is a time to clean up your garden in preparation for the winter's pause, which I think is good advice, if unlikely to be followed here. The one clean-up job that I actually consider doing at this time is leaf collection, but I have other things in mind than making the place look pristine. Leaf mould is a form of compost you can make from fallen leaves. Making leaf mould is a doddle compared to making regular compost and unlike regular composting, it is a 'cold' process – as you know, if you stick your hand into the centre of your compost heap it will be really warm (as well as disgusting). With leaf mould composting, it is fungi rather than bacteria that drive the decomposition process and so the whole thing remains cool. We collect a big pile of leaves, give them a good soaking with water, unless they are already wet, and put them into black sacks. Then we wait – leaf mould does not exactly provide instant gratification – it will take a year or two to rot down properly, but then again, what's the hurry? Once it has rotted down you can dig it into your beds as a soil improver or use it to 'dress' certain vegetables in the spring.

Of course, after the initial euphoria of having secured the manure, we were faced with the rather grim reality of having to move it from its location in front of the polytunnel to its final resting place out around the vegetable garden. Mrs Kelly was adamant that this needed to happen in short order, given the fact that we couldn't hang any clothes out on the line while it remained there. For about a week, I would pass it on my way to feed the hens and we would salute each other with great civility. 'Hello there, mountain of pooh,' I would say. Not much in return, but there you go; the mountain of pooh would just sit there steaming. Then, the following weekend we were lucky that there was beautiful weather and we rolled up the sleeves and got stuck in – loading the wheelbarrow with manure, hauling it to its destination and then unloading it. It's nasty, dirty work, but extremely satisfying, nonetheless – one of those days when your muscles are aching and you feel weary to the bone and yet, strangely, sorry that the day is over. You can see the manure teaming with worms and you know that over the winter they will be dragging nutrients down into the poor, exhausted soil, replenishing it and getting it ready for next year. With every barrow-load, our thoughts would get ahead of us and focus on a far-off day in the future – in spring, when, after the grim bareness of winter, we would lift the plastic and start growing afresh in fertile soil. We got most of the beds (one of them still had a few bits and pieces growing in it and the beds that will take the root crops next year don't need manuring) covered in manure and then covered down in black plastic. The beauty of doing this job so early was that the manure would have a minimum of five or six months to work its magic. (Though the growing season kicks off in February, very little is going into the soil outside until April). The bad news was that after two days of shovelling, and with all beds covered down, there was still a sizeable pile left under the clothes line. We continued to salute each other in the mornings, but for some reason the interaction was not as friendly as it had been.

COMPOST AND MANURE

All plants require macronutrients to grow and produce vegetables or fruit. The most important of these nutrients are nitrogen (N), phosphorus (P) and potassium or potash (K). If any of these nutrients is missing from soil, that will limit the growth rate of plants. Nitrogen is probably the most important of the three, since it encourages leaf growth, which in turn powers the plant's growth. The more leafy growth a plant produces the more nitrogen it will require – it will come as no surprise then that vegetables like brussels sprouts, cabbage, rhubarb, beetroot, celery and spinach have high nitrogen requirements. Other smaller-leafed plants have low nitrogen requirements, such as carrots and radishes, while legumes (such as peas and beans) do not require nitrogen at all because they actually take nitrogen from the air themselves and put it in the soil. This explains why we don't need to manure beds after we have grown pea and bean plants in them.

The goal of fertilisers, whether they are organic or artificial, is to make plants grow faster by supplying the elements that the plants need in readily available forms. Fertilisers generally focus on the big three minerals and are therefore usually known as N-P-K fertilisers – the numbers on a bag of fertiliser tell you the percentages of available nitrogen, phosphorus and potassium found inside, for example '10-10-20' has 10 percent nitrogen, 10 percent phosphorous and 20 percent potassium. In general, the nutrients in fertilisers are important to plants for the following purposes:

N: nitrogen, for producing leaf growth
P: phosphorus, to produce fruit and a strong root system
K: potassium (potash), for strength, flower colour and size.

Commercial fertilisers tend to be higher in NPK than both animal manure and garden compost, but it is worth bearing in mind that natural fertilisers have other benefits apart from their NPK rating. For example, compost also improves soil structure and its nutrients are released more slowly. There is much room for variation in the table below, since mineral quantities depend on the animal's diet, how long it has been rotted for, and so on, so this outline should be taken with a grain of salt – but it gives an idea. As you can see, pig manure is high in all three elements, as is chicken manure. Surprisingly, homemade garden compost has NPK values that are equivalent to or exceed animal manure. The main liquid feeds that you can make utilise comfrey, which is potash rich; nettle, which is rich in nitrogen and potash; and animal manure which has all three nutrients. The figures for the comfrey tea below look on the low side on the face of it, but because this is in liquid form it is more readily available to the plants. Leaf mould, which I mentioned earlier in this chapter, is a useful material for improving the structure of the soil but contains only tiny amounts of NPK. Seaweed is a good source of potash (K) and used by many growers to feed their potatoes or tomatoes (either as a foliage spray or as a root drench before planting). Only collect loose seaweed – never pull it off the rocks. Wash it in fresh water or leave it out in the rain for a few days to get rid of the salt. Half-fill a 45 litre drum with the seaweed and fill it up with water. Add about one cup of this to about 13 litres before applying it to plants. You can also put seaweed on the compost heap (it's an excellent activator) or use it to 'top dress' or mulch plants.

Fertiliser	% N (Nitrogen)	% P (Phosphorus)	% K (Potassium)
Compost	1.5	2	0.5
Cow Manure	0.6	0.2	1.0
Horse Manure	0.7	0.2	0.5
Pig Manure	0.8	0.7	0.5
Chicken Manure	1.5	1.0	0.5
Sheep Manure	0.7	0.3	0.9
Seaweed	0.25	0.25	0.5
Comfrey Liquid	0.014	0.0059	0.0340

NOVEMBER GROWER'S CALENDAR

Prep Work

- Yes indeed, our thoughts really are now starting to turn to next year's growing. Who would have thought it? If you are planning to cover down your beds for the winter (which will keep the worst of the bad weather off them, suppress weeds and prevent the rain from leaching nutrients from the soil), you need to get working on it.

- It's also a good time to prepare new ground for spring. Buy yourself a good spade if you don't already have one. Or alternatively, try cutting back the grass, then cover the area with about five layers of newspaper and then a layer of compost. Next spring you should be able to dig straight into this new patch and prepare it for planting.

- Start investigating seed catalogues for next year's sowing.

To-do List

- 'Earth up' vegetables that will be buffeted by the winds and storms over the winter, such as cabbage, cauliflower and particularly brussels sprouts. Tie brussels sprouts and sprouting broccoli to canes and apply mulch.

- Continue to tidy up beds, removing crops, digging in green manures etc.

- Divide up your rhubarb if you want to propagate it and cover it with a thick mulch of manure.

- If you grow perennial herbs outside, it's a good idea to move them to a sheltered spot. We grow most of our perennial herbs in the tunnel where the elements are not an issue.

- Continue to weed ground dug over since a crop has been removed – they say 'one year's seeding is seven years a-weeding' – but what would they know?

- Prune apple trees – you are aiming for a goblet-shaped, open tree. Prune any crossed and damaged branches, and those that are growing in towards the centre of the tree. The key is to improve circulation of air around the tree. Don't over-prune, as this will mean much leafy growth next year and little fruit.
- Mulch raspberry, loganberry and tayberry plants if you haven't already done so. Take cuttings of currant bushes from this season's wood to plant. A cutting should be 25cm long.

Sowing Seeds

- As per last month's calendar, you can sow broad beans outside now for an early crop next spring. It's important to use over-winter varieties such as Aquadulce. To avoid broad bean seeds rotting before germination, make small newspaper cups and germinate them indoors first.
- The polytunnel has its own microclimate – continue to sow carrots, red cabbage, rocket, mixed salad leaves, lamb's lettuce, perpetual spinach.

Planting Out

- Next summer's garlic does best if it's planted before Christmas – plant outdoors in well prepared soil in a sunny spot.
- Some varieties of onion seeds and sets can over-winter and will be ready to harvest in early summer. Again, choose a well drained soil, otherwise they will rot. Keep an eye on them for frost heave.

GRUB'S UP – WHAT'S IN SEASON?

Early frosts can kill off tender vegetables, but you can continue to harvest perpetual spinach, cabbage, cauliflower, potatoes, swede, parsnips, apples, pears.

Start harvesting: leeks (yum, if cut really fine and sautéed in some butter), winter cabbage, kale, artichokes, brussels sprouts.

Time to lift carrots and turnips, or at least cover them with a good layer of straw to keep them warm.

12

HAPPY SATURNALIA

MID-WINTER: DECEMBER

*the december garden – garlic – working horses – meitheals –
the final pitch!*

*'If we had no winter, the spring would not be so pleasant: if we did not some-
times taste of adversity, prosperity would not be so welcome.'*

Anne Bradstreet, *Meditations*

The shortest day of the year is on the twenty-first of this month and if
you're a ballsy, 'glass half-full' kind of person, you can take some
solace from the fact that from that day on the days are starting to get
longer. Just as the harvest brings with it both joy and a measure of
pathos at the impending winter, the arrival of winter brings,

strangely, a sense of hope that it will soon be spring. December is year's end – but we're also very close to a new beginning, so it's a good month to take stock, to add up the year's failures and successes and give yourself your Home Farm grade for the year. How did you fare? A-student? Could do better? The Home Farmer can and should find reason to celebrate at Christmas because, of course, the end of December has been a time of celebration for five millennia and perhaps even longer. Historians believe that the actual birth of Christ probably took place in September, approximately six months after the Passover – the evidence for this seems to be that the nativity story tells of shepherds minding their flocks in the fields at night time, which they were unlikely to be doing in December. One of the early popes (probably Pope Julius I) decided to celebrate the birthday of Jesus on 25 December because that date was already linked to an existing pagan feast day. This, the pope believed, would make the transition to Christianity easier for the pagans they were trying to convert.

In ancient Babylon, the feast of the Son of Isis, the Goddess of Nature, was celebrated on 25 December. In ancient Rome, the winter holiday was called Saturnalia, which honoured Saturn, the God of Agriculture. In January, Romans observed the Kalends of January, (*Kalendae Ianuariae*) which represented the triumph of life over death. The pagans of northern Europe celebrated their own winter solstice, known as Yule (from whence we get the word yule-tide) in honour of the pagan sun god Mithras, who appeared to them to be growing and maturing once the winter solstice had passed. The months of late summer and autumn were, apparently, terrifying for early pagans because they thought that the reason the days were growing shorter was because their sun god was slowly abandoning them. When they saw the length of the day increasing at the end of December, they celebrated his return with riotous drinking, gluttonous feasting and orgies of epic proportions – much like we do today.

So, regardless of your religious faith, come the end of December we have an ancient reason to celebrate as the days gradually become longer again. But in the meantime, things are pretty bleak. The hour has long since gone back, so it starts to get dark shortly after four o'clock these days – that means there are just eight short hours of daylight to enjoy, with the sun abysmally low in the sky. In some ways, perhaps, the short day is a good thing, because there's so little to do anyway. We think it's important to just enjoy this last month of the year, because really it's the only real month off for the Home Farmer – between one thing and another, we were kind of busy in November and come January our thoughts will turn once again to preparation for the growing year ahead. We could, of course, busy ourselves with such things in December if we wanted, but it wouldn't seem right to do so – better to kick back and enjoy the break. Perhaps even re-engage with the real world for a while and do things that normal people do – you know, like buying Christmas presents and so on.

The lack of light impacts on our hens' ability to lay eggs and at this time of the year we sometimes, very occasionally, even have to resort to the unthinkable – *buying* eggs. There is nothing I resent more than feeding hens only for them to fail to live up to their end of the bargain. The only joy I get at feeding time is watching the robins – each morning now, two little robins swoop in and loiter in the background waiting for their opportunity for a quick peck in the hens' bowl. They seem braver at this time of the year, often venturing in between the hens *while they eat* in a daring inter-leg hit and run. The duck continues to provide an egg a day, religiously, and at this time of the year we are tremendously grateful to have her.

There is very little growing in the December garden. Most of our raised beds are lying dormant. The ones that require manuring have been manured and are covered down to lie idle until March or April. Sometimes, if we have had a good year of it, some of our beds may well still have a few crops in them – it is now that the foresight and organisation skills displayed during the growing season just past start to pay dividends. If you thought of sowing them when they needed to be sown, you may well be lucky enough to be able to harvest cauliflower, winter cabbage, leeks, kale and Jerusalem artichokes this month. You will also hopefully have potatoes, carrots, parsnips and turnips in storage. The winter months are also, of course, the official time to eat brussels sprouts – though you can get early varieties that will start cropping in September. We couldn't be bothered with them that early in the year when there are other (nicer) things to eat. We have got some good crops over the years of this much-maligned vegetable and it stays cropping for about eight weeks – when you are finished harvesting the sprouts, you can even cut off the leaves and eat them like spinach. Brussels sprouts really are one of those things you either love or hate (hint: they are absolutely ruined by overcooking), but I think the plants look wonderful in the winter garden when there is so little else going on and, of course, Christmas dinner just wouldn't be Christmas dinner without sprouts.

One of the only mandatory chores for the December garden is the planting of garlic. Garlic, as you may already know, is traditionally planted before the shortest day of the year and harvested before the longest day (next June). If you love your garlic, you should do two sowings each year – the first one now before Christmas for harvesting in early summer, and then again in early spring for harvesting in autumn. Given how much of it we use in modern kitchens and the generally poor-quality product available to buy in the supermarket, it is one of those vegetables that is really worth trying to grow yourself. That's the real bonus about growing garlic – while you might be hard-pressed to tell the difference between your own onions and the onions you buy in the shop, you will have no such problem with your garlic. I won't go on and on about the garlic from China again as I did in my first book (yeah, okay, I would if I was let) but I just can't get my head around why supermarkets think people want to buy Chinese garlic, particularly when it has had to travel so far, its quality is poor, and garlic grows so well here.

Amazingly, many people still see it as a Mediterranean vegetable and consequently don't think it does well in colder climates, when, in fact, it does just as well here as onions do. The use of garlic in Irish and English kitchens is a relatively new thing, of course – before the 1990s it was seen as an impossibly exotic ingredient that only stinky-breathed 'Continentals' were into. I have a great vegetable-growing guide, first published in 1985 (just twenty-five years ago), that has just one short paragraph dedicated to garlic and it pretty much dismisses it as not worth growing unless 'you are a fan', or Italian.

Garlic is relatively easy to grow and it stores very successfully (some varieties will store for nearly a year), two factors that make it quite easy to become self-sufficient in. It is also a really thrifty vegetable to grow because, of course, once you get a crop going, each separate clove taken from a harvested bulb can be popped into the ground where it will turn into a bulb in its own right. So you don't even have to buy new seeds each year. Talk about economical! Garlic is also thought to have disinfectant qualities for the soil itself – in other words, while it is growing it is having a disinfecting impact on the soil. My sister, Niamh, swears by spraying other vegetable plants with a spray made from garlic and water, and someone else told me that it's a good idea to put some garlic in your hens' water to ward off parasites.

I was grumbling to a charming lady that I met at a book reading once about the fact that I wasn't able to source garlic for planting from my regular seed suppliers. She gave me a patient 'God you're clueless' smile and told me that each year just before Christmas she goes to her local supermarket and buys about ten or fifteen bulbs of good-quality European garlic and uses the cloves for planting. She reckons they are better than the ones you buy in a garden centre and has never had a bad crop.

GARLIC AND HEALTH

We may think that we discovered so-called superfoods, but our ancient ancestors knew about the health benefits of garlic, the 'stinking rose', five thousand years before the ridiculous term 'superfood' was even invented (it's ridiculous because, of course, all natural foods are superfoods). A recently discovered Egyptian scroll, dating back 3,500 years, shows that even then they believed that garlic could prevent cancer. It was consumed regularly by the populace when the plague ravaged Europe, and, given what we now know about its anti-bacterial qualities, it may well have worked too (or maybe the smell kept infected people away …). In 1858, Louis Pasteur stuck some garlic in a petri dish and found that one milligram of the stuff was as effective at killing germs and bacteria as 60 milligrams of penicillin. In fact, it was known as the 'Russian Penicillin' during World War II because those canny Rooskies used it to disinfect open wounds when their stock of real penicillin ran out. We now know that its healing powers come from sulfur compounds found in the vegetable. One of these in particular – allicin – can kill 23 types of bacteria, including salmonella and staphylococcus.

Incidentally, when it comes to the health benefits of garlic, most experts agree that fresh garlic is far better for you than supplements. Garlic is believed to reduce bad cholesterol (HDL) levels by up to 15 percent and systolic pressure in people with hypertension (high blood pressure) by 20-30mmHg. It is thought to be as effective an anti-clotting heart-attack preventer as aspirin. Garlic is also rich in vitamins A, B, and C, which have been shown to help the body to fight carcinogens and get rid of toxins. The sulphur compound in garlic stimulates the nervous system and blood circulation, regulates blood sugar metabolism and detoxifies the liver. In many cultures, it is also considered a powerful alternative to Viagra, if you catch my drift. So, if you've been avoiding it because it gives you bad breath my suggestion is, get over it!

Sowing garlic really couldn't be easier – all you do is shove cloves in the ground about 10cm–15cm apart, with the pointed tip facing upwards and just visible above the soil, and that's the job done. The only thing you need to be careful of is *where* you sow it, particularly at this time of the year. If you stick cloves into a sodden bed in a corner where they won't get any light, they will just rot. You need to put them in nice, free-draining soil somewhere where they will be able to access what little sunshine there is over the winter. We have got some of our best garlic from the polytunnel, but it likes a bit of a cold spell at the start of its growing so you don't need to worry about the impact of frosts on it. You can, incidentally, start the cloves off in modules if you prefer, but it is one of those very rare vegetables that we just find easier to put directly into the soil. Once it's in the ground, you can just leave it alone. There are unlikely to be any weeds at this time of the year, but in the spring you may need to weed to ensure the growing bulbs don't have any competition. It seems like a long way off now, but your garlic will give you a heart attack in late spring or early summer next year by appearing to wither and die – fear not, this is just its way of telling you that it's ready to be harvested. Lift up the bulbs carefully (this is among my favourite moments of the Home Farm year) and leave them somewhere dry and sunny to dry out. Traditionally, garlic is hung up in plaits, which look pretty cool in your kitchen – and you can show off when visitors call around by telling them that it's your own (though if you have a large volume of them, you should store them somewhere cool and dry like a shed).

Before we finish on garlic, I should mention wild garlic, which grows like a weed in wooded areas and, unlike regular garlic, is much sought after for its strongly flavoured leaves and flowers, as well as the bulbs growing underneath the ground – it is the trendy 'ingredient of the moment' in many posh restaurants. You should be able to recognise the plants from their distinctive garlic smell, and also from the pretty little white flowers they get in late spring. Wild garlic is just as good for the health as regular garlic and it too is believed to reduce cholesterol and high blood pressure.

PAULA MEE'S NUTRITION BITES: GARLIC

Many of the therapeutic effects of garlic are thought to be due to its volatile factors which are composed of the sulphur-containing compounds, high concentrations of trace minerals, glucosinolates and enzymes. Chopping or crushing the garlic stimulates the release of allicin, a compound to which many of garlic's health benefits are attributed, such as protecting against heart disease and lowering cholesterol and blood pressure. It is best to leave about fifteen minutes between crushing and cooking to maximise the health benefits of allicin.

Nutrition per Portion (2 cloves):

Calories	Fat (g)	Salt (g)	Saturated Fat (g)
10	0.1	0	0

If you find some, it's worth taking a cutting. It will never need cultivating as long as you give it a position in semi-shade, preferably under a tree. Some people are horrified at the notion of *introducing* wild garlic to a garden, as it is seen, in many quarters, as an aggressive weed. I would agree that you shouldn't consider putting it in a vegetable or flower bed, because once it's in there it's almost impossible to eradicate. But if you can find a corner of the garden where you don't mind it taking over, it's worth having because it's *really* good in the kitchen and very, very good for you.

Wild garlic grows over the winter, flowers in spring and is dead by summer. The best time to eat the leaves is in the spring, though you can eat the bulbs at any time of the year – given the size of them, though, they are a little fiddly to harvest and to cook with.

Here's a suggestion: instead of paying through the nose for little pots of pesto in the winter and spring, make your own with free wild garlic instead of basil. Throw 100g of washed wild garlic leaves into a blender with the same quantity of grated parmesan and pine nuts and blend till smooth; season well and add enough olive oil to cover. A cup of wild garlic leaves will also create a bit of interest in a standard vege-table soup and they are also a nice addition to a salad.

Every morning and evening, I feed the animals on the Home Farm and I take a good deal of satisfaction from doing so because I know it's essentially an investment in our own food security. The duck and hens provide us with their eggs, and, of course, earlier in the year the pigs and chickens made the ultimate sacrifice and provided us with meat. When I am buying their feed, it never feels like an expense per se, because, of course, it really is an investment. When I embark on a meat-rearing project, I always have a little spreadsheet in which I record how much it costs to feed and house the animals in question. I'm not a particularly well organised person, but keeping track of the costs like this, I think, makes sense, just so you can be absolutely sure that the whole thing makes some class of economic sense – it wouldn't do at all to be rearing chickens for the table only to discover that they are working out more expensive than the chicken on a menu at a Michelin star restaurant.

It's a different matter altogether when it comes to feeding our two dogs. We adore them both, of course, but, occasional captured rabbit aside, they are by a country mile the most useless animals on the Home Farm and as they devour their chow each day, that fact is thrown into sharp relief. Of course, they provide companionship, and Sam, the lovely Labrador, is perpetually cheerful, which always brings a smile to my face (the Red Setter looks like she is always disappointed in us, and perhaps she is). But really, when compared with the pigs, chickens, ducks and hens, they just ain't team players in terms of contributing to the Kelly family dinner. Before mankind completely domesticated dogs, and long before we started buying them little diamanté-encrusted outfits for their birthdays, dogs were essentially kept for a purpose – they were used for retrieving, hunting or working and they were cunning enough to keep themselves *off the dinner plate* by being instrumental in bringing food to it. That situation morphed into dogs becoming *pets,* kept only for the companionship they provide. Valuable and all as that may be, they remain a net draw on the Home Farm resources, when every other animal is contributing something (and some animals, of course, are contributing EVERYTHING).

Sometimes, as I watch Sam devour his food (it only takes him about twenty seconds), I find myself wondering whether there is some useful thing he could be put to doing around the place. He's a strong animal and eminently enthusiastic, so it's a great pity that we can't somehow harness that energy. I was discussing this idea of animals earning their keep with a friend of mine, Denis Shannon, recently. Denis is more smallholder than Home Farmer – he has twenty acres of land and rears cows, pigs, hens and geese as well as growing fruit and vegetables to sell to local restaurants and markets. I love calling to see Denis because he's basically living the dream, as far as I'm concerned, and he always has some fascinating new project on the cards. If I feel that things are getting a little staid here on the

Home Farm, I give Denis a call or go visit and I always come away feeling very much inspired and with a stack of harebrained projects in the back pocket. This year when I called him, he gleefully explained how he is now using horses to work his land – and, of course, I couldn't resist but get in the car to go visit and see what it was all about. There's something about turning the clock back fifty years that just attracts me like a magnet.

Anyway, Denis has had horses on his farm for years, but they were basically pets – much like our mutts – and he decided it was time for them to start paying their way. 'Working the horses is something that has been on my mind for years,' he said. 'When I was about nine or ten, we had a neighbour who had a pony and we used to borrow it to make the furrows for the potatoes. So there is that element of nostalgia about this for me.' Of course, working a horse is not easy if you don't know what you're doing, and Denis had to learn (or re-learn) the skills needed. What fascinates me about all this is that the philosophy behind working horses is practical as well as nostalgic – in other words, devotees believe that horses are better suited to particular jobs, such as preparing a seedbed, planting, cultivating and fertilising, and, indeed, are more effective at it than a tractor. They also claim that the animals have a more gentle impact on the land – while a tractor will compact soil, a horse steps lightly between furrows, leaving only footprints rather than long-lasting tracks. This is a particular advantage in sodden winters, when a horse can be deployed to do a job where a tractor would probably get stuck in the mud. There is something magical about the idea of these enormous animals being able to tread delicately between furrows – the classic French working horse, the Percheron, weighs about 800kg and stands up to 17 hands tall. Working horses also offer the small-holder a certain protection from the world of economics outside the gate: you don't need to worry about the price of diesel, for one thing. They also fit beautifully with the smallholding ethos that a farm should be a self-contained and self-sustaining ecosystem with little need for outside resources. The horses are fed from the land's produce and, in return, they work the land and fertilise it with their manure. For all the bells and whistles of the modern tractor, it is not that accommodating.

It's unlikely, of course, that many farmers would opt to abandon the tractor for the humble horse, but with rising fuel costs there is an emerging interest in the idea. For Denis, it has been an absolute revelation. His horses – a sixteen-year-old grey Connemara pony, called Beauty, and a twelve-year-old Cobb, called Blaze – are still in the early stages of their training, but he was confident enough in his (and their) ability after a month to sell off his tractor and other machinery. 'It took a while to drag the knowledge from the brain,' he said, 'but I just knew from the start that I could do the jobs I needed to do with them.' Interestingly, he doesn't miss the tractor either. 'I've spent days up on a smelly, noisy tractor and by the end of the day, I feel strung out – there's nothing satisfying about it. Certainly, working a horse is physically demanding, but it's far more satisfying. Tractors have a lot of drawbacks on a smallhold-ing. They are expensive to maintain and expensive to run. We can feed the horses from the smallholding so we basically have a free power supply. I go out in the morning and put the tack on them and they're there for the day, ready for whatever job I might be doing – weeding, hoeing, harrowing, ploughing.'

I couldn't leave without seeing them in action, and Denis was happy to tack Beauty up so that we could head off around the farm. Both horses love to work and Beauty *did* seem delighted to be going out, while Blaze was decidedly annoyed at being left behind, grunting dismissively as we headed off. A small timber cart was attached to the tack and we used it to pick stones in a paddock, while three cows looked on inquisitively. Denis told me that both the horses and their handler are fitter than they used to be, and, as if to prove the point, Beauty eagerly broke into a trot, even though she was hauling a substantial weight. 'She's that type of horse,' said Denis, as we walked along behind her. 'You are constantly reining her in. I work on my own mostly, but when I'm working with them, I don't feel that I am on my own. A horse is a thinking animal; they communicate with you.'

Beauty was impressively responsive, reacting instantly to voice commands such as 'Stand', 'Go on'. We brought the stones from the farm up to an alpine rockery in front of the house, where she swung around on the lawn, stopping beside the rockery while we unloaded. You could do all this on a tractor, of course, but the lawn would take a year to recover from the trauma – and it wouldn't be anywhere near as much fun. Next up, Denis attached a forecart to the tack and we sat in. He has been using the horses to collect feed and run errands at the local co-op – his neighbours think he's mad. I told him that my neighbours think the same about me. That night I had a strange dream (as if to prove they are right) – I had somehow managed to attach a tack and cart to Sam and I was running a taxi service in the local village called 'Mick's Rickshaws'. It was very profitable.

Ar mo ghabáil dom siar chun Droichead Uí Mhórdha,
Píce i m' dhóid is mé ag dul i meitheal,
Cé chasfaí orm i gcumar ceoidh
Ach pocán crón is é ar buile …

As I set out with me pike in hand
To old Dromore to join a meitheal,
Who should I meet but a tan puck goat
And he's roaring mad …

Lyrics from the Irish song 'An Poc ar Buile'

Feargal is a good pal of mine from the GIY group – he is a relentlessly and infectiously enthusiastic bloke, who approached me in advance of the first meeting with a list of ideas ('which you have probably already thought of,' he said – but I hadn't thought of any of them) that would just blow your mind. It was Feargal who came up with the idea of calling our small-group discussions 'PODs', but more importantly he came up with the idea of grower's *meitheals*, which were to have such a huge impact on the lives of all of us. A *meitheal* (pronounced *meh-hill*) is an Irish word and like many Irish words it doesn't really have a direct equivalent in English – it loosely translates as 'working gang' and describes the old Irish tradition where people in rural communities gathered together on a neighbour's farm to help save the hay or harvest crops. Each person would help their neighbour, who would in turn reciprocate – they acted as a team (much like the Amish tradition of getting together to construct a house) and everybody benefited in some way from the endeavours. As well as getting incredibly time-sensitive jobs completed in a hurry, the *meitheal* also builds up strong friendships and respect among those involved.

All of us are aware that modern life can be quite isolating at times, whether you are living in the depths of the countryside or in the middle of a five-hundred-house estate, which is why the sense of community that a *meitheal* implies is so appealing. Our plan for *meitheals* within the GIY group was to try to build small, local groups of people who would get together regularly in each other's gardens/veg plots to accomplish a particular job of work and at the same time (a) foster some community spirit, (b) make friends, (c) have some fun, and (d) learn from each other. Each *meitheal* consists of about five or six people who live near each other and each member of the group picks some task that they need to do in their garden – it could be anything: sowing, planting, harvesting, double digging, rotovating, making raised beds. We don't get too prescriptive about what work should be done or how long it should take. However, we do highlight the fact that it's probably a good idea to be reasonable and not to work fellow *meitheal* members into an early grave. Also, we have emphasised that it's very important to keep a growing/rearing theme to the *meitheal* work – it should be about food production and not some random chore that's been hanging around for years, like cleaning out a blocked drain or filling a skip. *Meitheal* members are encouraged to bring their own implements – spades, trowels etc – so that the person who is hosting doesn't have to go out and buy or borrow a collection of spades and so on for people to work with.

Breaking my no-work-in-December rule, last weekend our *meitheal* visited my garden on a beautiful, frosty December morning. There's something incredibly heartening about a gang of people showing up at your gaff on a Saturday morning to work on your vegetable garden. It's like being love-bombed or something – I promise you, you just can't help feeling good about yourself. All the *meitheal* members worked hard, but a special mention has to go to Feargal, who arrived on his bicycle with his spade tied to the cross-bar, and a plate of lovely apple and cinnamon sponge slices in the saddle bag. Kudos to you, Sir, for your impeccable carbon-free credentials (and delicious cooking)!

December is an interesting time of the year for a *meitheal* visit. There is obviously no harvesting to be done, but there are still plenty of heavy, boring or generally time-consuming chores that lend themselves well to this manner of work, and, of course, I still had the remnants of the mountain of pooh under the clothes lines to deal with. Rather than freak everyone out by introducing this as the first job, I decided to ease them in gently. My plan was to clear one of the long raised beds of remaining crops (a few) and weeds (a lot) and to plant some winter-hardy onions. To Mrs Kelly and myself, that would represent at least a day of hard toil, but the *meitheal* made short work of it (we sowed about a hundred onions, which I hope will survive the cold snap) and within an hour we were standing back, admiring our work and looking for something else to do. Well, as it happens, ladies and gentlemen …

To soften the blow of the unpleasant work to come we broke for some grub: Waterford bread rolls called 'blaas' and sausages cooked up on the barbecue. The sausages were from our own pigs and we opened a jar of precious, rare (as hen's teeth) green tomato chutney for the occasion. The smell of cooking bangers was irresistible in the frosty morning air (especially when you are ravenous with the hunger after working) and the grub was washed down with mugs of roasting hot tea. 'Enough guff,' says I when we had finished our food, switching from amiable chef to gruff foreman as quick as a flash. 'Back to work!'

We surveyed the mountain of pooh. I had hoped that if I ignored it for long enough it might just rot away into oblivion, but, in fact, it was pretty much unchanged since the mucky weekend in November when we distributed half of it. No problem to the *meitheal*. The wheelbarrows (people had brought their own, apart from Feargal, of course, who couldn't be expected to bring a wheelbarrow on a bike – though with him, you'd never know!) were filled and emptied God knows how many times and loads of manure were dispatched around the garden in double-quick time – to the polytunnel, where we will put a crop of early spuds in January, around fruit bushes and apple trees, and the balance to the compost heap. Perfect, if not particularly pleasant *meitheal* work. While we worked, people were exchanging gardening war-stories and talking about what works and what does not work in their own plots. All very valuable stuff for the novice grower. There was much banter about slave labour and how hard I was working them, but you got the impression that they were only messing (I think). At least, we know that as *meitheal* chores go, it can't get much worse than shovelling shit. We finished up by lunchtime and all hands departed, tired but much the happier for their endeavours. Whether it was the fresh air, the company, the sense of companionship and community, or perhaps just the fumes from the manure, I couldn't stop smiling for the rest of the day.

Of course, the essence of a *meitheal* is the need to reciprocate – much as you might like it, they can't just keep coming to your garden over and over again. At some point, you actually have to go do some work in someone else's garden! But the same principles always apply – you work your ass off for the day, get well fed, have a bit of a laugh and go home happy. Job done. One weekend, we got together in Feargal's garden and filled three raised beds with about ten tonnes of soil, ferrying it across the garden, one barrow at a time. That is a job that would have taken one person about a month to do. Another weekend, the *meitheal* convened to put up a polytunnel for Nicky – this is another perfect *meitheal* chore since you need loads of bodies to get involved in pulling the plastic over the tunnel frame, and, of course, a *meitheal* makes light work of digging the trench around the outside of the frame into which the plastic is buried. A *meitheal* always brings a good mix of talents to a job – some people are great at doing the hard lugging, while others are more cerebral, which, of course, has its benefits too. Some (me) have the 'Let's just start digging' mentality, while others like to plan things out a little better than that – the blend of expertise serves the *meitheal* well and provides many interesting moments!

In addition to the bigger jobs mentioned, we have also convened a *meitheal* for smaller, more pedestrian jobs. We have got together occasionally to sow seeds, for example, which, if I am honest, is a chance to have a bit of a natter more than anything else. It's like the horticultural equivalent of a knitting circle. I have also called on some members if I have a job to do and just need a little help – for example, when putting up extra fencing for the pigs. Back in the spring, we gathered in someone's garden for what we called 'Potty Sunday', where we all brought along seedlings in little pots to barter – absolutely brilliant fun. We have got together for what could be described as a garden visit rather than a *meitheal* – these are just excuses to snoop around someone's garden, drink gallons of tea and eat some nice cakes.

But you always pick up some little hint, some bit of advice, some new way of doing things to bring back home to your own little bit of heaven. And, of course, even if you didn't, it would still be worthwhile because of the incredible sense of satisfaction that comes from belonging to something – that, in itself, will warm the heart even on the coldest winter days.

It wouldn't be right to finish this book without making one final pitch to encourage those readers who have never grown anything at all to try growing something in the coming year. You may have read through this book and thought: Well now, that doesn't sound too painful, I think I might just give this whole Home Farming malarkey a go. But, then you might also be thinking: Yeah, but I really don't know where to start. Believe me, I know how you feel – it really can be daunting. I have been there. Plus, I have so many vegetable-growing books that if I put them all on top of one another, they would make a stack that would be taller than I am – I'm not particularly tall, but still, that's some stack of information. But, of course, access to information and having knowledge are two very different things. I've read some of those books from cover to cover, dipped into others on occasion, and some of them I haven't read at all. I've put some of the stuff I've learned into practice and completely ignored the rest. But let me put all that aside for a minute and focus on the things I have gleaned from our experience here, which might help you to get started.

The first thing to think about is where you are going to put your vegetable plot. In my experience, you often don't have a whole lot of choice in this (there's one particular area of the garden that's suitable, and that's pretty much that); but if you do have choice, then pick a sunny and sheltered spot rather than a shaded, wind-swept one. Vegetables and fruit generally enjoy sun and dislike wind, a bit like ourselves, I suppose. In our case, we situated the vegetable patch in a corner of the garden, and it gets shelter on two sides from a surrounding hedge, which is handy. If your garden is exposed, you will probably eventually need to introduce some form of wind-break for your vegetable patch, either natural (like a hedge, trees or shrubs) or otherwise (fence, dry stone wall). But I wouldn't worry about that for the moment – it's a job for when you're well and truly up and running. You will often read that it's a good idea to put the fruit/vegetables that you need most (like herbs, for example) near the back door, while putting the ones that you will be accessing the least (like an apple tree) furthest away down at the end of the garden – this is good advice, but may not be practical in the scheme of things. We grow everything down at the end of the garden, but it's not like it's a two-mile walk to the plot from the kitchen, so we don't mind.

As you are aware by now, in my opinion raised beds are the way to go – we simply could not get any good results without our beds. Vegetables like a type of soil which is called a 'loam', which is basically soil that is neither too sandy nor too sticky. Pick up a handful of your soil and concentrate on what you are feeling. Is it really fine, almost like sand? Or is it like a sticky potter's clay? Ideally, you want something in the middle of these two extremes – a crumbly soil that retains nutrients but which also drains well. You may not have that initially (we certainly didn't), but you will get there over time by adding lots of manure and compost to your soil each year. This will be far easier to achieve in raised beds because you can introduce good-quality topsoil from the start. Incidentally, you may as well get used to the fact that most things on the Home Farm take *time* – just go with it. Nature won't be rushed, so don't bother trying to rush her.

If you are starting from absolute scratch with a piece of lawn, now's the time to do the legwork so that you will have a vegetable patch ready for planting late next spring. Get your beds built. Four raised beds, each measuring 1m x 3m, for example, with surrounding paths 1m wide, will require a total area of just 45 square metres: 5m x 9m. Whether you go for tall or short beds is largely a matter of personal preference, and, of course, how much topsoil you have access to. Once you have your beds built and the topsoil in, you will need to beg, borrow, blag or steal some farmyard manure or good-quality compost. Cover the beds with about 10cm of this and then cover them down with black plastic. The plastic stops the nutrients from being washed away, prevents weeds growing and keeps the soil nice and warm until next spring. You should be in good shape then to get growing. Practise the simple crop rotation plan I talked about in Chapter 5 and allow for it from the start in terms of how many beds you build. It will make life so much easier in the long run, both in terms of improving your soil and preventing disease, but, equally important, you will know what you need to do in terms of soil preparation in the winter (ie whether you should manure/compost a particular bed) and you will never have any confusion about where you are supposed to plant things.

In January, get your hands on some good-quality module trays, some big pots (for growing herbs etc), some nice potting compost, and order some seeds in anticipation. What should you grow? Keep it simple. Do not try to grow every vegetable you can think of in your first year. I think one of the reasons why the whole project has been so appealing to us is that we started really small and expanded a little each year. We have tried not to get ahead of our ability too much. There is a huge amount to learn when it comes to growing vegetables – don't get me wrong, you will probably have a good deal of success in your first year and even more in your second. But you will still be learning in your fifth, sixth and probably twentieth year. So it makes sense to keep things at a manageable level for the first few years. Start with things that are easy to grow and that you like to eat. I've mentioned loads of them over the course of the twelve months – potatoes, peas, courgettes, broad beans, tomatoes etc. Pick a relatively small number of vegetables and focus your energies on them – you will be really successful and the joy you get from producing great crops of these will steel you for the inevitable problems that arise when you expand things out a little. Study the back of seed packets – they are a mine of information. Steer clear of the trickier vegetables, like cauliflower, for the moment.

If I were to recommend ten things that are easy to grow it would be the following (in no particular order):

1   **tomatoes**
2   **potatoes**
3   **herbs – particularly mint, parsley, thyme and basil**
4   **salad leaves like lettuce and rocket, and radishes**
5   **courgettes**

6   **peas**

7   **broad beans**

8   **onions (from sets)**

9   **leaf beets – perpetual spinach and chard**

10   **garlic.**

It can be daunting to take these first steps, particularly because growing vegetables is always made out to be so complex. In some ways it is, but in other ways it's very straightforward. Stick a seed in the ground, and it grows. That's the basic thing. The problem is that when you start, the straightforward parts seem to be in the minority and pretty much everything else about it appears mind-bogglingly complex. And, of course, it has a confounding vernacular all its own – cultivars, tilths, double-digging, broadcasting, sowing in blocks, ridges, drills, furrows, chitting, pruning, blanching, thinning, pricking out, heeling in, planting on. It's no wonder we're confused! Our approach while we have been learning, has been ostrich-like: we focus on what's straightforward and we pretty much ignore the rest. If you do that for a few years, the balance gradually shifts and, before you know it, there's a lot more that appears straightforward and a lot less that appears complex. I guess, if we keep marching forward rather blindly like this for another couple of decades it will *all* appear straightforward and we will become Monty Don.

After you get your first year under your belt, congratulate yourself on having caught the bug. Use the gentle pause in winter to learn new things. Go on a course. Recharge your batteries. Expand your growing activities to include other vegetables, herbs and fruit. Keep experimenting. Enjoy every morsel of your home-grown produce for its intensity of flavour, vibrancy and nutrition. Savour the story that Mother Nature will tell you during the year with the produce she provides – it's a fascinating culinary adventure. Each season has its place in the grand scheme of things and our place in life is to walk along in concert with them – savour their uniqueness. They all, every single one of them, come with their own set of wonders and challenges. You will derive great comfort and joy from living and eating seasonally rather than living in a staid, unnatural, homogenised commercial bubble. Forage for free stuff when you can – blackberries, wild garlic, sorrel, mushrooms, dandelions, nettles and elderberries. Maybe keep bees for honey. Join a food growers group if you are lucky enough to have one in your area, or at the very least try and find some people with whom you can share your passions. Go on a *meitheal* – you will be amazed how good it will make you feel to give your time and energy free of charge to other people. Consider getting some hens. It doesn't matter if you have a small garden – two or three hens will be quite happy in a little coop with a run attached, and they will provide you with an incredibly healthy, free food source for years to come. Ducks will do the same, with even more charm. If you have the space, think about a couple of pigs, or a goat (the name Geraldine is taken, by the way), or even some sheep or cows. There is no end to the number of fascinating, life-changing Home Farm experiences that are out there waiting for you. Start the journey now. You will very quickly discover just how simple and beautiful this life can really be.

DECEMBER GROWER'S CALENDAR

Prep Work

- Continue digging-over cleared vegetable beds and adding well rotted compost or manure.
- Get educated – book yourself on a course over the winter!
- Start a Gardening Diary.
- Start planning what you would like to grow next year; include at least one previously untried vegetable. Work out what crop rotation system you are going to use. Study and compare the various seed catalogues carefully before deciding on the best varieties to grow to suit your needs.
- Start a compost corner or heap.
- If you don't already have one, plan a fruit garden/area to include, at the very least, some soft fruit like raspberries, strawberries, gooseberries and currants; and some fruit trees like apple, plum and pear.

To-do List

- Good garden hygiene helps greatly in the prevention of disease carry-over from one year to the next, so remove yellowing leaves from any crops remaining and rake up fallen leaves.
- Slugs are a problem all year round, so slug control remains a necessity (though actual slug patrols probably don't). It's particularly important to keep them in check in the polytunnel or greenhouse. Maybe now is a good time to let the ducks loose in your vegetable patch – there is very little growing, so they can't do much damage, but they will do a good culling of slugs. Mice can be a problem at this time of the year and crops sown in the ground, like broad beans, garlic etc, can be vulnerable. Protect them under cloches.

- It's a good time of the year to add lime to your beds (particularly the ones that will take brassicas next year), so buy a pH testing kit if you don't already have one, and test your soil.
- Keep an eye on your stored veggies and discard anything that's rotting.
- Do interesting things with leaves! Store in bags to make leaf mould or use as cover for bare soil (keeps weeds down and prevents drying out).

Sowing Seeds

- No. Sorry. We're back to sowing the seeds of love again.

Planting Out

- If you haven't already done so, plant garlic – it should be in the soil by the shortest day of the year.
- Bring herbs like mint, chives, lemon balm, parsley, thyme indoors by lifting and potting them up.
- Chicory can be forced – dig up the roots, pot them up and place them in a dark, warm place. The chicons should appear in about a month.

GRUB'S UP – WHAT'S IN SEASON

In general terms, it's back to winter vegetables (and stores, if you have them) but you can try bucking the seasonal trend by continuing to harvest winter salad leaves (if you were canny enough to plant them!) like corn salad, land cress and mizuna.

You should still have at least some produce left in the December garden, for example, winter cabbages, brussels sprouts (of course), leeks, kale, Jerusalem artichokes, carrots, celery, turnips, parsnips, winter cauliflower, swedes and celeriac. Whether you have a good crop of these at this time of the year probably depends a lot on your experience and how much work you put into them earlier in the year.

Continue to harvest spinach and chard, and from your stores you can enjoy pumpkins and squashes, potatoes, onions, apples, beetroot and garlic.

Oh, and – Happy Christmas!

VEGETABLE GROWER'S GUIDE

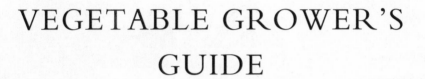

VEGETABLES	JANUARY	FEBRUARY	MARCH	APRIL	MAY
Aubergine	Sow	Sow	Sow		
Broad Bean	Sow	Sow	Sow	Sow	Sow
Broad Bean – Year 2					Harvest
Bean: Dwarf French				Sow	Sow
Bean: Climbing French				Sow	Sow
Bean: Runner				Sow	Sow
Beetroot			Sow	Sow	Sow
Broccoli: Calabrese			Sow	Sow	Sow
Broccoli: Sprouting				Sow	Sow
Broccoli: Sprouting – Year 2			Harvest	Harvest	
Brussels Sprouts			Sow	Sow	Sow
Brussels Sprouts – Year 2	Harvest	Harvest	Harvest		
Cabbage: Summer/Autumn	Sow	Sow	Sow	Sow	Sow
Cabbage: Winter				Sow	Sow
Cabbage: Spring					
Cabbage: Spring – Year 2				Harvest	Harvest
Carrot		Sow	Sow	Sow	Sow/Harvest
Cauliflower: Summer/Autumn			Sow	Sow	Sow
Cauliflower: Winter					Sow
Cauliflower: Winter – Year 2	Harvest				Harvest
Chilli-pepper		Sow	Sow	Sow	
Celeriac			Sow	Sow	
Celery	Sow	Sow	Sow		
Chicory					
Coriander/Cilantro		Sow	Sow	Sow	Sow
Courgette				Sow	Sow
Cucumber		Sow	Sow	Sow	Sow
Fennel (Florence)					Sow
Kale				Sow	Sow
Kale – Year 2	Harvest	Harvest	Harvest		

JUNE	JULY	AUGUST	SEPTEMBER	OCTOBER	NOVEMBER	DECEMBER
		Harvest	Harvest	Harvest		
Sow	Sow	Harvest	Harvest	Harvest	Sow	Sow
Sow	Sow	Harvest	Harvest	Harvest		
Sow	Harvest	Harvest	Harvest	Harvest		
Sow	Harvest	Harvest	Harvest	Harvest		
Sow/Harvest	Sow/Harvest	Harvest	Harvest	Harvest	Harvest	Harvest
Sow	Harvest	Harvest	Harvest	Harvest	Harvest	
				Harvest	Harvest	Harvest
Sow	Harvest	Harvest	Harvest	Harvest	Harvest	
				Harvest	Harvest	Harvest
Sow	Sow	Sow				
Sow/Harvest	Sow/Harvest	Harvest	Harvest	Harvest	Harvest	Harvest
		Harvest	Harvest	Harvest	Harvest	
Sow						Harvest
Harvest						
	Harvest	Harvest	Harvest	Harvest		
			Harvest	Harvest	Harvest	Harvest
	Harvest	Harvest	Harvest	Harvest	Harvest	
Sow	Sow	Sow	Harvest	Harvest	Harvest	Harvest
Sow	Harvest	Harvest	Harvest	Harvest		
		Harvest	Harvest	Harvest		
	Harvest	Harvest	Harvest			
Sow		Harvest	Harvest	Harvest		
Sow	Harvest	Harvest	Harvest	Harvest	Harvest	Harvest

VEGETABLES	JANUARY	FEBRUARY	MARCH	APRIL	MAY
Leek			Sow	Sow	
Leek – Year 2	Harvest	Harvest	Harvest		
Lettuce: Summer			Sow	Sow	Sow
Lettuce: Winter					
Lettuce: Winter – Year 2	Harvest	Harvest	Harvest		
Marrow				Sow	Sow
Melon				Sow	Sow
Onion: Spring			Sow	Sow	Sow
Onion: Bulb			Sow	Sow	
Onion: Bulb, Autumn					
Onion: Bulb, Autumn – Yr 2					
Parsnip		Sow	Sow	Sow	Sow
Parsnip – Year 2	Harvest	Harvest	Harvest		
Peas			Sow	Sow	Sow
Peppers (Bell etc.)	Sow	Sow	Sow	Sow	
Pumpkin				Sow	Sow
Radish			Sow	Sow	Sow/Harvest
Rocket			Sow	Sow	Sow
Shallot			Sow	Sow	
Spinach: Annual			Sow	Sow	Sow
Spinach: Leaf Beet			Sow	Sow	Sow
Spinach: Leaf Beet – Year 2	Harvest	Harvest	Harvest		
Swede				Sow	Sow
Swede – Year 2	Harvest	Harvest			
Sweet Corn				Sow	Sow
Tomato	Sow	Sow	Sow	Sow	
Turnip				Sow	Sow

JUNE	JULY	AUGUST	SEPTEMBER	OCTOBER	NOVEMBER	DECEMBER
		Harvest	Harvest	Harvest	Harvest	Harvest
Sow/Harvest	Sow/Harvest	Harvest	Harvest	Harvest		
	Sow	Sow	Sow	Sow	Sow	Harvest
		Harvest	Harvest			
		Harvest	Harvest			
Harvest	Harvest	Harvest	Harvest			
	Harvest	Harvest	Harvest	Harvest	Harvest	Harvest
		Sow				
	Harvest					
		Harvest	Harvest	Harvest	Harvest	Harvest
Sow	Sow	Harvest	Harvest	Harvest	Harvest	
	Harvest	Harvest	Harvest	Harvest		
			Harvest	Harvest		
Sow/Harvest	Sow/Harvest	Sow/Harvest	Sow/Harvest	Harvest	Harvest	
Sow/Harvest	Sow/Harvest	Sow/Harvest	Harvest	Harvest		
		Harvest	Harvest	Harvest		
	Harvest	Harvest				
Sow/Har.	Sow/Har.	Harvest	Harvest	Harvest	Harvest	Harvest
Sow			Harvest	Harvest	Harvest	Harvest
		Harvest	Harvest			
Harvest	Harvest	Harvest	Harvest	Harvest		
Sow	Sow	Sow	Harvest	Harvest	Harvest	Harvest

Read Michael Kelly's first book

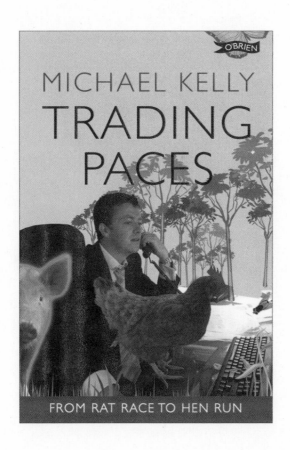